Awesome Families

Awesome Families

The Promise of Healing Relationships in the International Churches of Christ

Kathleen E. Jenkins

Rutgers University Press
New Brunswick, New Jersey, and London

Library of Congress Cataloging-in-Publication Data

Jenkins, Kathleen E.
Awesome families : the promise of healing family in the International Churches of Christ / Kathleen E. Jenkins.
p. cm.
Includes bibliographical references (p. TK) and index.
ISBN-13: 978-0-8135-3663-7 (hardcover : alk. paper)
ISBN-13: 978-0-8135-3664-4 (pbk. : alk. paper)
1. International Churches of Christ. 2. Christian sociology—International Churches of Christ. 3. Family—Religious aspects—International Churches of Christ. I. Title.
BX7990.I685J46 2005
261.8'3585'0882899—dc22 2005002581

A British Cataloging-in-Publication record for this book is available from the British Library

Manufactured in the United States of America

To my family

Contents

Acknowledgments

This ethnography would not be possible without the City Church of Christ (City COC) church members who welcomed me into their homes and lives. I am especially thankful to the major research participants who read this manuscript and commented with respect toward my commitment to a sociological perspective. My hope is that they and their church brothers and sisters are able to continue to foster a meaningful religious community through challenging times.

I am forever thankful for my training as an ethnographer in the Department of Sociology at Brandeis University. Karen V. Hansen provided constant inspiration, support, and critical feedback, as well as invaluable advice on balancing work and family. Stefan Timmermans helped shape this ethnography and offered wise direction through field dilemmas and the emotional tasks of doing fieldwork in challenging settings. Peter Conrad was a constant source of encouragement and critical reflection. Thanks to Debra Osnowitz who read multiple drafts of this book and whose sociological imagination, analytical insight, and friendship keep my spirit high. Thanks also to Claude for his therapeutic correspondence.

I am forever indebted to Lynn Davidman for her purple pen, encouragement of my work, friendship, and for awakening the sociologist in me. John Bartkowski's scholarship motivated me early in my career to pursue the dynamism of gender in the U.S. evangelical subculture. His advice and criticism helped shape *Awesome Families.* Michael Emerson has read my work on the ICOC over the years and helped shape, in particular, my analysis of multiculturalism and multiracialism in the movement. Thank you to the anonymous reviewers for their helpful comments and guidance. Thanks also to the sociology faculty and Diane at Clark University for providing a nurturing and supportive work environment as I wrote the book. Thanks to my dear friend and anthropologist,

Christa Little-Siebold, for reminding me of my voice and motivation early in the writing process.

Several friends and family members made this work possible. My stepbrother and his wife encouraged me to explore community in the ICOC and were willing, over the years, to talk with me about their experience in the church. My mother and stepfather maintained open minds and supported my efforts to understand the complex culture of the ICOC movement. My husband, Mark, offered constant understanding of the time and commitment it takes to conduct fieldwork and to write a dissertation and book. My young daughters, Kathryn Rae and Jackie Boyd, spent time with me in the field—in utero and out; their unconditional love and brightness of spirit feed my spirit. My long-term separation from my son was a constant reminder of the frustration and love that can lead parents to search for hope and peace in religious community. Judith O'Donnell and Tim Corkery convinced me long ago that what I thought were impossible goals, were well within my reach. Thanks to my mother-in-law, Lynn Lerman, for her constant support and reading and commenting on the introduction. Thank you to Julie VanNoppen for twelve years of loving friendship and our morning Dexter Park walk that has motivated me through the most difficult of times. Dawn Kerr offered much support, theological discussion, and coffee cake. A special thank-you to David Eliet for instilling a confidence and trust in my voice so many years ago.

Awesome Families

Introduction

"It's Like Free Counseling All the Time"

IMAGINE a church, a community of Christians who claim they are able to help people establish "awesome" families, who make up a fellowship where married couples share their most intimate fears and desires and develop fantastic sexual relationships, where children respect and enthusiastically follow the Christian life path set by their parents, and where sons and daughters are reunited with estranged parents and siblings. Within this church, interracial/ethnic marriages and biracial/ethnic children are fully embraced and members from disparate backgrounds become "real family," learning to love and care for each other in extraordinary ways. This is the picture of exceptional family that members of the International Churches of Christ (ICOC) claim to have and present to potential new members.

Member stories revolve around the restorative power of the church community to heal marriages on the brink of disaster. As one husband in the church relates: "There are many couples just here in our church of three hundred that have had their marriages saved because of the church. And there are countless testimonials that you can hear, worldwide." He credits successful marriages to the church's mandatory marriage counseling and community support, the DPI (ICOC's publishing house, Discipleship Publications International) marriage guidebook, *Friends and Lovers: Marriage as God Designed It*, and yearly ICOC marriage boosters like "Marriage Enrichment Day." In fact, before he and his wife joined the church, he claims they had one foot on the path to divorce. Other marriages healed in the church, he suggests, have been virtually resurrected:

> I know of one couple in our church who were actually at the point of signing divorce papers. They were separated for a long time,

> months, and I think the daughter got into the church and said, "You've got to see this," and it just went from there. And today they are one of the, as a couple, they are one of the elders, one of the leaders in our church, they are called shepherding couples. . . . They were on their way out and there was no reconciliation planned and it all came back together—so that was an *eleventh hour save* [my emphasis] and that's not that uncommon for that to happen.

Stories of members bringing biological families into the church and of all experiencing intense healing in their relationships with one another are also prevalent. Movies and videos produced by the church depict biological families reunited after destructive and dysfunctional family histories: families coming together in loving, caring ways as church members help them deal with past abuses resulting from alcoholism, conflicted divorce battles, and drug addiction. Turning biological kin into church kin seems a very real and desired ideal for most who have dedicated their lives to the ICOC's Kingdom of God. Christa, a twenty-two-year-old Guatemalan immigrant, notes: "God was there for me. Six months after I became a disciple God put me in the path of my sister and she became a member. It's awesome." Even those who do not manage to convert biological family express that they will keep on trying and that the church can help them, in therapeutic ways, to better understand why their mothers, fathers, siblings, and children cannot "open their hearts to the church." Members constantly praise and credit the church's Christian counseling structure for helping them to learn to forgive biological family members and to develop their own "awesome families" in the church community.

IMAGINE NOW, this very same healing community that most members describe as an awesome family portrayed as a "dangerous cult." Who makes such claims about this healing group? Ex-members, former leaders, anticult groups, and many university officials who have banned the group from campuses because of their "deceptive recruiting techniques" and authoritarian structure (Barnett 1989; Bauer 1994; Giambalvo and Rosedale 1996; Paulson 2001; Rodgers-Melnick 1996). Robert Watts Thornburg at Boston University charges that the International Church of Christ "discourages new prospects from associating with nonmembers, systematically cutting out any contact with family, friends, or outside sources of reality checks" (Giambalvo and Rosedale 1996, 21). College-age ex-members tell of being deprived of food and drink during all-night Bible studies, of being deceived into attending Bible study conversion sessions, of being "love bombed" and then psychologically "dumped," and of being cut off from their families of origin. A concerned parent of a member writes: "It is puzzling to me that my daughter no longer shows any signs of emotion. She has no laughter, no tears, and no anger. . . . Before her recruitment Karen was very open and honest, but now she seems to have many secrets and hidden thoughts" (Giambalvo and Rosedale 1996, 179–180).

Ex-members frequently tell stories of betrayal by church family members and of the dissolution of loving relationships within church boundaries. Accounts of marriages threatened and undermined by ICOC members are the subject of many ex-member narratives. One ex-member writes of her experiences in the church:

> Communication between Tom [husband] and me ceased. . . . In my eyes I was striving to rid my character of such things as deceit, prejudices, and unkindness, when in fact without my realizing it I had become arrogant and manipulative. . . . I was led to believe that the more difficult the trial, the more faithful and spiritual I was before God. . . . Many others [members] consistently tried to convince me that my husband was dangerous and had uncontrollable problems with his temper, and that the difficulties we were having would have occurred whether or not I had gotten involved with the church. (Giambalvo and Rosedale 1996, 97–98)

Another ex-member relates that upon joining the church in the early 1990s, she was counseled by members to break up with her boyfriend of two years because he did not want to become a disciple in the movement: "I left him. And I loved him. It was so heartless [her breaking up with him]. I mean without feeling. Just, no problem, I don't care if I never see you again."

Throwing away meaningful biological family relationships is also a frequent story of ex-members: many relate being coached by church members to "keep a distance" from fathers, mothers, and siblings, people whom "Satan" may be using as a medium to lure members from the church community. Narratives from mothers and fathers of members communicate biological family separation: "For five months, from March until August, we didn't see Karen [their daughter]. . . . She lived with a family who had been asked to help out in the San Francisco Church of Christ. . . . Karen slept on the sofa in the living room of the couple's rented home" (Giambalvo and Rosedale 1996, 177).

These examples of the church destroying intimate and loving relationships are only two of thousands of ex-member stories shared on websites, in anti-ICOC literature, and within ex-member support groups. These stories echo anti-cult movement rhetoric; they depict a radical religious group tearing families apart, of psychological victimization and loss of self, the very antithesis of the powerful therapeutic church family most members describe.

HOW DO WE understand the true nature of experience and attraction to a religious group that some claim is constructing awesome families and others charge is destroying loving and intimate relationships? Eight years ago, I was presented with this question as one of my step-siblings became a member of the International Churches of Christ. My family expressed great loss as my brother became more and more involved in the church community and they learned of ICOC cult charges from anti-cult organizations, university chaplains, and the news media. At the same time, my brother told me he was finally happy, fulfilled, that he and his girlfriend (now wife) had learned how to appreciate, love, and respect one another. Indeed, my brother seemed to be a changed person, but not in the zombielike way anti-cult rhetoric portrayed. Rather, he had tackled and overcome many personal issues that previously kept him from excelling in school, career, and relationships. As his life became filled with church activities and he grew closer and closer to his religious family, my parents feared for him and tried to find out as much information as they could about the ICOC. As a family member, I wanted to find a way for my brother and my parents to come to understand one another. As a sociologist of religion and family, my sociological imagination was stirred.

The puzzle ICOC members and ex-members presented—this picture of an ideal family community versus a dangerous and destructive one—is a sociological puzzle faced many times. How do we come to understand why individuals join religious groups that seem a direct affront to deeply held social values? How do we make sense of those who followed John Humphrey Noyes to the Oneida socialist Christian commune of the nineteenth century? How did Noyes's followers come to renounce monogamous heterosexual marriage and embrace a communal marriage arrangement that forbade romantic love? How do we understand the experience of hundreds of individuals who joined Jim Jones's People's Temple, giving up all their possessions to the community and ultimately participating in a mass suicide in Guyana in 1978? How do we understand the experience of those who joined the Family, or Children of God, in the 1960s, a movement widely criticized for its "sexual ministry" and sex sharing among adult members? Members of each of these groups described relational and spiritual experiences with their religious communities as deeply fulfilling; at the same time, others vilified group leaders and chastised members for deviant actions, beliefs, and submission to charismatic leaders and hierarchical, authoritative structures.

As sociologists have puzzled about how individuals come to join "extreme" religious groups, they have argued that part of the answer lies in the failure of dominant institutions, such as the family, to provide clear direction and answer individuals' needs. Solutions to this dilemma of understanding extreme religious experience are inevitably shaped then by social structure viewed in historical context. For example, the radical shifting of gender and family ideology ushered in by industrialization in the late nineteenth century gave Oneida group members reason to follow Noyes, just as the particular challenges to gender and sexual norms that rose from the countercultural movement of the 1960s shaped those who joined the Family. Those who followed Jim Jones were largely a group of socially disadvantaged individuals who had suffered years of extreme financial and relational consequences from living in a racialized society. The answer to the ICOC puzzle lies as well in dominant social institutions, paradoxes of gender, sexuality, and socioeconomic conditions. To understand why so many were attracted to the ICOC, we must look at the historically particular ways social institutions like the family, medicine, media, sports, religion, and therapeutic culture have come together at the turn of the twenty-first century. Their points of convergence hold the answer to the ICOC "cult" versus "awesome family" paradox.

This book is the story of the attraction of ICOC's therapeutic promise to heal, fortify, and construct kin in today's religious and spiritual marketplace: an ethnographic account of how a historically particular mixture of therapeutic ethos and practice, religious doctrine, and marriage and family ideology appealed to the over one hundred thousand individuals worldwide baptized into the ICOC since its formal founding in 1979 in Lexington, Massachusetts. It is also about the movement's high dropout rate and demise, exploring why this fast-growing international movement lost so many members along the way and ultimately fell apart in 2003–2004. In particular, "awesome families" is the vision of church community I heard while conducting fieldwork over several years (1995–2000), in a three-hundred-member New England congregation of the ICOC, the City Church of Christ (City COC).

When I first became interested in exploring the paradox of ICOC membership, I knew that to get any truthful picture of the movement and to confront the puzzle of destructive cult versus awesome family, I would need to collect data from a wide range of sources. I needed to listen carefully to the experiences and voices of members, former members, and outside critics (Beckford 1985; Richardson, Balch, and Melton 1993). I showed up one Sunday morning for the City COC services and asked leaders if I could spend time in their church observing and talking to members. I told them that I wanted to learn more about people's experiences in their church. They agreed. I attended over sixty City COC and ICOC regional group events and numerous in-home family group gatherings. During one year, I spent at least one day every other week attending a one-on-one, sometimes two-on-one, Bible study series in a member's home. I also interviewed formally and informally over fifty City COC members and several ICOC members from congregations across the country. These interviews took approximately ninety minutes, although many were greatly enhanced through informal conversation as I talked at length with some members over the years during City COC functions. To obtain a more balanced qualitative picture, I formally interviewed nine former members of the movement and attended an ex-member support group. I routinely monitored member and ex-member websites and analyzed more than forty ex-member testimonies from websites and ex-member and anti-cult literature. I also analyzed texts published by Discipleship Publications International (DPI), the movement's publishing house, and during my time in the field watched six Kingdom News Network (KNN) productions, ICOC's video/film company. In addition, I transcribed and analyzed fifteen audiotaped sermons and testimonies from leaders across the country. As the movement began to fall apart in 2003–2004, I continued to pay careful attention to the on-line ICOC-related websites, spoke several times with a City COC member whom I had grown close to, and conducted two formal and three informal interviews with members from different congregations across the United States.

My ethnographic story and analysis is based on careful and repeated review of each of these data sources for common themes, which informed coding categories that I then used to analyze data systematically (Glaser and Strauss 1967). Without exception, family rose to the forefront as a most prominent theme: healing families, destroying families, creating families, and dismantling families were the focus of numerous individual narratives, group rhetoric, and day-to-day social interaction.

A Portrait of "Awesome Families"

Ann, a thirty-five-year-old biracial woman (mother black, father white) and mother of four, and her husband Bob, a thirty-four-year-old African American former computer programmer, were paid church leaders in charge of City COC's Families Ministries. Sitting in Ann's living room, my eight-month-old daughter asleep in a car seat beside me and her seven-month-old daughter wide awake and smiling in Ann's arms, I asked her what was the first thing that came to mind when I said the word "family." Ann paused for a brief moment, took a deep breath, and then related a tragic loss the City COC community had recently experienced; a teenager had just died from an advanced stage of cancer only months after diagnosis. Ann's description of the events surrounding her young "church sister's" death exemplifies the way most members talked about their church relationships:

> Without God, there's no real family. Her family [biological] wasn't enough . . . to get her through that time. What really moved her family [biological] was the family [church family] that she had around her. On her casket, at the end of the casket . . . have you ever seen at the end of the casket they put a bouquet of flowers? Well, she had a living grandmother and grandfather and if the mom doesn't put the flowers there then the grandparents would, or you know,

> a godparent or aunts or uncles or whatever. So her mom decided, "I just want to give her a rose," and "I want it to be in her hand." So then the space [for the flowers on the casket] was left open and the shepherding couple in the church are very close to the family and have become like a substitute grandparent couple, and so they asked if "you [biological grandparents] would mind if we put the flowers at the end of the casket." And the grandparents were like, yeah, because you were the grandparents. You were there. You filled that spot in her life where they weren't able to. . . . She was so needy of that . . . so needy of a mom and a dad figure that were together because her mom was a single mom and just to see that role fulfilled. That's what God's family does. . . .
>
> It's hard, in breathing and dying and all of that . . . through the ups and downs in the hospital. . . . She really turned that hospital upside down. . . . I don't know if you heard about it but they are changing the policy at the hospital because of her and the way she died, the choices she made. All the people [church members] that were in her room, who sang to her when she died, and we sang to her all day long and then we took a break and then at the very end we sang again all of her favorite songs. She had told the doctors that morning, "I'm doing it [dying] my way. I'm doing it my way. This is the way I know God wants me to do it and I know it's an important hospital policy but I have to do it my way because this is what God wants me to do." That's an eighteen-year-old girl.
>
> You know, where so many people have come from broken homes, I mean who do we know that doesn't come from a broken home? And God's family fills that all in. You know, the pieces that are empty single parents, where there's a need for grandparents or in a marriage . . . that's what the family [church] does and it's like the *real* [her emphasis] family. Because I know family, everybody says I come from a family, but it's different to have a *real* [her emphasis] family, you know.

Ann's story of her young church sister's hospital experience presents an image of her church family as both soothing and challenging the medicalization of death: in her narrative, a heroic City COC family stepped in, broke prevailing institutional rules and regulations, and succeeded in returning a lonely and frightening medical experience into a family affair. Her "real" family soothed and healed in the face of death in a way that medical professionals and biological families could not.

Jeremy, a thirty-five-year-old white married electrician, told a similar story of community comfort in mourning. We sat in his wooded backyard at a picnic table while his wife, Alicia, cleaned the kitchen, waving to us periodically through the window over her kitchen sink. Jeremy confessed he was nervous about the interview. An hour passed and he said, "This isn't so bad." Soon after, this self-described "Mr. Spock" personality (a reference to the emotionless Vulcan character in the *Star Trek* television series) was in tears remembering a dear church "brother" who had recently died:

> We had a brother of ours die very suddenly around Christmastime. Boy, it was . . . (*he cries*) . . . he just turned forty a week prior. And he and I were discipling partners for a while, he and his wife. He has two kids. He came to our house, he and his family came to our house for dinner the night before it happened. So we were very grateful that we had the opportunity to really be with one another. Whenever I talk about it, I get a little choked up. But afterwards, he had a big family, a huge [biological] family, and one of his sisters volunteered her house as the reception place, and of course we had a lot of people to feed at that point so there was no problem. . . . The turnout, the support for that [from City COC members] was enormous. It was mind-boggling. I mean it boggled my mind and I'm sure it boggled the minds of the family members of John [the deceased] who were not disciples [church members] because, well just getting everything accomplished. . . . And the support doesn't stop there, we are still in her [the wife of the deceased] life.

Jeremy, like Ann, presented the involvement of his church family as extraordinary for a religious community today; he was taken aback by the closeness and caring that he understood as being absent in other congregations.

All members told stories of how church brothers and sisters filled "missing spaces," expanses created by what they bemoaned as the decay of truly intimate and caring familial relationships in outside society, physical and emotional distance resulting from geographic separation, widespread divorce, and a general dysfunction in secular family life. Jeremy said that before they joined the church he and his wife did not communicate well, that he often withdrew in silence when she confronted him with her concerns in what they both described as a verbally abusive manner. As his wife Alicia, a thirty-year-old white elementary school teacher, described it, their marriage was "stinkin' big time" before they became church family members.

Members also spoke frequently of how the church had helped heal biological/family of origin relationships and how they hoped to, with the help of their church community, create and sustain extraordinary relationships with their children. They spoke of raising children who would reach "awesome" life goals and remain faithful Christians in the ICOC movement. Their confidence echoed that of the movement's leader and founder, Kip McKean, who held his children up as examples of how influential church family counselors could be. In "Revolution through Restoration II," printed in a mid-1990s ICOC movement newsletter, McKean, who lived in Los Angeles, offered a description of his own family, an example of what God and the church could do:

> It seems incredible, but I am now the father of a teenager, Olivia, who turned 13 in May. My sons, Sean and Eric are 11 and 9 respectively. . . . I coached Eric's basketball team and the Lord blessed us with the championship and a 14–0 season. Eric averaged 18 points per game in the season and 25 points per game in the playoffs as he led the league in scoring. Sean played point guard and was selected in his league for the all-star basketball team the only fifth-grader among sixth-graders. Also, he was just elected president of his elementary school student council for next year. Olivia, student council president of her elementary school last year, went on to break the mile record at her junior high and tied the record for the 440-yard run. She also recently qualified for the national Miss Pre-Teen Pageant. All three have made straight A's this year and have been active in a tennis academy where they have reached out to and baptized their coach.

McKean presented his children as embodying a number of dearly held gendered values: his boys not only played sports but also were competitive and won; his daughter also excelled in sports, but at the same time she was considered beautiful enough to qualify for a national beauty pageant; all three achieved the highest marks in school—"straight A's." Several years later, I heard Elena McKean speak at a regional ICOC conference in New England to a crowd of over two thousand women. Dressed in a bright red business suit, she pointed out her daughter, Olivia, who continued to embody success as a young woman: she was a first semester freshman at Harvard University and a "nationally ranked tennis player," her mother boasted. Even though this Ivy League attendance meant that her daughter lived four thousand miles away from Los Angeles, Elena said she felt Olivia was safe with "brothers and sisters" in the "Kingdom" in New England.

Kip and Elena McKean are an interethnic married couple. Elena is a light-skinned Latina born in Cuba. Kip is white, born in Indianapolis in 1954. The McKeans presented the church family that they and a small group of Christians gave birth to in the late 1970s as a "multiracial, international community of believers" (McKean 1994). City COC interracial/ethnic married couples spoke of their church community as providing them with tangible emotional supports—a kind of built-in biracial, interracial, and interethnic support group. Church members described family healing experiences as possible because they had access to "free counseling all the time." Their counseling stories were of redemption from both sin and illness—of turning sinful, sick families into saved, healthy ones. The church family healing methods they spoke of were both religious and therapeutic—an alluring late twentieth-century combination of sacred family community, divine power, and therapeutic methods. Members painted portraits of families that could not be found anywhere else, families that could overcome the very worst of contemporary relational pitfalls.

Church Family Dysfunction—Another Portrait

Despite the general message of church family dysfunction that permeated most ex-member narratives, individual interviews I conducted with former members and my attendance at ex-member support groups revealed that many ex-members were ambivalent about the church. Most expressed that they felt they would always miss their "church brothers and sisters." One ex-member, a young white man, had tears in his eyes when speaking of a "black brother" whom he missed tremendously and who would not return his calls. Although these ex-members' narratives were about disengaging from the group and frequently included descriptions of uncomfortable and contentious breakups with church members, when I asked former members during formal interviews what they missed most about being a member of the ICOC, they expressed regret at the loss of intimate relationships, church friends, the "brothers and sisters" that they had grown so close to and had come to trust with their deepest hopes, dreams, and intimate relationships. They seemed in mourning, grieving the loss of a family dream left unfulfilled. The same feeling of loss and sorrow filled many members' reflections as the unified movement fell apart in 2003–2004.

In 2002, an ironic and significant incident of in-group family dysfunction developed. The group's founder and charismatic leader, Kip McKean, amid rumors of top leadership quarrels, admitted that his "leadership in recent years" had damaged both the ICOC and his own nuclear family household (ICOC official website: 12/2002): "My most significant sin is arrogance—thinking I am always right, not listening to the counsel of my brothers, and not seeking discipling [church counseling] for my life, ministry and family." He continued, "I have failed to build strong, mutually helpful relationships," and he listed his character sins as "anger," "arrogance," and "lack of respect" for other church leaders. These character sins, he confessed, have surfaced in his "family as well." So, he told the ICOC international community, "I have decided to resign." His daughter, Olivia, the supposedly perfect ICOC "Kingdom Kid," had discovered a life outside the church at Harvard and left the movement—a move that reflected badly on McKean, who had said more than once that if a child leaves the church, something is wrong with the parents. In the months after McKean's resignation and admission of family and character flaws, various ICOC congregations across the globe expressed doubt about whether or not the particular mandatory religio-therapeutic system McKean and other top leaders gave birth to, *discipling*, was potentially detrimental to their development of awesome families. Several leaders of congregations across the world posted resignation letters on-line, naming the ICOC's healing promise as failing and its practices as abusive. Leaders and members also came to seriously question the organization's exclusive claims: that to be saved one must be a practicing disciple in ICOC's Kingdom of God. Some leaders came to post serious and damning criticisms on ICOC-related websites. As I write in 2004, the unified movement has essentially fallen.

In 2004, the members that I came to know well in the City COC congregation are working hard to preserve the character of *real family* that they so deeply treasured as they try to understand how they could have believed so deeply in a church community based on submission to hierarchy and authority. They are in the process of shaping a democratic and autonomous church body, as are many of the church family communities to which the ICOC movement gave birth. This book captures a point in time, a time when these individuals were powerfully drawn to the ICOC's vision of Christian salvation and its quixotic promise of family and relational healing.

Religion and Medical Therapeutic Culture

Many have argued that our most dominant social institutions such as the family and religion, as well as our political, judicial, and educational systems, support and legitimate a therapeutic ethos (Rieff 1966; Bellah et al. 1985; Conrad and Schneider 1992; Nolan 1998; Lasch-Quinn 2001). How do we fix a dysfunctional family? We go to family counseling. How do we mend a troubled intimate sexual relationship or marriage? We go to couples' counseling. How do we heal our addictions and illnesses? We pledge allegiance to twelve-step programs, we go to psychologists' or psychiatrists' offices, we log on to web-based self-help communities, and we watch therapeutic television programs like the *Oprah Winfrey Show* and *Dr. Phil*. How do we make sure that our places of work or volunteer organizations are healthy environments for workers? We conduct surveys so that employees and members can express their feelings, we hold encounter groups so that employees, managers, and group members can be heard "honestly" and "truthfully." How do we deal with a young student who fidgets and cannot concentrate? We send the child to therapeutic "experts," who perhaps then suggest medication, psychiatric drugs like Ritalin and Adderall. We even see our animals and pets through a therapeutic lens: we certify select dogs with a therapeutic stamp of healing proficiency, "therapy dogs" ready to comfort the bereaved and emotionally disturbed. Expectations and legitimations of a therapeutic approach to self-improvement are everywhere today; so when ICOC members heard their church leaders promise to fix their "dysfunctional" families and heal their relational "cancers" by using various religio-therapeutic methods and practices, they were drawn to a familiar language and powerful cultural ethos that already pervaded their lives in late twentieth-century U.S. society.

Most valuable in ICOC's presentation of a sacred healing community was how the movement would help members address *particular* social relational ills at the turn of the twenty-first century. Managing gendered selves was a prominent group theme: shaping ideal Christian fathers and husbands, mothers and wives, and church sisters and brothers. Family and gender disease inside members was sometimes presented as the residue of parents who, confused by feminism and fluctuating gender expectations, failed to communicate well with their children and teach them how to be a fulfilled woman or man in today's society. Sometimes the sins ICOC therapists pledged to purge were family of origin acts of domestic violence—physical, sexual, and mental abuses perpetrated by parents that "ate away" at members and potential converts, inhibiting their ability to love others and themselves. The sins of parents and members that surfaced as illness and disease in ICOC discourse were specific to this historical period, an array of contemporary family problems and dilemmas that echoed conservative religious voices of the late twentieth and early twenty-first century: "dysfunctional" families, "broken homes," divorce, homosexuality, teen pregnancy, drug use, rising numbers of mothers entering the workforce, single motherhood, and "absent" fathers.

The ICOC, like other conservative Christian groups, strove to clarify gender in marriage and family, but their ideology was far from clear. Yet members were drawn to the extraordinary character of mandatory church marriage counseling that offered daily assistance and constant intervention in navigating complicated gender relationships. The ICOC promised resolution and management of several deeply felt cultural contradictions regarding families and kin through their "awesome" group family healing system. Ironically, as I come to argue in this ethnography, ICOC's promise to clarify contradictions often resulted in a higher state of confusion—a dizzying condition resulting from explicitly authoritative group practices and pressures to be extremely productive in bringing new converts to the Kingdom.

"Awesome Families"

One of the greatest benefits of doing ethnographic research in a tightly bound primary group like the City COC congregation is that it allows us to see particular kinds of micro-social relationships that would otherwise be difficult to capture. We hear and observe firsthand how members talk about and enact meaningful group experiences within potentially authoritarian structures. As other sociologists of religion have suggested (Beckford 1985), "deviant" religious groups like the ICOC, as they work to articulate radical new structures and ideas, bring into focus taken-for-granted routines and beliefs deeply embedded in our social structure—assumptions that may be otherwise difficult to see. The micro-social life I observed and recorded in this controversial movement indeed reveals a great deal about widespread social values and cultural practices at the end of the twentieth and beginning of the twenty-first century. This ethnography demonstrates the pervasive power of therapeutic beliefs and practices, the dilemmas of contemporary family life, and the limits of organizations that attempt to offer a structural panacea for building intimate relationships.

Chapter 1, "Sacred Counsel: 'Ambassadors for God,'" outlines ICOC's creation story and formal movement presentation of group purpose, history, and healing effectiveness. I describe here the architecture of the movement's controversial religio-therapeutic healing system. I explore the movement's extreme focus on "building the Kingdom" and its attempts to maintain a community where members were called to enact both submission to authority and individual choice. The ICOC structure was explicitly authoritative, members were called to submit daily to leaders and assigned counselors, yet they claimed their system was exceptionally committed to maintaining individuality. This chapter explores how a therapeutic group discourse and language managed to sustain such extreme systematic contradictions. I use Ann Swidler's (2001) work on "culture in action" to think about the creative ways that individual leaders and members pulled from family, religious, and therapeutic discourses to present and legitimate the ICOC system as an ideal and productive approach, despite such highly contradictory ideals and practices.

One of members' most vocalized fears was of living in a contemporary divorce culture where they perceived heterosexual marriage as a dying social institution. Chapter 2, "An Unsinkable Raft in a Foreboding Divorce Culture," illustrates members' presentation of discipling as the most foolproof marriage counseling system available. Members expressed a strong belief that marriage discipling, being assigned a mandatory husband/wife counseling team, would produce marriages that lasted forever, great sex, romance, and better marital communication skills. I show how individual narratives of heroic "marriage saves," shaped by ICOC's formal rhetoric and script, came to legitimate the movement's marriage counseling system. I also pay particular attention to the constant, inescapable social processes of gender construction, the particular challenges that contemporary society poses to these processes, and how ICOC disciplers were depicted as managing these constructions.

Chapter 3, "Collective Performances of Healing," demonstrates how members' stories of family healing were affirmed and made sacred through large regional ICOC events. This chapter takes us into the world of this movement's high-energy ritual performances and, drawing from classical and contemporary social theory, analyzes the power and meaning of such large-scale theatrical religious events and the use of media in contemporary religions.

Chapter 4, "In with the Old and the New," explores the various ways that discipling was talked about as a cure for "dysfunctional" families of origin. The idea that each member should be unwavering in his or her long-term commitment to evangelizing family members was prevalent. Underlying our culture's most basic understandings of the concept of family and kin is the notion that a family is supposed to be able to take care of its members. Members were exceptionally attached to the idea that one day their biological family/family of origin would join them as new family members, brothers and sisters in the ICOC Kingdom of God. Implicit in this goal was the effort of members to heal relational wounds with their family and kin. I show how many members tried to reconcile their faith in ICOC's healing power with the reality of continued estrangement and how widespread therapeutic practices and ideals fueled their presentation of selves as loyal biological/family of origin members.

Chapter 5, "Awesome Kids," illustrates how the ICOC presented its discipling community as exceptionally able to help members raise their children. Group stories presented the discipling community as able to keep children close to their parents and safe from a dangerous outside culture of "sex," "drugs," "suicide," and "consumerism." The ICOC community argued that as members of God's modern-day movement, children would shed consumer identities, abstain from sex and drugs, engage in peacemaking among their peers, and develop lifelong positive and communicative relationships with their parents. I discuss how ICOC congregations maintained therapeutic (each teen was assigned a church counselor) teen and preteen youth groups, as well as a "Kingdom Kids" ministry (ICOC Sunday School/child ministries program). ICOC's therapeutic model did a great deal to alleviate parental concerns. Like other evangelical parents today, ICOC parents talked about how the church enabled them to discipline and raise their children without outside intervention or appeals to secular "therapeutic experts." Ironically, by pledging submission to an authoritative church counseling system intimately involved in their children's lives, they potentially gave up a great deal of parental control and involvement.

Chapter 6, "Brothers and Sisters for the Kingdom of God," illustrates the constant construction of church family as *real* family. Members, in narratives and through social interaction, shaped their relationships with other church members as family. Naming community members as "brothers and sisters," as it has in many religious groups throughout history, established ties of reciprocity and duties to movement goals. I explore here the highly complex gendered nature of church roles as brothers and sisters. To be a true brother in the church was to be engaged in a constant effort to become a physically and spiritually strong and sensitive Kingdom worker, winning converts for the Kingdom of God and counseling other church brothers. Sisters in the Kingdom were called to be physically fit and spiritually strong evangelical workers as well. Like Christians involved in early twentieth-century organizations like the YMCA, YWCA, and the Christian Endeavor Society, ICOC family members were, both men and women, called to be church "warriors," winning souls for Christ. I explore how the pressures of living as warrior-like evangelical sisters and brothers intensified the contradictions members felt in their loyalties and gendered roles in church and nuclear family relationships.

In the final chapter, "A Kingdom That Promised Too Much," I offer an explanation for the growth and downfall of the ICOC movement.

I point to several individual and organizational forces at work in both the construction and dissolution of the unified ICOC churches. Most important, I stress how many members were pushed to a point where they were trying to balance too many contradictory cultural ideas and practices; in their search for relational clarity, they too often felt torn between conflicting notions of gender, family, and Christian purpose. They were constantly balancing, in narrative presentation and everyday interactions, leaderships' demands for submission to church authority and group ideals of individualism and personal choice. Church brothers and sisters also became seriously overburdened in their efforts to provide family and marriage therapy, live up to leaders' unrealistic expectations for converting large numbers of new members, and maintain their own wage work and nuclear family responsibilities. These heightened contradictions and responsibilities left the movement ripe for dissension and dissolution.

Chapter 1

Sacred Counsel: "Ambassadors for God"

> "Miracle" is the defining word of the decade and a half since our attack against the darkness was launched. In Boston scarcely more than fourteen years ago, 30 would-be disciples gathered in the living room of Bob and Pat Gempel. They came together bounded by the blood of Jesus, the Spirit of our God, the Bible as the only inspired and inerrant Scriptures and a conviction that the only totally committed could be members of the Lexington Church of Christ (later renamed Boston). In the next few months the Bible doctrine from Acts 11:26 of Saved=Christian=Disciple was crystallized. The Spirit then gave us a deep conviction that only these baptized disciples comprise God's kingdom on earth. This was and still is the true church of Jesus.
>
> — Evangelization Proclamation, signed by movement leaders 2/4/94

Most organizations have a creation story, a founder's vision that drives goals and ideals. Organizations benefit from telling these stories, members like to hear them; for both they serve as a sacred ritual of legitimation (Berger 1967; Berger and Luckmann 1966). They tell these stories frequently. In religious community, the story takes on a sacred life, made real, powerful, and often credited to divine design. These creation stories are told over and over again, in different settings, through various mediums and with creative variation. The story gives life to group symbols and worldview, their practices and beliefs articulated in the retelling of origins of faith-bound community. For some communities, group legend details the experiences and motivations of a charismatic leader, a divinely chosen inventor. In the ICOC, Kip McKean was this voice and character, and his divinely inspired story of movement construction supported his charismatic authority and legitimized the movement.[1]

The ICOC birthing story, wrapped in a myth of unmatched evangelical growth, was in the forefront of group discourse. McKean told the story himself, from pulpits and in group publications, and members and leaders recounted the birth during services, interviews, Bible studies, and more informal social events. The organization performed the story using various mediums: through music, their publishing house, Discipleship Publications International (DPI), and their video/film production company, Kingdom News Network (KNN).

In 1992, McKean recaps the history of the movement in his famous movement essay entitled "Revolution through Restoration: From Jerusalem to Rome: From Boston to Moscow" (RR). In a section entitled "Seeds of Faith," McKean lays ground with an autobiographical sketch worthy of charismatic devotion:

> I was born in Indianapolis, Indiana, on May 31, 1954. Like many young men of the '60s, I was inspired by those who refused to compromise and were willing to sacrifice everything for "the worthy cause." This conviction was also deep in my family's heritage as we have always been called higher by the courage of one of our ancestors, Thomas McKean. He not only signed the Declaration of Independence, but also was the President of the Congress of Confederation, the highest office in the land, when news arrived from General Washington that the British had surrendered. My father, serving as an admiral in the U.S. Navy, not only became a strong influence, but also my early role model for leadership and excellence. Always very outgoing and warm, my mother gave me a great passion for life. My heroes became John F. Kennedy and Dr. Martin Luther King, Jr. who paid the ultimate price for their dreams. In time, my greatest hero became Jesus.

In this brief description of personal motivation and construction of self, McKean locates his passion in several powerful cultural symbols. He invokes the will and mission of the civil rights movement, the bravery of the "founding fathers," the valor and status afforded a military officer, and the reverence and respect of political and social figures who died for their beliefs. McKean's intent and effect is a defense of moral ground and purpose that drove ICOC vision and shaped a charismatic character.

Armed with his legacy of moral uprightness, in RR McKean recounts his educational and theological pursuits, his work with the Crossroads campus outreach program in the 1970s, and his disillusionment with what he saw as a lethargic Mainline Church of Christ community in "slow decline." McKean came to form his own vision of a "Bible church." Accepting a ministerial position in Lexington Church of Christ in Lexington, Massachusetts, in the late 1970s, he challenged his new congregation to follow his vision: "I told the people in that congregation that in order for me to come, every member must vow to be (in the terminology of that day) 'totally committed.' *On June 1, 1979, history was made as 30 would-be disciples gathered on a Friday night in the living room of Bob and Pat Gempel.* Our collective vision was a church where not only the college students were totally committed, but also the teens, singles, marrieds and senior citizens. This was a radical concept not witnessed in any other church or movement in my experience to this day." This "radical" beginning, the birthing of the movement in the Gempels' living room, was told and retold in the community, each repetition cushioned in a rhetoric of phenomenal evangelical growth and success. The strong emphasis on church growth touted alongside early vision was especially prominent in group discourse in the mid- to late 1990s at the height of the movement.

In 1994, the leaders of the movement gathered for a historic moment, the signing of their "Evangelization Proclamation." This document was printed in script lettering with the signatures of major men and women church leaders at the bottom and distributed to members through various publications over the years. The document's title and style bring to mind important U.S. historical documents like the Emancipation Proclamation and the Declaration of Independence—a visual legitimation of democratic revolution. ICOC's proclamation begins, *"On this fourth day of February, in the year of our Lord on thousand nine hundred and ninety-four, we the World Sector Leaders issue this proclamation."* And continues, *"As God's modern-day movement, the time is now for each true disciple to go far beyond any feat of faith or deeds of daring witnessed to this hour. In this proclamation, we issue such a challenge."* The proclamation goes on to tell that familiar story of the thirty would-be disciples in the Gemples' living room planting a movement that had grown significantly: "God in his grace and mercy has blessed his modern-day movement of true Christians as our churches now number 146 with an attendance of over 75,000!" The document also notes significant points in the history of the church and world affairs—depictions of ICOC evangelical effort coinciding with world narratives of the conquering of "evil" political forces. For example: *"Eight years ago a miracle happened in Johannesburg, where in the church blacks and whites did not merely coexist, but for the first time hugged one another in the midst of apartheid and under the threat of extremists."* And, *"Three short years ago God melted the Iron Curtain. The Moscow Church of Christ was planted and already has over 2,000 in attendance."* The proclamation ends with a financial commitment to evangelizing the world, and a passionate appeal to church members: *"Nationals must ready themselves to return to their homelands. Of ultimate necessity for all of us is fervent prayer unseen in our day. Only zealous prayer will allow God to empower, embolden, and employ each of us to fulfill our individual destiny, and thus this global proclamation."*

Sermons and official DPI and KNN movement propaganda frequently featured charts and graphs highlighting impressive statistics and images that supported the idea of "radical," "awesome," and "mind-blowing" growth. Any accurate accounting of ICOC membership, dropout rate, and growth is beyond reach here. Critics of the movement claimed a large dropout rate, and ex-members told me that people were "heading out the back door as fast as members were baptizing new ones." The small three-hundred-member congregation where I conducted field studies through the years boasted of international movement growth in the mid- to late 1990s, but the number of local members stayed fairly constant. I saw new faces here and there, but certainly not the growth touted in formal group rhetoric. Former members from other sectors around the country voiced similar observations in my formal interviews. In addition, the "mind-blowing" numbers that supported the idea of awesome ICOC growth and were showcased in group literature and promotions were based on Sunday church attendance, which would include members and their guests. Actual membership numbers were rarely printed in DPI and KNN publications. Regardless of the lack of a true count of membership and dropout rate, it is clear that McKean and church leaders were somewhat successful in their use of media and publications to create at least an *illusion* of exceptional growth until the fall of the unified movement in 2003–2004.

KNN produced video newsreels resembling a local news and television magazine format. These videos highlighted the growth and establishment of the ICOC movement across the nation and the world, and were shown during weekly services and in the privacy of members' homes to potential converts and members. I saw several of these videos, and each stressed the exceptional growth of the movement across the globe, telling the legend of McKean and his thirty would-be disciples.

I sat in the living room of a City COC leader during my first month in the field and watched one of these KNN news programs. In this video, the makers stressed church growth, noting that MTV had called them the "fastest growing alternative religion in the country today." Leadership couples from around the nation and world were interviewed about their "awesome" experiences in the church. A shot of the famous Gempel living room where McKean, his wife, and the other disciples met to discuss the "plan" held our attention for a moment. All images presented a passionate and active ICOC evangelical mission, each member depicted as a team player on the winning side. The team was one that would change the world: a KNN newscaster announced that the Johannesburg church was planted in South Africa *before* (my emphasis) the end of segregation. They showed a picture of a South African church with blacks and whites worshipping together, hugging each other—an image reinforcing formal group rhetoric that promoted the ICOC community as extraordinarily racially diverse (Jenkins 2003). The video message seemed to be that the ICOC's planting a church in South Africa was in some way related to the end of apartheid. With similar intent, the video stressed that the church was planted in Berlin "one month" before the fall of the Berlin Wall. We saw photos of the Berlin ICOC church and then people chopping away at the wall victoriously. The message throughout the newsreel was clear: the ICOC movement was part of some divine plan to save the world from a host of evils. The video ended with clips of members all over the world being baptized in pools, oceans, and rivers.

Each DPI and KNN print and video representation of the creation of the movement, its exceptional multiracial/cultural character, and its evangelical success fueled the divinely inspired authority of McKean's discipling movement and his corps of charismatic evangelists. In KNN's *Jubilee 2000*, a printed brochure, a prominent movement leader, Roger Lamb, promotes the ICOC memoir of exceptional growth with evangelical fervor:

> When God laid on the heart of Kip McKean to challenge the 30 would-be disciples in the Gempels living room in Boston to be totally committed to God and to be evangelistic, who would have dreamed that we would see 403 churches of disciples in 171 nations of the world today? Who would have dreamed that the Cold War, apartheid, the Bamboo Curtain and the wall between North and South Korea would all be removed so that God's Kingdom could forcefully advance the message of salvation and discipleship to people forbidden from hearing the Scriptures? The middle of a miracle may be where people appreciate it the least. . . . Let us see how uniquely and powerfully God has moved in only 21 years and how he continues the miracle in his modern-day movement. Let us see and "be utterly amazed."

ICOC leaders consistently stressed the exclusive nature of racial/ethnic diversity in their church. Gordon Ferguson, a longtime white leader and church author, writes: "I've never before experienced relationships like these [discipling relationships among diverse members], nor have I seen them. Politics has not produced them; education has not; sports has not; and the arts have not. Divisions in our society are as dramatic as ever. Only Jesus in the heart of disciples, who share his love for God and for the lost, can cultivate such love for one another" (Ferguson 1997, 85). McKean describes his movement as unique: "In the L.A. Church, we have 17% Asian, 18% Black, 41% Caucasian, 23% Latin and 1% Native American. . . . Most denominational congregations are predominantly one skin color or one nationality or one economic group. . . . Other 'churches' often only pay lip service to the multiracial, international communion of believers" (1994). In fact, most Christian congregations in the United States are composed of individuals from similar racial and ethnic backgrounds (Chaves 1998; Emerson and Smith 2000). The City COC (and ICOC movement) were clearly multiracial/ethic. My visual estimate of the racial and ethnic makeup of the City COC congregation was 55 percent white, 25 percent black, 17 percent Hispanic, and 3 percent Asian and Native American. McKean and other leaders used this multiracial/ethnic quality to argue that their movement was divinely inspired and "radical."

An important chapter in the movement's creation story was the genesis of McKean's version of Christian discipleship, ICOC's "radical," as he and members called it, Christian counseling and evangelical system. McKean's interpretation of Christian discipleship was a group feature that set the movement apart from the Mainline Churches of Christ and other evangelical Christian movements. It was an institutional structure that members and leaders credited as providing both exceptional relational counseling for church members and producing church growth. In RR, McKean recounts the generation of his ICOC discipling structure:

> In the Crossroads movement, one another Christianity was expressed in a buddy system called "prayer partners," where each person chose their own "buddy." . . . Building on this concept, I came up with "discipleship partners." In these relationships, the evangelists, elders and women's counselors after discussion and prayer, arranged for an older, stronger Christian to give direction to each of the younger, weaker ones. They were to meet weekly, but have daily contact (Hebrews 3:12, 13). (Obviously, the younger discipleship partner also gives input and advice to the stronger disciple, as in any healthy relationship.) We also saw in Scripture that Jesus primarily trained men through groups—the apostles and the 72 (Luke 10:1–24). Therefore, we began discipleship groups for every Christian. (This group would usually meet at the midweek service.)

McKean argues that these discipling relationships would build healthy selves, healthy families, and church community, but that they would also serve to fashion a prodigious evangelical team. Discipling was the most efficient way to achieve the movement's stated goal: "to evangelize the world in one generation." McKean proclaims, "Through this approach, each Christian could naturally build relationships with other Christians in addition to their discipleship partner," and that "Studies were done by several church growth experts that proved the greater the number of relationships in the church a new Christian possesses is directly proportional to his likelihood of remaining faithful to God" (McKean RR). McKean further legitimates ICOC discipling growth and sacred status by invoking the status of an outside church growth and missiological expert: "Dr. Donald McGavran (considered the father of church growth by the denominational world) told me many years ago, 'You are the only church with a plan to plant churches in every nation of the world in one generation.' Once more, I believe this marks us as God's true and only modern movement" (McKean RR II).

McKean constructs his thriving discipling movement using language like "revolutionary" and "radical." To emphasize the revolutionary zeal of the movement he presents himself as a descendant of a signer of the Declaration of Independence, he identifies with leaders of the civil rights movement, and he draws on images of the movement as divinely placed to witness and take advantage of the end of apartheid and other significant worldly events. Members, too, constantly used the words "radical" and "revolutionary" to describe their movement. Formal live performances of this revolutionary character were made through music and theatrical presentations.

I attended a large outdoor regional gathering early in my field studies. Approximately two thousand members had gathered for services and to see the Radicals, the movement's own Christian rock band, film their new music video. Video cameras on scaffolding swung in and out of view, and a large blue stage backdrop with a map of the world read, in large red letters, "Radical Love, it's a love that's heard around the world." The theme song was titled "It's a Radical Love." The song began with images of evangelical revolution and the birth of Christ. Instead of a little town in Bethlehem, it began "in a little town called Lexington, in 1985." "It's a Radical Love" then told a story of phenomenal ICOC movement growth ending with the lyric "Now fifteen years have come and gone and see what God has done." In the middle of the song, Kip McKean's nephew (the son of Randy McKean, another charismatic ICOC lead evangelist), who appeared to be approximately twelve, took a position downstage left. He was dressed in an American revolutionary soldier's costume, a drum was strapped around his shoulder, and a bloodied bandage was pasted across his forehead. He played a marching beat as the song continued, "It's a radical love that we share, a love that's heard around the world, shows how much God cares." The crowd cheered, teenagers sang along in front waving arms high in the air. All joined in singing. A revolutionary fervor filled the large outdoor concert stadium, the energy documented in a music video that could be distributed throughout the "Kingdom of God."

The ICOC movement used various contemporary media venues to convey growth and sacralize McKean's vision.[2] Religion and media are closely interrelated in our contemporary setting; people find and express religion through technology daily. Brenda Brasher (2001, 6), for example, reports that she found "more than one million on-line religion websites in operation." The ICOC had an active website as well that highlighted church growth and movement goals. ICOC twenty-first-century technological productions of church birth and growth are not surprising; many religious groups make much use of these powerful evangelical and commitment tools. Video, film, on-line sites, music, and print have enormous potential for reaching great numbers of individuals. Successful media mobilization—the use of video, on-line promotion, and so on—is no doubt a key factor to the success of any social movement in our contemporary world.

Almost all religious communities and organizations use various forms of media in group rituals and presentations of beliefs and practices. They do so because print, film, video, television, and web images have the cultural power to legitimate religious worldview and beliefs, just as they have the power to convince people that a certain product is the best on the market, or that our cities and towns are dangerous places. As one of my major research participants told me, the ICOC switched from written newsletter publication form to the video KNN news program because the video was "more real." Contemporary media forms (video, computer web, burgeoning evangelical publishing industry, music) are late twentieth-, early twenty-first-century evangelical tools of conversion and commitment that have incredible potential for the social production of reality. These contemporary forms are not just a new way of religious expression; they have "profound" meaning. As Jesús Martín-Barbero (1997, 109) argues, "Some churches have been able to transform radio and television into a new, fundamental 'mediation' for the religious experience. That is, the medium is not simply a physical amplification of the voice, but rather adds a quite new dimension to religious contact, religious celebration, and personal religious experience." As we will see throughout this ethnography, use of media served a crucial function in ICOC individual experience, religious identification, community solidarity, the promotion of the movement as exceptional and unique, and ultimately, in its downfall.

McKean and other movement leaders, as charismatic speakers and media-savvy evangelists, employed a wealth of cultural values, beliefs, ideals, and practices as they communicated their legend of unprecedented evangelical success. They framed organizational success through widely recognized narratives of victorious and justified revolution and social change. They told their story with vague, yet powerful, symbolic reference to familiar cultural stories of regimes falling, wars and walls crumbling: the persecution and persistence of first-century Christians, the American Revolution symbolizing freedom from British oppression in the eighteenth century, and twentieth-century victories over communism and racism worldwide. Their story was familiar. It was a story of good versus evil, of righteous resistance and revolution. The validity of their Christian revolution was supported with an organizational "discourse repertoire" that provided an ideological "frame," an interpretive schematic that leaders and members drew from as they constructed discipling as sacred (Gamson 1992; Goffman 1974; Snow and Benford 1988, 1992). The repertoire included, among many other values and practices detailed throughout this ethnography: a strong emphasis on biblical purpose, evangelical productivity, submission to church authority, family and heterosexual marriage as the building blocks of a good society, a therapeutic ethos as a driving force of healthy selves and relationships, and Christian free will and salvation.

THE GRAND MCKEAN evangelical mission, told through ICOC's birth story and myth of exceptional success, was an essential and frequent organizational performance. Complementing this magnificent global vision of a church changing the world, and perhaps even more important to understanding conversion and group commitment, was the day-to-day depiction of the discipling movement as an intimate church family. Most members presented themselves and their fellow church members as friends, counselors, and family members. To be a member of the "Family of God," meeting disciples' needs in intimate and therapeutic ways, was paramount in members' articulation of group experience. What did it mean to live as members of this family that believed so strongly in McKean's vision, his creation story, his commitment to exceptional evangelical growth, and his unique system for healing and constructing family and obtaining salvation and grace? What exactly did local members see and experience in discipling's promises? What cultural problems and moral solutions drove McKean's vision and made sense to thousands of individuals dedicated to improving their selves and intimate relationships? To answer these questions, it is first important to confront the ideological breadth of the movement's discourse repertoire, and the resulting contradictions that built and ultimately helped break apart the unified movement.

Discipling: Commitment, Accountability, and Authority

> Early on I developed a series consisting of nine Bible studies on the "first principles" (Hebrews 6:1–3). The members of the church were called to memorize these studies and then teach others to become Christians. The most impacting was called "Discipleship" where, from my study of the Scripture, I taught was clear in Acts 11:26: SAVED=CHRISTIAN=DISCIPLE, simply meaning that you cannot be saved and you cannot be a true Christian without being a disciple also. I purposely developed this study to draw a sharp biblical distinction between the Lexington (later renamed Boston) Church of Christ and all other groups.
>
> —Kip McKean, RR

ICOC group presentations of discipling resonated clearly with members' cultural "tool kits": the "symbols, stories, rituals, and worldviews" that they understood as significant for actions aimed at improving family relationships in our society (Swidler 1986, 273). Discipling's stress on enduring and extensive family commitment, accountability, and submission to discipline and authority made sense as essential components of intimate church kin relationships. To become part of this growing and highly committed church "family," an individual had to pledge to be a faithful disciple, adhering without reservation to the ideas and practices supporting McKean's discipling system.

The first step on the road to ICOC commitment was to complete an intensive Bible study series called the First Principles study. McKean and group leaders were clear on this order of conversion: "I taught that to be baptized, you must first make a decision to be a disciple and then be baptized" (McKean RR). Potential converts engaged in this Bible study in primarily two-on-one sessions (two current members with one potential convert). I attempted the First Principles study twice during my time in the field. I was forthright about my interest in studying the Bible. I told members I wanted to learn about how they studied with people and why the Bible study series was so integral to becoming a disciple. We acknowledged that this would not be an easy task; they would proceed with the purpose of conversion, and I would participate with the aim of learning and a clear intent not to convert.[3]

My initial attempt was with Natalie, a married white woman in her late twenties with one child. Natalie's husband took care of the congregation's financial affairs and had the church office in his basement. I met Natalie during my first ICOC service where she introduced me to the group leaders who gave me permission to conduct field studies in their congregation. I spent a great deal of my participant observation time during my first year and half at services and events with Natalie by my side. When she moved to an ICOC region far away, I then came to know Pat, a married white woman with three children, who invited me to attend church events with her and volunteered to help with my research. My First Principles study with Natalie did not go very well. We had completed only a few of the studies when she voiced that it was too difficult for her to study the Bible with me if she knew my intent was only to learn more about how the study proceeds. Natalie felt that she could only continue if I had serious motivation to convert. I did not and felt uncomfortable as well. I found Natalie's teaching approach harsh, my answers regarding my vision of God and sacred life created tension, not open debate and conversation.

My experience with Pat, on the other hand, was almost completely different. Our Bible studies were primarily an open exchange of ideas and beliefs. Pat's approach to studying the Bible was much less rigid: she did not always follow the scripted study and was willing to engage in honest debate about images of God and the meaning of religious practice and faith. She was willing to listen to how I combined my background as a Presbyterian, a conservative Jew by choice, and a sociologist of religion. My meetings with Pat and Jill, another white married woman with two small children and the other member present to help Pat teach me, were also part coffee klatch and child care (we all had our children with us, and they played together while we studied). Other members would drop by now and then to join in; on occasion, the study became an informal counseling (discipling) session for Jill.

My sessions with Pat and Jill, rather than ending purposefully as with Natalie, slowly faded without much acknowledgment. The moment at which my studies languished, however, is significant: the point in the First Principles study when I was asked to compose and share what ex-members have called a "sin list." This was supposed to be a list of acts, instances in my life that I was most ashamed of, my biggest "sins." Unlike Pat, Jill, and many of the other members with whom I spent time, I was not willing to reveal what I would consider my major life sins; to do so would have made me feel too vulnerable. I considered my most unfortunate life choices and circumstances private. Given the relaxed and conversational nature of our Bible studies, and probably the fact that she knew my ultimate purpose was to write a book about her church, Pat did not pressure me to detail my deepest regrets or "sins." Some ex-members have argued that this ICOC "sin list" was "dangerous." These lists of personal sins, they reported, would float around the top leadership in ICOC congregations and be used to make members feel guilty, essentially an invasive mechanism of social control. Social theorists have called attention to the ways in which confession has served as a powerful form of social control in various social institutions. One of the most prominent social theorists of the later half of the twentieth century, Michel Foucault (1978, 98), in his major work on the history of sexuality, draws attention to the production of power in "local centers" through the one-on-one relationships of "penitents," and "confessors," and their "directors of conscience." Some former members reported that the leadership was "stuck on sin," that even as disciples made progress in relationships and life problems, leaders persisted in demanding that members admit sinful thoughts and actions.

If you made it through the First Principles Bible study series, which highlighted a number of biblical scriptures presented as proof for McKean's version of discipleship—for example, Matthew 28:19–20, "Therefore go and make disciples of all nations, baptizing them in the name of the Father and of the Son and of the Holy Spirit" (NIV)—you would then be baptized in front of other members. Baptisms were generally performed by your discipler, the member you had studied the Bible with, in a baptismal during services, in a river, a pool, or, as I heard from some, in a leader's Jacuzzi. Once you became a disciple you were then held accountable to living as an ICOC discipler and responsible for, among other things, bringing potential converts to church services with you and always "studying the Bible" with at least one potential convert. Thus, the verb phrase "to disciple" entailed proselytizing—the key, as clearly emphasized by McKean and other top leaders, to the movement's "awesome" growth.

Commitment to discipling had a rudimentary daily expectation in addition to proselytizing: the mandatory, formal interaction of members with their elder "prayer partners" or disciplers. Many members presented this mandatory nature of discipling as unique, echoing Jeremy's sentiment: "In normal life, I don't know of any kind of regular system in place where there is an expectation as to getting counseling." Discipling partners were of the same sex, came from similar life situations, and were assigned by leaders. As a participant observer (and potential convert), I suspect that leaders thought Pat, who was from a similar class, life course position, race, and gender, was a good match for me. Disciplers gave daily advice regarding relationship and life issues; such acts of counseling and advising were called discipling; thus discipling relationships were composed of both the discipled and a discipler. Disciples were told to "confess all" to their disciplers, and leaders stressed often that confession was a key part of these counseling sessions. A clear commitment to voicing all concerns and sins to your discipler was presented as a necessary and nonnegotiable part of being a disciple. Members and leaders offered biblical legitimation for this mandatory confession in verses such as James 5:16: "Therefore confess your sins to each other and pray for each other so that you may be healed. The prayer of a righteous man is powerful and effective."

Disciples were also directly committed to smaller discipleship groups (D-groups) composed of approximately three to four people. Members would meet regularly in these small groups and also weekly in their discipleship family groups (in the City COC congregation, approximately eleven members) of like individuals (e.g., members with children, singles, and young married adults). Married couples were also assigned formal "marriage disciplers," husband and wife teams who routinely counseled and intervened in marriages (the subject of chapter 2 here). ICOC discipleship, to reiterate, having a discipler, being in a discipleship group (a D-group), and participating in a discipleship family group were not optional.

Discipling clearly supported hierarchies of position and knowledge, constantly reinforcing a church "family" with clearly defined distinctions between parental leaders and childlike followers (new converts were named "baby Christians"). "Older Christians," those who had been members for several years, took on the role of spiritual parents responsible for "disciplining" and "guiding" younger members. Each congregation was led by a married evangelist couple and had several paid ministerial leadership positions (such as in the family ministry and singles ministry). The wife of the lead evangelist couple was the head of the congregation's "women's ministry," a formal structure set up by McKean and other core leaders in the early years. Congregations also had nonpaid ministerial leadership positions such as those in charge of the teen and youth ministries, and a number of "shepherding couples," married couples who did a great deal of the congregation's family and marriage counseling. Members and official church publications insisted that all leaders were discipled by "older Christians" (meaning number of years as an ICOC disciple). Even Kip McKean and other top leaders in the organization talked about being discipled by one another.

Formal group presentations and individual member and ex-member narratives made clear that submission and accountability to the authority of disciplers and church leaders was key if you were to reap the benefits of discipling as a healing system. Gordon Ferguson, longtime ICOC author and charismatic evangelist, in his DPI text, *Discipling: God's Plan to Train and Transform His People*, draws from cultural values and ideals of relationship in family, work, and school to legitimate this authority: "There is really nothing here [in discipling] that is surprising. Can you imagine any business in the world without some form of accountability? Can you imagine any school without it, or any family? In areas outside of religion, accountability is absolutely expected" (Ferguson 1997, 102). Here, Ferguson presents commitment and accountability to the discipling system as no different from any other core social institution where you should maintain loyalty and accountability; submission to authority is just the way things are. Ferguson adds that authority is a necessary ground for social life on biblical grounds: "God placed leadership in the church in order to lead his people to maturity and productivity (Ephesians 4:11–16)" (Ferguson 1997, 189). Furthermore, he notes that "God has designated authority in several areas, including the church. The broad list would be: 1. Government (Romans 13:1–7; 1 Peter 2:13–17; 2. Masters (Employers)—Colossians 3:22–24; 1 Peter 2:18–20; 3. Husbands—Ephesians 5:22–25; 1 Peter 3:1–6; 4. Parents—Ephesians 6:1–3; 5. Church leaders—1 Thessalonians 5:12–13" (1997, 190).

Ferguson further describes the breakdown of disciplers' authority and power in ways that resonated with members' cultural tool kits—an understanding of the inevitability and necessity of authoritative relationships in various institutional worlds: "Relational authority occurs when a family member or trusted friend has some influence on our decisions. Knowledge authority is present when we allow people with training and experience to exercise the influence of their expertise. Positional authority is that exerted by a designated official, such as an officer in the military or a manager in the workplace" (Ferguson 1997, 189). In each of these social realms, submission is presented as a natural part of our social world, as a real and necessary part of family and other primary institutional relationships.

One way that a strong commitment to one's discipler, D-group, and the discipling family group was routinely performed was in the frequent interaction and absorption of members in each other's daily lives. Kip McKean and other church leaders explicitly called for members to be in "daily contact" (physical or phone) with formal discipling partners and to interact frequently with D-groups and discipling family groups (weekly Bible studies, prayer groups, and dinners). They were also held accountable to attending group worship services on Sunday mornings and Wednesday evenings with their entire church family. My observations also show that this frequent interaction took place on an informal basis as well; disciples in the family group and larger congregational network dropped by without notice several times while I was in members' homes. Members were constantly on the phone with one another, and cared for each other's children as needs arose. Members talked about this frequent informal church family network as a good thing; someone was always there to help out with household projects or help with a child care crisis.

Members and leaders named this frequent interaction and network construction as something that was missing in outside society and as a clear sign of commitment to the ICOC family of God. This extraordinary commitment to being present in one another's lives had strong cultural resonance for members in a society where loss of community, high geographic mobility, and families separated by great distances have been promoted by many social researchers, local governments, and media as threatening American democracy, family, and civic engagement (Fischer 1991; Putnam 2000). Despite the empirical reality of loss of community, social mobility, and family, the idea that community is an endangered species, and the world of cyberspace and television taking the place of much face-to-face interaction, is perceived by many as a very real social problem.[4] ICOC's discipling community presented a contrary image, a vision of close church kin interacting and forming a reliable community of disciples that was no doubt very appealing.

Lisa's description of a typical week in her life was indicative of how almost all members and ex-members described their day-to-day experiences as members of the church community, a schedule that left limited time for non-church-related activities.[5] Lisa emphasized that she had a "very busy" schedule and suggested that, to save time, we conduct our first interview at the bakery across from her office. She had to leave soon after we began because she and her husband needed to travel to a city one hour away to meet with ICOC youth counselors across their region to discuss how the teen ministries were going and "come up with new ideas for teens." Before Lisa rushed away, we scheduled another meeting at her home, and she answered one last question: "What's a typical week like in your life?" "Well," she took a deep breath and sighed, "it's full." She then went on to describe a week structured by her 8:30 to 4:30 job and her late afternoon, evening, and weekend church responsibilities and activities. Monday evenings were the one night that she and her husband either "sat down with their weekly calendars" or went out on a date or, quite frequently, met with their church marriage counselors. Tuesday after work she held a "study group" at the local library for several young women she discipled in the teen ministries. Wednesday night she, along with three hundred other church members, attended midweek services held in either a high school auditorium or a local hotel conference room. Every other Thursday night she traveled to a city an hour away with her husband and four other local youth counselors to attend the ICOC regional teen ministry leader meeting. On Thursday evenings that she was not out of town, she held an "extra study night" for her teen girls. Friday night she called "teen night," when she, her husband, the other youth counselor couples, and a "big group of teens" did something "fun" like "bowling or a movie." Saturday during the day she and her husband visited either her family, who were also ICOC members, or her husband's family, whom Lisa described as strict Catholics who were "resistant" to their son and daughter-in-law's active ICOC membership. Saturday evening Lisa and her husband went on "double" or "triple" dates with the teens and taught them "how to date" and "talk to each other." On Sunday morning she and her husband then went to church services, which lasted for at least a couple of hours. Sunday evening, Lisa and her husband had a meeting with other "church team (ministry) leader groups."

Ex-members validated the busy schedules and church responsibilities of an ICOC member. One ex-member writes in an apostate newsletter:

> After church, I was expected to fellowship extensively, study the Bible, and attend the leadership meetings which very often last for 2–4 hours. . . . Monday, I was expected to spend time with the men in my bible study. . . . Tuesday, I had my Bible talk meetings, Wednesday, mid-week service, Thursday, I tried to disciple [church counseling] my own men as well as receive my own discipling. Friday, I was expected to go to Campus Devotional and on Saturday, I dated. Where in this schedule does one see enough time for me to be a full-time student, work 30 hours per week, study for school, study the Bible with people, and "share my faith" adequately? (*Right Side Up!* 3)

Ex-members also reported that time demands were especially heavy for local nonpaid female ministry staff, those with huge numbers of church families to oversee, paying jobs, and their own household and children to care for. Three such couples, two current City COC member couples and another former ICOC couple, reported the hefty time and emotional demands they felt as the unpaid congregation, what they called "mom and pop."

The high contact/frequent interaction and group commitment was also validated in my field research by members' need to label "free time."

Members and ex-members recounted schedules that had only one or two (on rare occasions) days of what they called free time. Yet, even free time was somewhat monitored by the group. Leaders would recast members' free time as their "prayer quiet time with God" or a time to sit at a coffee shop and reach out to potential converts. Free time was certainly not talked about by leadership as time to cultivate friendships outside of the church or spend with family of origin (unless an evangelical aim was there). Free time was, most clearly, best used as time to display commitment to the church, to God, and to the evangelical mission of the ICOC.

Although members talked of their church community as "free counseling all the time," such mandatory group commitment rendered therapeutic assistance expensive. Membership came with high time demands as well as extensive monetary commitment (members and ex-members reported donating anywhere from 20 to 30 percent of their yearly income). Monthly church offerings and routine "special donations" were collected at services—not in a plate passed through the pew as is the case in many congregations, but gathered in D-groups that met after the service so that D-group leaders could keep track of offerings. I sat in on a couple of these D-group offering circles, feeling slightly guilty that everyone else was giving their monthly check and I gave nothing (although I did donate a small amount to the "benevolent" wing of the church, HOPE International, on a couple of occasions). The social control this monitored monthly church contribution interaction created was palpable; to not write a check would require explanation in front of others in your D-group.

Congregational leadership meetings were closed, and a careful accounting of church funds was not made available to members. While the group did publish "reports" (for example, of HOPE International's activities), they did not appear to give a detailed financial accounting of donations. Therefore, the fate of high member contributions was often the subject of in-group dissension and ex-member fodder. Some ex-members who had been local leaders told me that less than half the money that they were told was to go to missions did, and that they saw most of the funds go to the salaries of McKean and other top leaders in California. During one ex-member support group meeting, a former member argued that his congregations' donations went to support a local leader's art collection.

Reciprocity in therapeutic effort, serious submission to the authority of disciplers and church leaders, constant evangelical outreach, and monetary giving were not negotiable. To fail on any of these points, members and former members noted, meant the possibility of serious social sanctions: being "marked" and kicked out of the community, shunned by members, gossiped about, and/or being harshly "disciplined" by your discipler. But these costs of membership somehow made sense to many members; they seemed reasonable because they were cast in familiar discourses of institutional authority, therapeutic ethos, family commitment, biblical story, and community building—all beliefs and points of social legitimacy that signaled the development of moral selves and community. Still, the high level of commitment and accountability to fellow disciples and the ICOC movement could (and did for many) translate into the loss of individual choice and will. For many, the ICOC became a community where group members relied too much on each other, an undemocratic church body where ultimate power lay in the hands of lead evangelists and Kip McKean, who made unrealistic evangelical demands. Leaders and members had to work hard to keep this negative vision at bay.

As much as community accountability, commitment, submission to authority, and major monetary giving was a large part of ICOC's discourse repertoire, so was a language of love, mutuality, expressivity, relationality, healthy interdependence, and utilitarian individualism. Such formal and informal presentations worked hard to push back dangerous "cult" labels hurled at the group by ex-members, psychologists, the media, and other church critics. Group discourse stressed the caring, loving, therapeutic side of discipling, a community where individual members were able to better themselves and relationships, and a church where individuals *chose* to engage in relationships of mutual healing and respect. Despite the mandatory and authoritative nature of discipling, members argued, in the words of one disciple, that "the church gives you freedom, security to be who you are and it also gives you incentive to want to change."

Healthy Sacred Selves: Discipling as a Therapeutic Choice

Members named their discipling relationships and community as a superior, sacred, therapeutic choice that enabled positive change in self and relationships. Therapeutic discourse was pervasive in group, as was the likening of church leaders and disciplers to medical and psychological "experts." We live in a society where involvement in therapeutic relationships, turning to therapeutic experts to guide and heal intimate relationships, is seen as a positive and necessary step on the road to healing self and family. Engaging seriously in religio-therapeutic relationships resonated deeply then with members' understanding of bettering themselves in a culture of the self (Bellah et al. 1985; Nolan 1998; Rieff 1966). Therapeutic language, practices, and beliefs were prominent in ICOC's discourse repertoire. To understand such a religious commitment to therapeutic ethos, it is necessary first to explore the historical relationship between religion, medicine, and therapeutic culture.

American Protestantism provided seeds for our concentration on bettering the self. In particular, the brand of Christianity brought to Massachusetts in the seventeenth century by the Puritans supported a more individualistic form of Christianity than the Catholic, Anglican, and Orthodox institutions at the time in Europe. Grounded in Calvinist Reformation theology and influenced by Enlightenment emphasis on individualism, these early Puritans saw the elaborate ritual of the church as getting in the way of their relationship with God, and stressed a more intimate, individual experience of grace as most important. ICOC church members, like those early Puritans, were preoccupied with personal salvation and betterment, as well as the success of their own twentieth-century City on a Hill.

Expressions of individual sin and what to do about it are historically specific. In Puritan minister John Winthrop's seventeenth-century world, association with the "devil" might result in harsh punishments like banishment, the loss of an ear, or even death. In the ICOC, those suffering from contemporary social relational ills like "marriage cancers" were assigned church counselors who proposed religio-therapeutic treatment. ICOC members' and leaders' frequent use of medical and therapeutic metaphor is predictable; religion has historically shaped and been shaped by medical and therapeutic approaches to morality, just as medical and therapeutic endeavors have shaped and been shaped by religious approaches to salvation and moral accountability.[6] For example, a major prescription of modern-day therapeutic mental health intervention, *expressivity*, a practice whereby individuals are to express emotions, feelings, and thoughts in social relationships, can be seen as religious in origin.

The belief that emoting is a major step in healing has been a primary focus of much religious endeavor, seen clearly, for example, in the emotionality of the great evangelical awakenings in this country and the worship style of the Shakers. When hundreds of thousands of individuals in this country today sit in counselors' offices recalling, reflecting, and emoting, or sit in church basements and conference rooms in self-help and twelve-step meetings sharing their histories, hopes, and fears, they are, essentially, engaged in a practice that is not so different from age-old expressive religious healing rituals.

Both physical and emotional expression were encouraged in the ICOC discipling community. Expressivity was a major part of individual and group performance during ICOC events large and small: tearful confessions, physical expressions of love and caring like hugging and kissing. As a participant observer, I had to get used to this norm of physical expression in everyday worship and social interaction. Members I had met only a couple of times would greet me with a hug or kiss, or place an arm around my shoulder or waist as we sang in services. Members talked about discipling and its regular demand for expression of all feelings and issues as a method for bringing about wellness: from healing depression, to improving intimate relationships, to weight management. A major ICOC regional leader, Gordon Ferguson (1997, 37), in arguing the importance of the confession of feeling and emotions in discipling relationships, states that "confession and prayer brings healing. It may well improve physical health, for our spiritual condition definitely affects our bodies. . . . [D]on't wait until an illness and the presence of church leaders motivates you. Be in the habit of doing it, for surely confession is good for the soul."

Over the years, many religious leaders have incorporated medical scientific language and symbol as they work to legitimize their prescriptions for personal salvation. Late nineteenth-century metaphysical groups like Mary Baker Eddy's Christian Science directly challenged the fast-rising authority of scientific medicine with assertions that doctors combat sickness in vain with "material remedies," and that a true path to healing sin and illness through God far surpassed regular doctors' efforts (Eddy 1875, viii). Today's priests, from mainstream denominational leaders to Scientology's L. Ron Hubbard to ICOC top leaders, all adapt religious conceptions of sin, illness, and health to medical paradigms and therapeutic language in specific ways. For example, L. Ron Hubbard's Scientology borrows heavily from psychology and mental health frames, *Dianetics* hailed as the "modern science of mental health" (Hubbard 1950). Like the ICOC, Scientology promises individual betterment through intense one-on-one counseling with a Scientology "auditor," and proposes a "purification program" to right the wrongs of medicine and its coconspirators, a program that claims to literally push toxins from the body, sweating them out from pores so that individuals can experience sound mental and spiritual health (Hubbard 1990). The following message delivered by ICOC leaders exemplifies the medical model at work:[7] "It's not society messing you up, it's that you have sin. . . . [I]f you deal with it, you'll be fine . . . but if you hide it . . . sin will *always come oozing out of your pores, it will be known* [my emphasis]." Like a viral infection ready to surface in an unwelcome bloom of pox, leaders underscored the danger of sin ignored. The cure? Members must throw themselves completely into McKean's discipling system.

The ICOC was born in a social climate where the lines distinguishing "new priests" from "old priests" had blurred. ICOC leaders worked to legitimate discipling as a valid therapeutic choice. Just as other religions must, they had to acknowledge the taken-for-granted status and power of medical and therapeutic professionals, those "new priests" who have risen to power in the past century (Rieff 1966; Zola 1972). Christopher Lasch (1977, 97) emphasizes the implicitly religious character of medical psychology as it rose to prominence in the twentieth century:

> Having attained the status of a full-fledged social science, as the bolder members of the profession now insisted, psychiatry simultaneously claimed, as the modern successor to religion, to represent a comprehensive worldview—in the words of John Money, a scientific "philosophy of life" that replaced discredited beliefs, superstitions, "absolutist" orthodoxies, "ready-made philosophies." Psychiatrists now proposed not merely to treat patients but to change "cultural patterns" as Money put it—to spread the gospel of relativism, tolerance, personal growth, and psychic maturity.

A redefining of religion as a kind of psychotherapy resulted from this "rapprochement between religion and psychiatry." Those who supported "existential and humanistic therapies," notes Lasch (1977, 98), argued that theologians and religious thinkers such as "Martin Buber, and Paul Tillich, had redefined religion as a form of psychotherapy." As the century progressed and the line between religion and psychotherapy blurred, sociologists introduced a number of conceptual categories to account for this confounding: for example, "spiritual groups," "New Age," "healing groups," "human potential movements," and "quasi-religions"—all representations of religio-therapeutic organizations, groups that incorporate both religious and therapeutic symbols and practices.

The ICOC gained momentum during the later decades of the twentieth century, a time when our society experienced a proliferation of mental health and psychological approaches to healing self and relationships, followed by a decline in financial support for such clinical relationships. The numbers of individuals involved in family and individual therapy grew significantly in the 1970s and early 1980s, as did the authority of therapeutic professionals and the number of doctorates in psychology (Herman 1995; Irvine 1999, 37). However, insurance cutbacks and the policies of HMOs at end of century have brought about a decline in clinical psychology and the advancement of support for pharmaceutical alternatives and limited clinical treatment periods. Participation in self-help groups, health and wellness movement alternatives, and quasi-religious healing groups have risen in number to fill the void (Irvine 1999; Philipson 1993; Wuthnow 1994).

ICOC leaders appropriated the discourse and status of psychiatric clergy, our cultural emphasis on health and wellness, and the acceptability of drug therapy for treating depression. The movement had some members who had been trained as medical and psychiatric professionals, who then combined this training with ICOC's own brand of Christian counseling (as is true in many contemporary religious organizations).[8] Disciplers and church leaders spoke of sending disciples who they thought had "serious" problems to these individuals for "extra help." City COC members talked of members who needed medications and were sent to a nearby city to see an ICOC "psychiatric nurse," who they claimed was certified to write prescriptions for depression medication. One woman I came to know in the City COC community had some previous training in a clinical psychology program and saw her work in the church with depressed women as a divinely sanctioned use for her professional counseling skills and knowledge. A few members and ex-members who served as disciplers and local ICOC marriage and family counselors reported, to what they said was the dismay of lead evangelists and top church leadership, that they sent members to professionals outside the church if they felt they had "severe problems."

The ability of ICOC discipling to heal and create healthy sacred selves was legitimated through the rhetorical and practical employment of a pervasive interpersonal ideal of interaction in our therapeutic culture, relationality. Relationality is essentially a belief that individuals will express their needs, emotions, concerns, and issues to another individual or group of individuals who are then responsible for listening and taking into consideration others' feelings, ideas, concerns, and needs as legitimate. The idea that the ICOC discipling family embodied this relational skill was used to signify that relationships within the church were therapeutically productive. This was a community portrayed by members and leaders as responsible for working things out and listening to one another, no "giving up." Relationality was a core group ethic and practice.

Like widespread cultural assumptions about what family should be, disciples were depicted as church family who persisted in relationality. As one member told me, "If we don't work it out, there's a problem. It's not, I don't like it, I'm outta here. So, it's a healthy environment. We listen to each other." Another related this stick-to-itiveness to cultural assumptions of family: "I think what we have is a family. I think what the church is is a family. We go through bumps, we stick together, we believe in each other." Ann Swidler (2001, 77) names this form of loving relationality as a late twentieth-, early twenty-first-century cultural expectation, a "new social skill and style" of social interaction, "accepting oneself and non-judgementally loving others." The capacity to perform relationality has become deeply engrained as a cultural good.

In descriptions and performances of ICOC discipling, members and leaders worked hard to emulate this social skill and interactional style. Sherie delivered a half hour defense during one informal family group function, making sure I understood that discipling was based foremost in mutuality; it is a "give and take" relationship," she insisted. Having an "open heart," she claimed, was being able to tell your discipler if you disagreed with him or her and knowing that your discipler would "listen faithfully" to your concerns. Longtime City COC member Ronny noted, "It is a privilege to have relationships where you don't pay for counseling. I get it for free. I get to give it for free." Discipling was presented by members as firmly grounded in an ethic of relationality. This relationality, as communicated to me by members, appeared to somewhat successfully mute the mandatory, authoritative demands that members, and especially formal movement discourse, stressed were important for discipling to function well. Relationality, as a rising and highly valued social skill and expectation, had the cultural weight to soften authority and submission.

Our present expectations of relationality are ubiquitous. Relationality, as a concept, has grown similar to diversity and multiculturalism, in that we expect individuals and organizations will, at least rhetorically, commit to it. In a very real sense, relationality then has become a widespread social value, an ethic of reciprocal expression and listening with respect that permeates places of business, religious institutions, educational institutions, and our judicial system (Nolan 1998). Perhaps most convincing that an expressive relationality has become a pervasive U.S. social value is the location of such discourse in political rhetoric, language that aims to persuade and impress a broad range of citizens. An example can be found in President Bush's statement to reporters about the possibility of a war with Iraq: "Some very intelligent people are expressing their opinions about Saddam Hussein. . . . I listen very carefully to what they have to say. . . . [I]t's a healthy debate for people to express their opinion" (Bumiller 2002). Former president Bill Clinton's much referenced phrase "I feel your pain" and his touting of the "town meeting" approach to hearing citizens' concerns are representative of this political approach. Present-day politicians, like new religious priests at the turn of the twenty-first century, understand very well that a commitment to relationality will resonate with their constituency.

Ann (the woman who, in the introduction, told the story of her young City COC sister dying) exemplifies this commitment to relationality and an expectation of interdependence in her understanding of how one is meant to progress, grow, and develop a healthy moral self through discipling relationships:

> I think it's [discipling] a combination of learning tools. You know, actually having the tools and then being very sensitive and allowing

> other people to—it's more of a learning how to be interdependent. You know, working hard to develop yourself at the same time knowing that the people around you also influence how you do it. Develop yourself and utilizing what you know. As someone who is in the leadership role, it's a very hard thing because you constantly have to be looked at a certain level. Though what I've realized is I think people have helped me as much as I've helped myself in this sense.

Ann, in her paid church position with her husband as family ministry leaders, held herself to an ethic of relationality that necessitated interdependence, even though, at the same time, she routinely told members that they must submit to "older Christians" and follow disciplers' prescriptions.

The institution of family is an icon of relationality. Social scientists, medical and psychological professionals, government officials and politicians, and religious leaders have often held family up as a model of interdependence. They have promoted family as a primary social relationship where members are disciplined and socialized, where they persevere together through the good and the bad, and most especially, in the later half of the twentieth century, where they are to listen, express emotions, and be willing to seek counseling. Pat's husband, Tom, told me, "My image of family today is what I see in the church, where I have relationships where I am completely vulnerable with other people and they are completely vulnerable to me. To me, that's family—true friends who know each other totally." Presenting the discipling community and practice as embodying relationality resonated with members' interpretation of cultural standards, what family should be and do for one another.

When ICOC potential converts presented themselves to members as coming from a "dysfunctional" or "broken home," leaders and members responded by legitimating their claim to family victim status and promised that their church community would help them "express their pain," and liberate their true Christian loving and forgiving selves. When members and potential converts who struggled in their marriages were told by ICOC leaders that trained church counselors could heal failing "cancerous" unions by encouraging good "listening" and "communication" in marriage, this made an impact. When ICOC leaders told potential converts that they must "tell all their feelings" to "older and wiser" Christians in the church, the objectified goodness of the emotive act rang true. When ICOC leaders told potential converts not only that they must express their deepest feelings, but also that those listening were held accountable to taking their feelings, concerns, and issues as genuine and significant in their own right, a strong belief born of the emotive in our therapeutic culture, relationality, resonated with members' moral understandings of ultimate virtue. An understanding of the individual as ultimately responsible for bettering the self through relationality was at work as well.

Our therapeutic culture supports a curious dialectic: submission to therapeutic experts and interdependence alongside a model of individual power and choice. The idea that through therapeutic practice all individuals are capable of making "good" choices and constructing morally sound selves, relationships, and healthy bodies is at the forefront of discourse in many of our medical, state, educational, and religious rehabilitative institutional efforts. Such voluntarism, "the assumption that individuals create social ties by their free choices, has long been considered a central feature of American culture" (Swidler 2001, 136). Individual choice, motivation, and will has been a driving force and a core U.S. value for centuries, most specifically, a belief in utilitarian individualism, the expectation that all individuals, if they try hard enough, can pull themselves up and succeed. Freewill individualism is a strong and prevalent value in the contemporary U.S. evangelical subculture (Emerson and Smith 2000; Smith et al. 1998).

A Christian model of free will supports utilitarian individualism and group dependence. God gave humans the free will to choose good from evil, to make the most of their own lives, and to determine success and failure. On the other hand, the Christian tradition, and especially the evangelical tradition, supports the idea that individual change and personal salvation take place within a community of believers. When ICOC members and leaders stressed individual choice and free will as driving the success of the discipling system, they were tapping a wealth of Christian and widespread cultural beliefs and expectations, as well as speaking to individuals who had been deeply socialized to value individualism alongside collective achievement in various social institutions. Being a disciple and participating in the discipling system was presented as an individual religious and therapeutic group choice in a number of ways.

First, members and local leaders talked of making a *choice* to be healers. As Pat told me, "It's rewarding to watch people change. God has used you as a vessel. We are ambassadors of God." Making a decision to be a vessel for God and willfully bring about healing in others' lives was a major topic for most of the City COC members I spoke with. Members and leaders also talked a great deal about accepting discipling as a well-thought-out therapeutic choice. In a society where therapy is often a fee for service endeavor, disciples were making a wise consumer choice among the abundance of self-help and wellness products and services in the religious and secular marketplace. Second, members also talked about enacting choice and individual will through discipling by pushing for change in their discipling partner and group assignments. Even though leadership claimed to have final say over who discipled whom, members frequently told stories of successful assertive attempts to switch discipling partners and groups. Third, leadership promoted discipling as an individualized healing process, crafted to cater to the particular needs of each disciple. Gordon Ferguson (1997, 179) advised: "Our expectations in discipling should be . . . individualized. We are all born with different capacities and we have had different influences in our lives shaping those capacities. We have different needs and respond differently to events in our lives, to failures and corrections. Disciplers have to learn what each person he disciples needs and figure out what motivates him best." Ferguson (1997, 181) names this practice "situational discipling," which allows "life situations to determine when we deal more heavily with character issues." Members told stories of tailored discipling techniques, depictions of an individualized approach that worked to balance and justify membership in an authoritative, heavily dependent group as a valid therapeutic choice.

McKean, top movement leaders, local evangelists, group leaders, and individual disciples understood the power of therapeutic cultural values and skills like relationality, interdependence, and individual choice and will to resonate with members' understandings of how they should proceed on journeys to better self and relationships. The resulting paradox of which they sought to make sense, gaining individual control through submission to authority, was a magnified version of a long-standing Christian and secular practice. Given the mandatory and extreme authoritative demands of McKean's discipling system, leaders and members had to engage in a constant balancing of an authoritative ethic with individual choice and relationality—and, as we shall see throughout this ethnography, many other familiar, magnified, and new contradictory approaches aimed at improving self and intimate relationships. In order to successfully legitimate discipling then, the organization and individual members had to work hard to create some measure of coherence in high cultural opposition.

Creating Cohesion in Contradiction

Creating an appearance of a uniform ICOC approach to family life and relationships in the face of multiple contradictions was constant organizational and individual work. How was discipling, in member and leader presentations, able to both embody and resolve contradictions? Part of the answer lies in the presentation of the discipling system as the ultimate way to control and manage ambiguities that already touched individuals' lives in profound ways—familiar cultural paradox cast as more manageable within the community.

Most members were socialized in a U.S. society that sustained various confusing cultural assumptions and expectations through a variety of institutional relationships. This is a culture where we talk of choosing to enter into our most intimate relationships, of freely creating marriage unions and family ties while at the same time believing deeply that we are powerless in the face of "love at first sight" and biological family links. This is a culture where utilitarian individualism, the idea that people can make the most of their resources, can pull themselves up and achieve high ends, exists alongside an ethic of relational interdependence, the reality of poverty, and vast social stratification. This is a culture where we are to submit to various forms of institutional authority and rule, yet never give up our individual voice and will. This is a country where we believe in the First Amendment's separation of church and state, yet where we sustain images of God and a Christian nation in many government rituals, language, and symbol. This is a culture where women are seen by many as strong, independent, capable of achieving any ends, yet a society where women are oft portrayed as highly emotional, unpredictable, natural caretakers of small children, and inherently domestic. This is a culture where men are thought of as breadwinners, responsible for taking care of families, where they are seen by many as emotionally distant, driven by logic, and yet where they are held to an ideal of involved fatherhood and emotional connection with their children. Cultural paradox is relentless.

That culture sustains contradictory ideals is not a new anthropological or sociological puzzle. Classical social theorists saw individuals as living among contradictory social forces that produced ambivalent relationships between the individual and society. Max Weber, for example, illustrated how individuals in modern society are driven by rational systems that produce irrational consequences.[9] Kai Erikson (1976, 249–250), expresses the force of contradictory cultural beliefs and orientation succinctly: "Any culture . . . can be visualized as a kind of gravitational field in which people are sometimes made more alike by the values they share in common but are sometimes set apart, differentiated, by contrary pulls built into the texture of that field. Every culture, then, is characterized by a number of continua, or 'axes of variation.' " Erikson further suggests that we "can learn something about the cultural history of a people by watching the way they cope with the ambiguities built into their cultural terrain and by tracing the way they move along the axes thus formed." He applies this to his investigation of the mountain culture and ethos of the people of Appalachia, where he locates a familiar cultural ambiguity "characterized by continuing tensions between a longing for individual freedom and a longing for conventional forms of authority, between a sense of assertion and a sense of resignation . . . above all, between a need for independence and a need for dependency" (250). ICOC discipling was, in so many ways, an exaggerated representation of this long-standing cultural tension.

Classical theorists, like Emile Durkheim (1893), suggested that the modern world, born from Enlightenment ideals and industrialization, was inevitably less coherent than more "traditional" societies—traditional in the sense that of a society where conceptions of family, gender, and labor relations are long established, primarily unchallenged, and religious power and authority provides most explanations for relationships in the natural and social world. Enlightenment ideals, scientific authority, and vast changes in the nature of work challenged traditional understandings and led to major shifts and changes in social relationships as industrialization took hold. Charles Lemert (1999, 26) notes ambiguity and contradiction as a condition of modernity: "Life in the modern world is a split life. Modern persons are torn—by their conflicting passions, by the contradictory messages of the culture, by the improbable divorce between what is promised and what is actually given." Some suggest that a "postmodern" self in U.S. society, individuals at the end of the twentieth and beginning of the twenty-first century, are faced with an unprecedented number of cultural ambiguities, tensions, and continual change (Bauman 2000; Giddens 1991): a unique condition resulting from the processes of a new world order, globalization, media, rising numbers of new immigrant populations, religious pluralism, and ever-changing competing morality and worldview. In this social environment, we draw from various social worlds to construct ourselves, to tell stories to ourselves and others that make sense (Bauman 2000; Giddens 1991). The extent to which this historical period presents more ambiguity and cultural variation than any other remains an interesting and debatable sociological question (Hewitt 1989). Clearly premodern societies experienced upheaval and ambiguity that may have seemed, to those at the time, just as uncertain and confusing. What we can say with confidence is that we confront the "axes of variation" in our cultural terrain in historically particular ways. Our responses and approaches to cultural contradiction are shaped by particular social problems, contemporary religious and moral dilemmas, and the rising influence of powerful social institutions like the media, medicine, and our therapeutic culture.

Ann Swidler (1986, 2001) offers useful concepts to help us think about how, in a contemporary world that sustains multiple contradictory ideals, beliefs, and practices, individuals manage to make sense of and use culture. Culture, she stresses, does not necessarily push us to set and achieve particular goals; rather, use of culture has a much more dependent relationship on the "strategies of action" that social institutions make available and plausible to individuals in particular circumstances. In contemporary U.S. society, individuals are not faced with one complete and "settled" worldview. They are, as Geertz (1973, 94–98) suggested, involved in the production of "symbolic formations" that "establish powerful, pervasive, and long-lasting moods and motivations"; but the life of the ordered existence produced by ritual and symbolic formulation is limited. Culture is always shifting, changing, used by individuals and organizations in particular ways to achieve certain goals.

Creating ordered lives can be confusing and chaotic as individuals are faced with multiple methods of approach and contradictory goals. Social institutions like marriage, religion, and education provide institutional ideological frames and concrete practices that are capable of embracing and making sense of contradictions. For example, Swidler (2001) notes that through the institution of marriage we are both independent beings and deeply dependent on one another; we choose our mates freely, yet are prisoners to mythic romance and love at first sight. For some reason, we accept these contradictions and use cultural tools available to us (provided by institutions and related social structures) to make sense of the resulting ambiguities. As Berger and Luckmann (1966) articulated, institutional worlds provide "legitimations," stories offered to represent why we pursue specific ends and behavior in particular ways, the reasons we are given over and again when a paradox or deep contradiction presents. We are told that a marriage based on love is stronger if we maintain our individuality. We read and see films where characters perform scenarios of individuality through all-consuming romantic love. The news media offer a daily assortment of stories to help us make sense of puzzling current events and social relationships. We accept contradictions because they are cast in familiar stories. In fact, contradictory ideals can and do coexist all around us in ways that make sense, very simply because our most deeply felt social institutions provide legitimating stories and explanations that make these inconsistencies appear normal.

Those studying religious and spiritual therapeutic groups and individual journeys therein have found Swidler's tool kit analogy and attention to culture in action extremely helpful (Bartkowski 2004; Emerson and Smith 2000; Gallagher 2003; Irvine 1999). Their use of her concepts for making sense of a religious landscape that, at a glance, seems fractured and complex is understandable. I turn here to Swidler's work on culture in my analysis of the ICOC as well. Her concepts are extremely useful when looking at individuals who join groups that claim to help members make sense of disruptions and inconsistencies in their lives.

Swidler (2001) distinguishes between "settled" and "unsettled" lives: there are times in a person's life when culture makes sense and seems to work. For example, cultural beliefs about what it means to be a woman or man, husband or wife, come together in a seemingly ordered and sound approach for many as they live their day-to-day lives. In settled lives, internalized cultural norms, beliefs, and practices make sense as enacted in one's intimate relationships and wider social interaction. There are "unsettled" periods as well, periods when one's internalized beliefs and strategies of action seem unable to tackle the problems and inconsistencies that arise through social relationships: perhaps after divorce, as a career unfolds, when family members suffer illness, violence, or substance abuse, when a husband and wife both work long hours and yet still long for funds to be able to afford food and health insurance, and crave time with their children.

There is much evidence that people who join new religious and spiritual therapeutic movements are looking for ways to settle what they feel is an unsettled existence. For whatever reason, any previous therapeutic, religious, or other institutional structures have either failed them or not provided enough of the tools and approaches needed to bring the desired order to their lives. Wade Roof (1999, 9–10) argues that many of the changes in cultural norms and a rise in religious/spiritual therapeutic culture have created a "quest culture" post–World War II, "a search for certainty, but also the hope for a more authentic, intrinsically satisfying life." The conceptual religious marketplace of Berger's (1967) *Sacred Canopy* develops in Roof's contemporary study into a "spiritual marketplace," where individuals choose from a variety of organizational and ideological quest choices: religious, spiritual, self-help, environmentalist, New Age, feminist, men's liberationist. We are a nation where many are involved in an active search, searching from positions of disturbing life experiences. Irvine (1999, 88) notes in her study of the codependent self-help movement, Codependents Anonymous (CoDA), that members "come to CoDA during unsettled periods, when much of the structure has gone out of their lives." Lynn Davidman (1991) found that many of the women who came to the Jewish Orthodox Lubavitch community were in unsettled periods. R. Marie Griffith (1997) in her study of narratives of women in Aglow, an interdenominational evangelical women's prayer group, found a heavy emphasis in narratives on a desire to heal and make sense of family "dysfunction" and abuses. Robert Wuthnow's (1994) edited volume, *"I Come Away Stronger": How Small Groups Are Shaping American Religion*, also provides evidence of the unsettled character of religio-therapeutic community participants' lives. He argues that part of the contribution of the rising number and popularity of small self-help-like groups in religious communities (1994, 353) is that they provide spaces, relationships, and approaches for individuals who wish to enact life and relational change, to use faith and culture to "put their faith into practice." For example, "Some groups encourage members to be better mothers or fathers, to have the patience, for example, to read a story to their son or daughter at bedtime, or the courage to set a better example. For others, putting faith into practice means staying sober . . . groups nurture practical applications by discussing them, by praying about them, by communicating information about needs and opportunities." Indeed, many of the narratives and descriptions I collected during my time in the field were from folks who seemed intent on making sense of lives that did not seem ordered or fair—stories of lives trampled by family dissolution, estrangement, separation, drug abuse, alcohol abuse, divorce conflict, trying to balance work/family, loss of job, inability to make ends meet, and illness. Their ICOC success stories represented a wide variety of situations that were likely to provoke "unsettled" lives.

High boundary religious groups offer a distinct case in our spiritual/religious marketplace as they are extremely active in constructing and rendering absolute worldview and practices meant to order cultural chaos and produce settled lives (Berger 1967; Davidman 1991; Kanter 1972). I use the descriptive term "high boundary" here to represent a group with high levels of social and ideological encapsulation (Greil and Rudy 1984), groups where, as Kanter (1972, 52) suggests, members "have a clear sense of their own boundaries" and construct a "strong distinction between the inside and the outside." The ICOC, as one such high boundary religious organization, worked hard to erect social and ideological walls, and to distinguish itself from secular society and other Christian churches while supporting cultural values, beliefs, and practices that these outside institutions embraced. They were actively committed to developing and presenting a novel Christian approach to making sense of life's contradictions, rabid assemblers of culture for evangelical and therapeutic purpose.

Swidler (2001, 89) notes that "in unsettled lives . . . culture is more visible—indeed, because there appears to be 'more' culture—because people actively use culture to learn new ways of being." Aggressive appropriation and use of culture in high boundary new religious movements render the complexities of culture even more visible. In the ICOC, disciplers and church leaders were presented as "ideological specialists"

(Swidler 2001, 65), institutional experts applying, prescribing, and sifting through various moral approaches, relational skills, and cultural beliefs as those they discipled confronted various social experiences and relational challenges. The ICOC was an example of highly "intensified use of culture" to construct and make sense of lives (Swidler 2001, 90). They provided, or tried to provide, an institutional structure meant to make much use of culture and ideological specialists adept at balancing contradictions for members. These ideological specialists, in Pat's words, were able to teach appropriate moral and relational skills because they were divinely inspired—they were "ambassadors of God." Disciplers' abilities to reconcile contradiction and embrace ambiguity were rendered sacred through individual member and formal church narratives as well as observations of disciplers at work in members' daily lives.

Part of the perceived power of disciplers' ability to resolve cultural ambiguity was in the observation of discipling itself. Individuals witnessed, as I did on several occasions, discipling relational trauma counseling. In the City COC congregation, the act of discipling was not bound by formal daily or weekly sessions with one's discipler; discipling often happened informally, and sometimes among those who were not official discipling partners. Because the congregation was composed of a community of informal disciplers, if you were in emotional crisis you did not have to wait for your formal discipler to receive intervention. Members often spoke of this as an in-group therapeutic advantage. In action, disciplers were often present at the moment of crisis, holding hands, on the phone, present in some way to apply cultural meaning and action to a particular relational crisis. My field log observations of on-the-spot discipling are significant here:

> A member breaks down during a late night Bible study because a child has left home and left the church. She is in tears and cannot continue with Bible study. One of the shepherding couples is present to take her away for a private counseling session. We watch from a distance as she is held, comforted, and counseled. Shepherding couple spends at least an hour with the woman.

> During one Bible study a woman admits that she is consumed with feeling selfish in her marriage. Members join in to disciple her on the spot, helping her decide when she is being harmfully selfish and

> when she is being a strong Christian woman and how she can tell the difference . . . when she should be submissive and when she should speak her mind.

> A woman breaks down after viewing a KNN film about father/daughter relationships. She is having a difficult time resolving her relationship with her own father. Her discipler is present and embraces her as she sobs. We watch her leave with her discipler to go to a coffee shop for a discipling session.

Even though in two of these examples we were not privy to the exact advice given, those present did witness a clear performance of on-the-spot discipling. Members and ex-members report that this was certainly not always the case, that providing such constant help in figuring out how to approach a difficult moral/relational problem was a very difficult task and taxing on members and nonpaid staff leadership. No doubt this is true; however, the power was in the *performance*, the image that the community was able to create, if only for a limited number of years, of at-your-fingertips counseling and management of life's problems. Those who showed extreme emotion and vulnerability during church gatherings were not alone; they seemed to receive quick attention and in-depth therapeutic assistance. Members and ex-members also told many stories of on-the-spot discipling intervention, calling disciplers at all hours of the night and receiving help, which also fueled the group image of disciplers as always there to help members tackle difficult situations, to serve as ideological specialists.

Unlike many Christians, who may turn to a pastor or religious authority as an ideological specialist, ICOC members saw that they were susceptible to serious social sanctions if they did not confront their life situations using the individualized cultural prescriptions disciplers and leaders routinely and promptly assembled for them. In fact, they knew of members who were asked to leave the community and "marked," members who were shunned, gossiped about, and received harsh words from disciplers and leaders if they did not welcome and follow advice. Balancing these harsh mechanisms of social control with individual choice and will was a constant chore for members and leaders, but a necessary one if they were to construct discipling as a sound and extraordinarily successful therapeutic instrument for making sense of a number of cultural contradictions. Relationality was the rhetorical ground that members returned to as they told stories of balancing authority, individual choice, and therapeutic ideals.

A great deal of this balancing work in the presentation and method of discipling took place through metaphors of the heart. This symbolic tool in the organizational repertoire provided a powerful cultural symbol that legitimated ambiguity. To benefit from discipling, members and leaders talked about having to have an "open heart," a heart willing to shift from one moral stance to the next and see the goodness in disciplers' prescriptions, a heart with the capacity to embody and make use of multiple ideals and practices. "Soft hearts," "teachable hearts," "open hearts," "expressive hearts," and "totally honest hearts" were featured in group discourse as safely giving in to and trusting in the authority of discipling relationships because these relationships were mediated through hearts (of fellow disciplers) that were committed to mutuality and relationality. During my time in the field, disciples referred many times to Jeremiah 29:11–13 as they told me of sitting down to study the Bible for the first time and having the Word (the Christian Bible) cut like a "knife" into their hearts.

Heart is a long-standing powerful cultural and biblical symbol, a long-standing rhetorical trademark of evangelical "born-again" Christians who speak of Christ changing their hearts upon conversion. Contemporary author John Eldredge's (2003, 150) book, *Waking the Dead: The Glory of a Heart Fully Alive*, is just one example of the evangelical emphasis on heart as the site of a battle for soul: "We are at war. The war is against your heart, your glory. . . . Our hearts—they are the treasures hidden by darkness . . . held away in secret places like a hostage held for ransom. Prisoners of war." For those members who came to the ICOC from the evangelical subculture, the heart as a symbol of contestation was familiar.

Harper's Bible Dictionary (Achtemeier 1985, 377) names "heart" as "probably the most important anthropological word in the Hebrew scriptures, referring almost exclusively to the human heart (814 times; cf. 'the heart of God,' 26 times)." Biblically, the heart is seen as both the center of emotions and the "source of thought and reflection. . . . Isa. 6:10; Mark 7:21–13)." Furthermore, the "heart understands (Deut. 8:5; Isa. 42:25), provides wisdom to rule justly and wisely (1 Kings 3:12; 10:24), and discerns good and evil (1 Kings 2:49)."[10] Biblically, the heart sustains a familiar cultural contradiction; the location of submission to God's authority and individual will. The heart is where True emotions are hidden and thus a point of revelation and salvation in Christianity.

If a member came to the ICOC from a primarily secular background, the heart was still a meaningful symbol. We hear, through various social institutions (e.g., media, family) that our hearts fall in love, our hearts drive hard choices, and that home is where the heart is. We may be asked when faced with an important decision, "What does your heart say?" We may be told to follow our hearts and to give our hearts to others, and that those we have loved and have died live on in our hearts. As a cultural symbol, hearts are malleable and capable of sustaining great joy and pain, the ultimate bed of life's most painful contradictions.

In painting self-portraits of autonomy and individuality in discipling relationships, members told me stories of having felt unable to follow their individual disciplers' advice for a particular reason, and so having an "open heart" meant that they needed to express their reservations truthfully. These recountings seemed proudly stated, performances that their individual moral compasses, their "hearts," were ultimately in charge. Pat and other members I interviewed stressed over and over again that it was "important and biblically right for Christians to question disciplers and do what they feel is right in their hearts." "I, for instance," she insisted, "as Kay's discipler, would never want Kay to do something that bothered Kay." Another member insisted that he took what disciplers told him and "went off" and figured out for himself, in his own "heart," what he should do.

To balance authoritative edicts with individual choice and relationality, leaders worked hard rhetorically to soften discipling's mandatory submissive quality. For example, Kip McKean (1992, 8), lightens "positional" authority (to use Gordon Ferguson's term) of disciplers by qualifying the discipling relationship as mutual, as each disciple "listening" and helping the other: "Obviously, the younger discipleship partner also gives input and advice to the stronger disciple, as in any healthy relationship." Ferguson (1997, 191) tells disciples that "obey" really means to "be persuaded," which implies that an individual who goes along with a discipler's advice is not doing what she/he is told, but rather making a "decision" (a personal *choice*) to follow advice: "The word 'authority' in the NIV (New International Version) is not in the Greek, so the literal translation would be 'obey and submit to them' (as leaders). The word 'obey' is from the Greek *peitho*, and the literal meaning is 'be persuaded.'"

Another rhetorical method for balancing contradictions when the scales tipped too dangerously on the side of submission to authority and loss of personal freedom was formal apologetic gesture. Leaders "apologized" as a display of relationality, a performance of listening well to fellow disciples and taking member criticisms and concerns seriously. Al Baird, a longtime powerful ICOC church leader, voiced regret in an attempt to soften images of the ICOC as an authoritative organization:

> I wrote a series of articles published in the Boston Bulletin (from September 6 through October 18, 1987) about authority and submission. In retrospect I wish that I had taken more time in prayer and consideration on the subject because the wrong emphasis was given for discipling relationships. There was too much emphasis put on authority and too little emphasis on motivating out of love for God and persuasion from a "What would Jesus do?" approach. This allowed some insecure leaders to say, "Do it because I tell you to, and don't question me about it." The Bible teaches that authority is from God and therefore is good, but it can be abused and misused. When a person has to appeal to the use of his authority to accomplish God's purposes, he has usually lost the battle." (www.icoc.org, "A Look at Authority," posted 9/20/1999)

Baird's depiction of his own wrongheaded advice did little to undermine the healing power of discipling; if authority were practiced properly, he argues, disciplers would not abuse it. But his willingness to admit wrong in placing undue emphasis on authority fueled the idea that ICOC leaders and disciplers were able and ready to admit fault, thus giving the impression that ICOC's top leadership were not bullies, but a group of leaders with "open hearts" willing to own mistakes and apologize. Apologizing, as a social skill, is a cultural expectation, a familiar salve in our therapeutic nation; politicians, clergy, and government officials have apologized for slavery, unethical medical testing of racial minorities and national service folks, lies and sex in the Oval Office, priestly pedophilia . . . the list could go on. In each case the expectation has been that the apology represented some genuine regret on the part of those who had abused power.

Anti-group rhetoric posed a particular balancing challenge. Ex-members presented the mandatory nature of counseling as infringing on individual rights, questioned the ability of the organization to provide such "awesome" counselors given the lack of formal training for disciplers and church leaders, and, along with other outside critics, many labeled the group a dangerous "cult." Leaders frequently confronted readily accessible ex-member web-based rhetoric, what they called "spiritual pornography." They argued on-line, in the pulpit, and in DPI publications that discipling did not take away individuals' free will but promoted relationality by engaging cult discourse head-on. In Ferguson's discipling book, leader Thomas A. Jones writes: "People [in the ICOC] are specifically taught . . . that no one should ever do anything they are told to do if (1) it violates the word of God, or (2) it violates one's conscience that is being trained by the word of God. This is a message you will not hear from the dangerous cults of our day and age" (Ferguson 1997, 246). Furthermore, he writes, "No true disciple wants to have any control over the person he is discipling . . . any efforts to weaken a person emotionally or physically are totally rejected. Being a disciple is all about making a clear minded and completely voluntary decision to follow Jesus Christ. Biblical discipleship is either completely from the heart or it is not real at all" (Ferguson 1997, 245–246).

Church leaders confronted ex-member and critic cult accusations head-on in services as well. During one local City COC Sunday morning service, a leader read from the book of Acts in the New Testament:

> They devoted themselves to the apostles' teaching and to the fellowship, to the breaking of bread and to prayer. Everyone was filled with awe, and many wonders and miraculous signs were done by the apostles. All the believers were together and had everything in common. Selling their possessions and goods, they gave to anyone as he had need. Every day they continued to meet together in the temple courts. They broke bread in their homes and ate together with glad and sincere hearts, praising God and enjoying the favor of all the people. And the Lord added to their number daily those who were being saved. (Acts 2:42–47, New International Version)

"In our society," he told us, "this reads as how to spot a cult." People in cults, he laughs, "help one another. We get our needs met, we are devoted to one another." He qualified that God was not asking them to sell all their possessions, but to be there for each other, to be willing to sacrifice when others needed it. We don't need to give up everything, he told us, but we need to "use our influence to help meet people's needs." Do what this passage says, he argued. "They were radical," he told us, "they like being around each other and supporting each other, and if that's what a cult is, then so be it!" His words brought applause from the congregation. He confronted the disputed value and character of discipling with a strong emphasis on relationality, using scriptural justification to soften the cult label in a bed of family commitment and therapeutic ethos. His direct use of "cult" accusations to legitimate the movement was common in formal group discourse.

"It Covers Every Part of My Life"

The City COC members I met and the ICOC members whose testimonies and narratives I read on-line and in movement publications came from a variety of religious and ethnic backgrounds. They self-identified as former Catholics, Evangelicals, Baptists, Presbyterians, Muslims, and as members of other religious traditions; some identified as pre-movement secular humanists, atheists, and feminists. Regardless of their particular religious/spiritual/political experiences and efforts in our spiritual marketplace before identification as an ICOC disciple, they were all, already, deeply committed to a therapeutic ethos. They were primarily U.S. citizens grounded in democratic values and individualism, and surrounded by a therapeutic consumer culture that stressed individual choice and the primacy of bettering the self. Therefore, successfully balancing ICOC's authoritative qualities and high time and monetary commitment with individual choice, will, and therapeutic ethos was essential to movement viability. The movement would likely not sustain membership if the scales tipped too heavily on the authority/commitment side.

Sustaining equilibrium was an essential and difficult organizational chore. Some sociologists argue that such high boundary groups, churches they name as "strict," have the potential to elicit high member devotion, but are likely to lose membership if they demand too much from members (Iannaccone 1994). This appears to be true for both ideological and practical demands. As I explore in the final chapter, failure to maintain a cohesive balance between individual will and submission to authority no doubt ultimately contributed to the downfall of the movement. For over twenty years, though, to a significant number of people, the balance held strong, and ICOC discipling was rendered a sound and exceptionally sacred therapeutic option. Many members believed that discipling would help them approach and conquer personal dilemmas and reach goals: discipling would help them understand when submission to authority was appropriate, to whom they should submit, when they should speak up, how to stand strong in individual choice, how to learn better communication skills, how to listen and express honestly, how to be a woman/man, when to discipline children, how to balance work and family, how to fulfill obligations to biological/family of origin, how to be a Christian in a world driven by science, medical knowledge, and expertise, and how to find time in busy lives to proselytize and turn "hearts" to God.

Ann, the woman in the introduction here who offered the story about her young church sister's death and the community support surrounding the event, told me: "The church gives me security. It covers every part of my life, my marriage, my children. It trains me to be happy, gives values. It creates a real family bond. It makes me complete." How were disciplers depicted as embodying and teaching such a thorough and cohesive approach to gender and family life? How did they become convincing ideological specialists who aided members in sifting through the inconsistencies of U.S. culture at the turn of the twenty-first century? What function did the telling of individual stories and collective group rituals of "awesome family" have in the life and death of the unified movement?

Through my observations and analysis of narratives of discipling's healing power, disciplers emerge as successfully navigating messy cultural waters of gender and family ambiguity, holding members' hands as they point them in one moral direction and then another, naming relational sins, and teaching and enacting relationality. In the next few chapters, I focus on how disciplers were talked about by members and leaders as managing and providing ideological coherence and relational skills for different aspects of members' lives: marriage, biological/family of origin, children, community, and church family relationships. Disciplers emerge in individual and group presentations as "covering every part of life," of making members feel "complete" and settled through a performance of secure ideological and practical approach. At the same time, their stories, and the narratives of former members, make clear that full participation in ICOC's discipling system introduced new relational dilemmas and ideological confusion.

CHAPTER 2

An Unsinkable Raft in a Foreboding Divorce Culture

> Best friends. Exciting lovers. Rarely has the heart and soul of marriage been summed up any better. Friendship and romantic love are the two essential ingredients of a great marriage, the qualities that will make it grow ever richer, deeper and more fulfilling. Although this should be the norm, few of us grew up seeing such marriages, and perhaps even fewer of us believed that we could experience such a relationship ourselves. Many have seen marriage as a drain rather than a fountainhead, a battleground instead of a refuge, and a pit stop rather than a permanent home.
>
> —Sam and Geri Laing,
> *Friends and Lovers* (1996, 21)

LONGTIME ICOC LEADERS Sam and Geri Laing's formal pronouncement is familiar. From Jerry Falwell's Moral Majority born in the 1970s, to the 1996 federal Defense of Marriage Act and recent attempts to constitutionalize heterosexual marriage, hundreds of private, religious, and government-backed movements have and are actively promoting and working to revitalize heterosexual marriage as an enduring and necessary institution. Conservative mainstream and religious efforts to reinforce heterosexual marriage in what is presented as a "traditional" family model clearly clashes with contemporary values of gender egalitarianism and the day-to-day realities of an economy where both mothers and fathers must work to try and make ends meet.[1] Even though momentum has waxed and waned over the years, conservative religious and political concerns over the condition of the American family remain strong. Even seemingly liberal voices have legitimated the fear that families in this country are in a state of disaster and that the solution to child safety and social betterment is to raise children in two-parent heterosexual households (Stacey 1994). The notion (and what at times may even seem like a moral panic) that family in the United States is in serious trouble is deeply entrenched in our cultural discourse and individual consciousness.

It is amid this culturally perceived social problem of the decline of the American family that religio-therapeutic "experts" claim to heal and strengthen intimate relationships through therapeutic, spiritual, and divine mechanisms. There are various contemporary religious approaches to fixing family: one-on-one clinical religious marriage counseling, small group self-help religious meetings and marriage renewal retreats, the large church-based interdenominational Marriage Encounter movement, and interdenominational groups like Promise Keepers and Women's Aglow (Bartkowski 2004; Griffith 1997; Swidler 2001, 18). The ICOC's efforts to heal marriages must be understood in this wider context. The ICOC was offering a similar religio-therapeutic good; however, support and guidance in most other secular and religious fee-for-service counseling does not necessitate individuals' *explicit* submission to an authoritative system of healing. Just as individual ICOC members were required to submit to regular discipling, married members were expected to engage in weekly marriage discipling sessions with another "older" married couple, a mandatory ICOC practice instituted in the early 1990s. Through mandatory submission, leaders promised extraordinary marriage therapeutic techniques to the point where, as one ICOC evangelist put it, "in God's modern-day movement [meaning ICOC movement] there are no divorces."

The ICOC members I spent the majority of my time with in the field presented themselves as individuals awash in a dangerous social climate, living in a contemporary world where their marriages and those around them were seriously at risk. They understood heterosexual marriage as a threatened institution. It is no wonder that they felt this way; they heard the misleading statistical warning frequently from church leaders and the mainstream media: "50 percent of marriages end in divorce," a figure that often compares the number of marriages yearly to number of divorces, a statistic that reveals little about an individual's chances for divorce. Member expressions of marital anxiety were further fed by media reports of rising numbers of single parents (both women and men), increasing visibility of gay and lesbian couples, cohabitation, and census reports that marriage rates are dropping. These transformations in marriage and family have fueled fears nationwide that a large proportion of young women and men are abandoning the institution of marriage. It is this contingent nature of marriage in our culture today that the ICOC and other conservative groups try to belie.

Sociologist Karla Hackstaff (1999, 2) argues that we form intimate relationships in our society today in the "midst of contesting ideologies," yet another point of—to use Erikson's (1976, 249) term for cultural tensions and contrary forces—"axes of variation." On the one hand, we live in a divorce culture that promotes the idea that we do not have to stay in a marriage if we are not happy, a culture that sees divorce as an often necessary gateway to the self-fulfillment we all deserve. On the other hand, we are deeply grounded in a "marriage culture," composed of a "cluster of beliefs, symbols and practices, framed by material conditions, that reinforce marriage and deter divorce." Marriage culture is grounded in a belief that the union is meant to last forever and that spouses should be held to a strong marriage "work ethic." Marriage culture promotes the idea that marriage, while based on sex and romance, has important functional elements as well, and requires great effort. Hackstaff's work highlights an important institutional paradox: even though divorce is seen by many in our society as a legitimate and often necessary action, a model of heterosexual marriage remains a desirable ideal. ICOC members were very much caught in the middle of these contesting ideologies and told of how marriage discipling would help them navigate and master this postmodern cultural cleavage.

The stories members told me during formal private interviews and extended informal conversations, and the stories they told in formal witnessing to the congregation, were performances of married selves who had found a divine therapeutic method for promoting what they named "awesome" companionship, romance, and sex in marriage relationships. Member stories detailed how their church family repaired, constructed, and rejuvenated marriages even as the possibility of divorce loomed. These stories and the beliefs they represented brought members a kind of relational confidence. Spouses were held accountable by other church members to attending weekly counseling sessions (marriage discipling).

Divorce remained a distant option, permitted in group only in the case of adultery or physical abuse, or if a spouse decided to leave and speak against the church (thus the claim by leaders that there were no divorces *in* the Kingdom). Like covenant marriages,[2] ICOC married couples were told by leaders that they were bound and held accountable to working out problems and not to even consider divorce. Therefore, members came to understand that if they, and their spouses, remained faithful disciples in the church and allowed marriage disciplers to guide their unions, their marriages would be for a lifetime.

Most secular, spiritual, and religious therapeutic approaches to healing and assisting marriage and intimate relationships lack this mandatory quality of ICOC marriage discipling; members understood this difference and spoke of the compulsory nature of marriage discipling as reassuring. In a society where multiple models of relational marital ethics coexist, members were presented with and talked about what seemed a clear-cut marriage management system—one that allowed them to embody a marital "work ethic" where mutuality and egalitarianism prevailed, but one that also embraced cultural values embedded in divorce culture, like the expectation of self-respect and self-fulfillment.

Individual and organizational performances of this forever-after certainty were indeed attractive. Single members talked of their dream of being married "in the Kingdom," a dream that outside the church would be fraught with doubt. Members whose spouses were not disciples reported feeling intense pressure and labels of group deviance. They feared that their non-Christian spouses would leave them—fall prey to the temptations and depravity of secular culture. No one ever explicitly told me my marriage may be headed for disaster. They may have thought that such an affront could taint my presentation of the church. The closest I came to an explicit denouncing of my marriage was at the end of my interview with Jeremy, whose story of marriage in the church is detailed later in this chapter. Jeremy asked to meet my husband, and when I told him my husband would not attend City COC functions with me, he let me know that my making new "friends" in the church without my husband meeting these friends was too "dangerous." My position bore similarities to those female City COC members who were labeled as "Sarah's Daughters" or in some congregations "Esthers" or "Bravehearts," labels of difference bestowed on women married to men who were not in the church, women whose unions were cast by leaders and other members as precarious.[3]

Member narratives of ICOC marriage saves are a powerful source for understanding individual attraction to and experience in the movement. They do not provide concrete variables for measurement, and they are retrospective understandings of experience, yet they reveal a great deal about members' construction of religious identity and how they found meaning in church relationships (Ammerman 2003; Roof 1993, 1999; Yamane 2000). Member narratives provide important clues toward understanding how members resolved participation in authoritative discipling relationships driven by an ethic of relationality, individual choice, and freedom, and how they came to accept discipling as an essential tool navigating the construction of moral selves in a world of cultural ambiguity. Anthony Giddens (1991, 54) stresses that "a person's identity is not to be found in behaviour, nor—important though this is—in the reaction of others, but in the capacity *to keep a particular narrative going.* The individual's biography, if she is to maintain regular interaction with others in the day-to-day world, cannot be wholly fictive. It must continually integrate events which occur in the external world, and sort them into the ongoing 'story' about the self." The telling and retelling of journeys from a dangerous, morally bereft divorce culture to "amazing" and secure marriage in the ICOC community was essential in many members' understandings of self as morally sound. They presented themselves as actively pursuing growth in intimate relationships through daily interaction in a discipling community that demanded submission and allegiance. ICOC's community of "ideological specialists," sacred counselors armed with an abundance of cultural tools, were major characters in member narratives of marital healing—stories of marriage work, self-fulfillment, and submission to a sacred religio-therapeutic authority.

City COC member marriage stories, like the following from Ronny, Julie, Alicia, and Jeremy, were symbolic, concise, and oft-repeated recountings of miraculous marriage saves, stories that continually objectified discipling and their construction of marriage as morally sound and sacred. These patterned performances, while endowed with particular meaning and qualitative detail that represented each couple's life history and current relationships, all echoed the formal ICOC marriage save script. Individual performances of heroic discipler interventions followed this organizational pattern: descriptions of pre-church marriages that were dull, lacked communication, and threatened by divorce turned into fulfilling unions, or performances by members who were afraid to marry and then developed confident and extraordinary marriages in the church. These feats were accomplished by: (1) disciplers teaching couples how to balance ambiguous gender roles and ideals; (2) constant and mandatory counseling and submission to disciplers' prescriptions and interventions; (3) round-the-clock discipler availability and on-the-spot intervention; and (4) matching couples with marriage disciplers who had been through similar relationship issues.

Members seemed at ease telling stories of marriage discipling saves, stressing the mandatory and authoritative interactions as well as the more relational and intimate encounters. Some of the information they offered and that I detail below—for example, discussions of sexual expression and experience—I, and others, may perceive as private. Yet, in a culture where media showcase the sex lives of the rich and famous, where television talk shows tackle sexuality explicitly and with regularity, where expression of sexuality in self-help groups and counselors' offices fulfills a respected therapeutic practice, expressivity, such disclosure by these supporters of Christian "traditional" family is not surprising. This expectation of open discussion regarding sexuality and other intimate details of marriage relationships was uncomfortable for me as an ethnographer. As I developed close relationships in the field and interviewed members, I maintained my own culturally received ideas about the private nature of my sexual relationship with my husband. While many of these women talked with me about being "led" in bed by husbands and taught how to have orgasms by disciplers, I did not share my sexual preferences and experience. I was, to some extent, breaking the ethic of relationality they demonstrated in their openness.

Telling stories of successful marriage discipling to me and during group services and events no doubt served individual members by constantly reminding them of how their marriages were in safe and secure hands: they were reassuring stories in a culture with multiple ideals of marriage and intimate relationships. Repeating these stories served the ICOC organization as well. Each time a member told a story (to me or during a formal service or event), he or she strengthened the collective belief that the discipling community had exceptional therapeutic healing powers, and that disciplers had *new* approaches for them in navigating a divorce/marriage culture. The more members performed these abbreviated scenarios, the more they came to believe that their marriages would be exceptional, and the more ICOC's organizational portrait of skilled and successful marriage counselors as hard disciplinarians and thoughtful, engaged listeners was legitimated and secured.

Heroic Interventions: Individual Performances and Formal Scripts

Ronny and Julie

I spoke with Julie and Ronny on several occasions during my time with the City COC congregation. Ronny was a twenty-five-year-old black man from Trinidad who had been a member of the church for nine years. He and his wife, Julie, a twenty-two-year-old black graduate student from Nigeria, were married in the church. Like most members, they faithfully attended services Sunday mornings and Wednesday evenings. They were also present at several of the Bible study and home social events I attended. As longtime church members, their stories of church healing and relationships were also present in the narratives of other members in this closely knit congregation; I had heard Ronny and Julie's story of marital healing in some detail from others. During formal interviews, Ronny and Julie told me a story of heightened romance, healing, and exceptional marriage, and how they had helped save member marriages through discipling. Both described a dangerous world of divorce and family dysfunction outside the church that had led them to, until encountering married ICOC couples, give up on the possibility of ever being happily married. They told a story of choosing to submit to disciplers' advice, of hearts made soft (submissive) and strong (individual will and effort) at the same time.

Julie, a member of the City COC for six years, proclaimed that before she became a disciple she "never wanted to be married. Never! I was like, be married, no one stays married! Everyone gets a divorce, three, four years, not even. And my whole family, I can't even think of one person who is still married . . . so it [marriage] just turned me off." When she observed couples in the church actually staying together and "in love," she said it "blew her away." "I wouldn't even be married if it weren't for watching these people, if I didn't see how they were living.

By going to their homes and seeing that." Julie stressed that she was most impressed with the way couples she spent time with in the City COC seemed to "work out" their marriage and family problems rather than "running away." She had told herself pre-ICOC membership: "If I do get married some day, which I don't want to, but if I do, then I'll be in control of my life." "In control" was how she interpreted the married lives of her new extended church family that she had come to know intimately over several years. Divorce culture was out of control and the ICOC marriage work ethic, combined with constant access to skilled and experienced Christian marriage counselors, she felt, offered her great control. "I feel like now that I'm married I have trusted friends that I can talk to. . . . When I talk to her [her marriage discipler] she is so understanding. She has been through similar situations. She is honest about her marriage. She is honest about what her weaknesses are. She is honest about her strengths."

Ronny was from a divorced family as well. His parents separated in Trinidad right before he moved to the United States with his father and stepmother. He had a falling out with his father as a young teenager and moved in with his maternal grandmother as a young teen. He met ICOC disciplers soon after at the age of sixteen. Ronny described a similar fear of marriage pre–church membership: "If I wasn't part of the church and learning how to trust and how to be trustworthy then I don't think I'd be married because my family, my entire family, there is not a successful marriage in my family. It starts out, the first few years, you know functional, deteriorates, then divorce." Ronny went on to include his entire network of friends and family as representative of divorce culture and dysfunctional family: "I don't think I'd be a husband because of all the things that I saw. There wasn't a good example of a good male role model first of all in my family and people that I knew. There are a lot of, everybody had broken homes and messed up families as far as I could tell. I never really had a friend that goes, oh, mom and dad are doing great. It was weird stuff going on all over the place, so." His story so clearly communicated a total lack of positive marriage examples outside the church. He even described his mother's second marriage as "nothing you'd be, oh, I want that! Give me some of that stuff, mmm—no." However, like his wife, Ronny described experiencing long-term exposure to an entirely different kind of marriage and family relationship in the City COC congregation: "I've seen marriages when they were dating, when they get married and I've seen those apply the Bible a lot. They apply those principles and you see the result, *you get to see the result*." He offered examples of the kind of care, attention, Christian love, and discipline that he and Julie had received from pre-marriage disciplers as young singles dating in the Kingdom.

Ronny has had to deal with health problems over the years due to a serious back injury; he is tired a great deal of the time and cannot always engage in physical activity. When I interviewed Ronny he was feeling well and working full-time, but for months during his courtship with Julie, he had not been able to work: "I lost my health. I was a young, strong, healthy looking guy collecting welfare, can't work. I was very frustrated." But, he stressed, Julie stuck with him through these unhealthy times, she cared for him and believed in him. Her care and unselfishness "was a convincing time for me that if God made me able to marry this woman, that's the person I want to be with." Disciplers and premarital counselors helped mold their relationship. He described disciplers as helping them to learn to care for one another and counselors who intervened time and again in their relationship; for example, disciplers had helped them balance emotionality and build communication techniques.

Ronny presented himself to me as emotional and high-strung and described Julie as "very patient . . . and peaceful." "She doesn't react the way I would react to a situation. I am very emotional, very high-strung and ah, she would not respond to a situation the way I would and, in my mind, how can you keep yourself so calm?" Ronny also identified as the more affectionate spouse and cast his wife as more practical: "She's very laid back and pragmatic, so . . . but I'm very much hugs, kiss, touch. Love all that stuff. . . . I love to hug and there are times where I feel like, could she initiate some of the hugs?" Julie's descriptions of disciplers' efforts in their marriage centered around her struggle to eradicate what she called the "sin of selfishness" and learn to be more open and expressive: "What I would talk with my discipler about is just making sure that I'm not being selfish. By nature, I'm a very selfish person. I want to be able to do my own thing and when I want to do my own thing . . . sometimes I'm just so rude to him."

"What do you mean by selfish?" I asked. She explained that "there have been situations where, you know, intimacy, at times I'm just, you know, tired, and I don't want to give of myself and she's [discipler] helped me to be, you know . . . if God didn't make you for that purpose, then what is the purpose of being able to give yourself to each other?" Once Julie was able to deal with this "selfishness" and "give herself" to her husband even if she was tired, she said their sexual relationship improved. A lesson in learning submission in marriage through submission to discipler intervention.

Ronny offered another example of how marriage disciplers helped negotiate marital conflict: "I'm extremely paranoid by nature," he told me. "I am suspicious of everybody, so I am extremely animated in my mind and I will blow things way out of proportion. . . . So I'm insecure. I'm working on my insecurity." Ron's health concerns would arise from time to time to "test" his faith and efforts to deal with insecurity, and disciplers were there to guide him. He explained:

> Julie came home one day when I was sick and I'd been thinking I really wanted to go out to church with her, to be with my family, but my health . . . and so she came home telling me about church service and in my mind I'm thinking, you think I'm not committed don't you? So I said all those things to her, you think I'm sick blah, blah, blah. I just dumped on her [Julie] all this stuff and she started crying. I was hollering, and so, when I find myself getting that way, actually *at that moment* [my emphasis] when I go that way I called him [marriage discipler] and I said, "She's crying right now as we speak," and he said I was a jerk. He asked if she had ever said anything, if she had ever done anything that would make me think that. "No," I said, "she's never said anything." "So what would make you think that?" he said.

Ronny apologized, and then he and Julie were able to calm down and talk. He said that marriage disciplers "have been crucial at times like that."

Ronny, like so many other members recounting ICOC marriage saves, ended with descriptions of romance. "She was always there for me . . . as we dated we just grew to like each other, wrote each other tons of poetry and cards and . . . all over the place." Ronny pointed to the shelves to our right in his living room.

"You have them framed up there," I said.

"Yeah um, you know, long-term plans, short-term plans. I like that one in particular." He took down the frame and continued, "It's from our two-year anniversary of dating and then we got married that next year. It spells out Julie's name and after each letter I say something about her starting with that letter. I was looking for a word that I could use to describe her."

He showed the framed poem to me. "I'm looking and I'm trying to spell her name so I'm looking up in the dictionary and I'm like God, come on, show me a word, show me a word. And I, the word I spelled," he said smiling and pointing.

"Ineffable," I read aloud.

"Yeah, and I never knew what that word meant. Definitely, beyond the ability to communicate and I said, that's it! I found the word! She was just, a piece of God really. He was just giving me a piece of himself."

Alicia and Jeremy

I saw Alicia and Jeremy a couple of times during services and conducted formal interviews separately in their home. Like Ronny and Julie, I had heard stories of their marriage from other church leaders before the interview. Alicia, a college-educated thirty-year-old white married woman with two children, began her story of church marital healing by telling me that "the marriage was stinking big time!" Like most other member stories of marriage saves, she presented her pre-ICOC life as existing in an alienating and "heartless" divorce culture. As we sipped tea at her dining room table, she told me of a divorced friend in the Congregationalist church she attended before becoming a disciple. She said that having such a divorced friend made her feel that divorce was an acceptable option. Lost and feeling helpless in her marriage, she had searched for comfort and guidance in her Congregational church but had found "no help" there. Alicia described her five-year marriage to Jeremy, a thirty-five-year-old white male insurance salesman, in those pre-ICOC membership years as lacking "communication and honesty." She emphasized that they were on an inevitable path toward divorce: "We were growing apart. I went to visit my family one summer and I decided while I was there that I was probably going to leave Jeremy." Jeremy confirmed during his interview that they were on a clear path to divorce at that time. The threat of divorce had left Alicia "very scared" and feeling "alone with no one to talk to"; she felt no one truly cared about her problems and that only bad advice surrounded her efforts to heal her wounded relationship.

Alicia's voice then lifted as she told me of the miraculous relationships she developed with City COC disciples, relationships that saved her marriage that was "stinkin' big time" (a phrase she used several times). She had anxiously studied the Bible with an ICOC woman, a family group leader, even though Jeremy had no desire to become involved with the church. Alicia recalled that his resistance to studying the Bible led her to feel even more like she "wanted to split up," that she wanted to pretend her marriage had never happened. Divorcing him would have "killed him and it would have killed me and destroyed our son." Luckily, City COC disciples, she emphasized, would not let her "give up." It did not matter, she said, that Jeremy was not yet a disciple, City COC marriage disciplers still "worked hard" to help her fix her marriage. "These disciples," she stressed, "were trying to teach me to love him again. They were teaching me submission. They were a shoulder when I had a problem. They were like, tell us what you are feeling in your heart. I could call them with anything." And she did, from on-the-spot crisis intervention when an argument got out of hand, to advice on which spouse should be the sexual "leader" on a particular evening. Alicia described marriage disciplers as on call, round the clock, ready and eager to wipe out her relational sins. Her story turned course as she made a definite choice to submit to these effective church counselors.

In describing how he and his wife learned to better communicate and listen to one another openly, Jeremy presented his pre-discipled self as guided by an essentialist masculinity that drove him to be "silent" and "distant." I'm not as prone [as his wife] to expressing my emotions." He depicted his wife, Alicia, using an essentialist vision of females as more "emotional," but at the same time, blamed their pre-disciple suffering marriage on Alicia's anger and her inability to live up to a feminine ideal of "openness" and "warmth." He cast his male silence and distance as sinful: "By nature, we [men] grow up to be very self-centered." This self-centeredness, Jeremy emphasized, was partly from the "social thing" where "men are the ones to make all the decisions."

Alicia, however, cast her pre-discipled self as emotionally disconnected from Jeremy. She identified as an extremely emotional person whose angry outbursts were the sinful force behind their marital "bumps": "I'm the more emotional one, even though we both have our faults, mine show up more because I tend to be emotional and very verbal and he tends to pull away. . . . I'm very emotional. If it's there it's got to come out. I can't always control it. Sometimes I'll say it in front of the kids. I get discipled on that all the time." Both Jeremy and Alicia described disciplers as helping them learn to find the right degree of expressivity and emotionality. For Alicia, disciplers taught her how to "tone down" her emotions, to integrate a more logical practice by "thinking through" complaints and issues before "throwing" them in anger on Jeremy. For Jeremy, disciplers brought him out of his silent, "Spock-like shell." At the end of our interview Jeremy offered proof of ease with his newfound expressive masculinity; he cried while recounting the death and funeral of a close church brother.

Alicia and Jeremy decided to have a second wedding ceremony because before joining the church they "almost didn't make it." They rented a small clubhouse event room at an apartment complex and invited everyone in the congregation. "About 150 people showed up, we renewed our vows, and we taped something that we read to each other." They also made an audiotape for each other that Alicia wanted me to hear. She searched the house for the tape and grew upset when she could not find it. "I'll probably find it as soon as you walk out the door!" She had to settle for a description: "It [what he said about her on tape] was just so awesome and I shared about him, too, on a tape. It was almost as if everything that could be said was said, it was so perfect. . . . Both of our hearts had to be that we wanted to change to be better for our spouse and that was our heart, we did it."

In the end, as with most stories of heroic marriage discipling, Alicia and Jeremy stressed that they had made a choice to learn how to better communicate, how to balance emotional release with logical thinking, how to have a romantic marriage and, as they put it so many times, an "awesome marriage." "I was in shock," Alicia told me, "in shock because we were both babies growing up together in the faith. We still made mistakes, but we were getting help from disciples. There were people in our marriage helping us to learn to express ourselves."

RONNY, JULIE, ALICIA, JEREMY, and many other members I interviewed and heard testify stressed the power of making a choice to open their hearts to marriage disciplers and praised the ability of marriage disciplers to clinically confront and resolve marriage issues. In their narratives, disciplers embodied relationality and applied on-the-spot marital counseling. In Alicia's words, "They were a shoulder when I had a problem." Money, communication, sex, and romance were frequent targets of marriage discipling interventions. Therapeutic concentration in these areas is not unique. ICOC's discourse of relational hot spots reflected those promoted by outside marriage "experts" in clinical counseling, self-help marriage texts, and grocery store magazine racks. Disciplers and leaders naming these issues as important points of therapy resonated then with members' cultural understanding of what marital topics should take center focus.

Performances of heroic marriage interventions were always framed in romantic language and gesture. Ronny searched for a word to complete his love poem. Alicia wanted me to hear a romantic tape. Another wife read me a list that her husband had composed for her that noted everything he loved about her: "love," "strength," and "patience," followed by "your little red nighty" and "the way you kiss." Most married members who told me their stories of relational healing closed with cards, poems, and romantic stories and/or gestures—images of ICOC-healed marriages as exceptionally romantic and fulfilling. This should not be surprising; our therapeutic culture is full of venues for helping individuals secure romantic marriage: sex counselors, couples' therapists, and bookshelves of marriage and romance advice self-help guides. These efforts and products construct and reaffirm long-standing cultural beliefs about what romance is: a list of idealized notions that include love at first sight, altruism, forever after, expensive gifts, companionship, great sex, and interdependence. Romance is a moral ideal; marriage and intimate relationships are perceived as morally sound when they are represented through romantic discourse and language. Images of what romance is confront individuals frequently in various media forms—in magazines, on television, in movies and literature, and through fashion. The ICOC is not alone in its Christian approach and outreach through promotion of romance in love and marriage; 'Christian romances' and sex manuals are part of a booming religious publishing industry (Ferré 1990).[4]

Even though member stories of romance and successful discipling were grounded in an individual's own experiences—for example, Ronny's poems on his shelves were his poems, written to reflect how he felt about Julie and describe their life together—individual stories of saved marriages were shaped by formal organizational discourse. DPI's marriage advice text, *Friends and Lovers: Marriage as God Designed It*, was a book prominently displayed on bookshelves and left out on countertops in many of the City COC homes I visited. I noticed that some members carried this text and other DPI guidebooks with their Bible to services and group events. DPI texts such as *Friends and Lovers* were, in many ways, crucial elements of ICOC boundary making—they were books that members could keep in their homes, and carry with them and refer to as they ventured out into the diseased secular relational world. These books were symbols of ICOC therapeutic power, constant reminders of the ICOC community as a sacred healing place. Greil and Rudy (1984), in their essay on structural components of identity transforming institutions (ITOs), break down the idea of social encapsulation into three types: physical, social, and ideological. They suggest that some ITOs create a kind of "ideological encapsulation," meaning a kind of "space capsule" that enables members to "venture beyond the boundaries of the group for short periods of time without damage to their 'identity support systems.' " These space capsules are composed of learned symbolic physical behaviors, rituals, and/or memorization of ideological precepts—such as when Alcoholics Anonymous members memorize the " 'Twelve Steps' which codify the AA outlook and program" (267–268). The walls of these capsules are further strengthened when members have material group symbols to carry with them: for example, a sheet of paper with the twelve steps on it, a piece of jewelry in the shape of a group sacred object, an item of clothing that distinguishes, or a book that represents the ideals and beliefs of the religious community. *Friends and Lovers*, like other DPI texts, were tangible reminders that the ICOC movement had extraordinary powers to heal marriage relationships and that in order to access that power, couples must be fully committed to a marriage discipling relationship. They were also literary guideposts for individual performances of marital healing.

Friends and Lovers encourages framing ICOC marriage success narratives in romantic language and gesture. Authors Sam and Geri Laing (Laing and Laing 1996, 45–46) suggest: "Write down your feelings of love, thanksgiving and affection in cards and notes. . . . Surprise him or her with a note scrawled on a scrap of paper and left taped on the mirror, tucked under the pillow, or stashed away in a briefcase or purse. These are small, thoughtful expressions that make marriage a joy and can rekindle a dying love." In preparation for one yearly marriage retreat, City COC leaders distributed a flyer to the congregation requesting church couples to "write a story describing the time they got engaged." City COC leaders were to choose and honor winning stories "in categories such as most romantic, most elaborate, least expected, largest audience and 'It's about time! I've been waiting for years!' " The romantic stories submitted would legitimate ICOC marriage in future publications and performances.

In *Friends and Lovers*, Sam and Geri Laing also offer examples of "real people" whom they have "worked with" in their ministries, models of heroic discipler interventions. Like Jeremy and Alicia's story, the Laings began with a description of a marriage in imminent relational danger: "When we came to know John and Michelle, they both had a vacant, dead look in their eyes. They were discouraged, depressed and weary. It seemed they had everything to be happy about: healthy children, a beautiful home and a solid position in the full-time ministry [ICOC]" (Laing and Laing 1996, 157–158). The Laings tell us that John experienced the death of his father and failure at work, feeling that he was "ineffective in leading others because he knew he was not close to his wife and was failing in leading his own family." His wife, Michelle, possessed "a positive and outgoing personality" but was "unhappy with herself, her marriage and her children." John would reach out to her "through his longings for sexual affection," but felt "unloved and alone . . . dying slowly from within." Michelle was unresponsive sexually partly because she "knew she was many pounds overweight (as was John)." Being overweight "embarrassed her and made her sexually indifferent." The Laings intervened as marriage disciplers.

"Talking to John and Michelle separately and then comparing notes," the Laings wrote, "was quite an experience." They seemed to have a very different "recounting" of the "simplest situations." The Laings' diagnosis: "We realized . . . both of them were so completely self-focused that they could not begin to comprehend the other's point of view." Their prescription: relationality, mutual compassion, and expressivity: "They could learn to resolve conflict only if they began to make serious efforts to understand and empathize with each other." Through making each of them "face up to their individual deficiencies," and learn to "speak openly to each other," the Laings managed to help them save their marriage. "Today," the Laings professed, "John and Michelle are happily in love . . . communication has radically improved, as has their romantic life. All of this has taken much work, patience and self-examination, but they are now much more aware of what they need to do to meet one another's needs."

Sexual satisfaction in marriage is a widespread cultural good. When it comes to heterosexual marital sex and romance, ICOC leaders, and conservative Christians in general, have been quite explicit about how to perform romance and achieve sexual satisfaction. This approach reflects a society where sex therapy and guidebooks that offer explicit understanding of biology and sexual stimulation are not deviant but considered appropriate methods of improving selves. ICOC leaders promoted consultation of the mainstream Christian text *The Gift of Sex*, written by Clifford and Joyce Penner (1981), a couple raised as Mennonites who have practiced Christianity in Baptist, Presbyterian, and Congregational church communities. *The Gift of Sex* is a good example of the clinical prescriptive nature of such righteous romance pedagogy. Penner and Penner's (1981, 72–73) chapter entitled "Discovering and Sharing Our Bodies" guides readers through an " 'I'll show you mine, if you'll show me yours' kind of sharing time." City COC members described marriage disciplers as intimately invested in whether or not those they discipled were content with their sex lives and as applying an individualized and detailed approach to sex counseling. One church member said her discipler gave her a chart that showed erotic points and exercises to do with her husband so that they could come to understand each other's bodies. Another church member, who was having difficulty becoming aroused with her husband, talked about her discipler showing her a diagram of her vagina and talking through how to achieve an orgasm step-by-step. This practice, she claimed, helped her learn to "finally have orgasms." These intimate and explicit attempts to help individuals achieve sexual satisfaction made sense to members; they seemed a sound therapeutic practice as secular sex counselors and publications promoted similar approaches and interventions.

Almost all member narratives of exceptional marriage through discipling described sex inside the church as the best they had ever had. Here again, this emphasis in individual narratives is seen at work in formal literature and group discourse. The Laings write, in *Friends and Lovers* (Laing and Laing 1996, 80–84), "It seems everyone is hungry for sex, yet few are satisfied. . . . *God has a plan.* It is not just a good plan. It is the best plan, and it works without fail. We can understand it, and we can follow it. We can check out of the striptease scene and get into the real action!" How can members get this "real action"? Well, "The best sex is married sex. The most exciting, fulfilling and thrilling sex takes place in the marriage bed, not the bed of illicit sex." "Married sex," the Laings note, "gets better as the years go by. It becomes increasingly intimate, pleasurable and satisfying. . . . As we know each other longer and better, we become more comfortable in our lovemaking." With the predictable humor of ICOC leaders Sam Laing adds, "Honeymoons are wasted on amateurs. . . . They [older marriages] not only still have the fire—it burns brighter and hotter!" Implicit in Laing's message is the understanding that to get this kind of hot sex one needs to seek the advice and counsel of married couples in the church: *God's plan*, in the ICOC, is the marriage discipling relationship.

Members' stories, in addition to stressing sex and romance, included the discipling community and disciplers as helping them improve physical health and body, thus improving marital sex lives. (Recall Michelle and John's sexual relationship was described by the Laings as threatened by unwanted pounds.) During one Wednesday night ICOC service, the prayer theme was losing weight, and "church sisters" witnessed to others of how God had helped them shed pounds and improve relationships with their husbands. Weight loss was salvation not just for women; it was prescribed for men too. Sam Laing, during an all-male regional event, told a group of men: "I don't want to hear about metabolism. I don't want to hear about genetics. I want you to go with an infallible weight loss program. You can lose weight. I know some of you need medical help, but some of us, as men, have allowed our bodies to degenerate. We are prematurely old." He related this sinful state of being overweight to the weakening of intimate relationships, suggesting that an unhealthy lifestyle is a sin that can potentially destroy marriages: "And you wonder why your sex life is nowhere? Well, your wife's not really fired up looking at you with your shirt off anymore!" In the ICOC, and many other contemporary religious movements, the promise of "looking good," an end goal of many health and wellness practices, is a significant and alluring organizational commodity. As Griffith (1997, 141–150) notes, weight loss under a Christian rubric, as in secular practices, often involves submission and discipline alongside individual will. Health and wellness discourses support the idea that individuals must take responsibility for being "good," consuming medically labeled "healthy" foods and exercising while staying away from "bad" food and behaviors such as munching on candy bars and chips while lounging on the couch (couch potato sin). The "infallible weight loss program" promoted above is the discipling relationship—disciplers are there to help you, monitor your progress, and scowl if you were "bad," like routine weigh-ins at Weight Watchers or any number of other monitored weight loss pay-for-service programs. Such monitored health and wellness practices and relationships made sense to members as a sound and culturally acceptable method for improving self, body, and intimate relationships. The ICOC formal message was clear: "thin" and "in shape" spouses had healthy marriages; "overweight," "obese," or "flabby" spouses risked unhealthy marriages.

In addition to divorce and extramarital affairs, domestic violence was another worldly relational disease, a more recently publicized social problem that ICOC formal narratives showcased as threatening couples in the secular world. The story of disciplers changing abusers' hearts was a powerful moral narrative. During one Sunday morning regional event, a white married couple in their early thirties offered a formal testimony to approximately three hundred members that showcased how the church had saved their marriage from its violent existence. Even though this couple was from another ICOC congregation, during my time in the field I heard the wife tell this marriage save story twice. The couple's story followed an awesome marriage formal script: their marriage was seriously threatened and subsequently saved by choosing to submit to ICOC marriage disciplers and their therapeutic skills.

The wife spoke first. Tearfully, she related how her husband, when first married, had hit her and even thrown her body across rooms into walls. She related how his abuse and her empty forgiveness became a pattern, and how her silence and inability to communicate her true feelings often instigated his attacks. When the husband spoke to the congregation, he confirmed his sinful actions as a non-Christian. She told us that she never would have believed that her husband could have changed into the "loving, caring, and awesome man he is today." But he did change, she insisted, when he met church "brothers" and began studying the Bible and becoming open with his discipler. She changed too, she insisted, and stopped "provoking" his anger by learning how to better communicate. As they both studied the Bible and opened their "hearts" to disciplers, their marriage became stronger and the physical abuse ended. Like Alicia and Ronny's heroic saves that concluded with displays of poetic romantic gesture, this couple read us a loving and romantic anniversary card that he had recently given to her—a symbol of how their relationship had been changed from a violent nightmare to a fulfilling and caring marriage. This couple, in *both* admitting fault, had taken the first step encouraged by disciplers on the road to successful Christian marriage counseling.

In all narratives of heroic marriage saves, disciplers and other members, "older Christians" with congregational status, named and identified sin in other couples. In this way, among others, the organization had some hand in crafting the relational "problems" that were addressed in marriages and thus the marriage save stories told by members. I was informed several times by members and congregational leaders that if they saw or heard a problem going on in a marriage, whether it was the tone that one spouse took with another, the husband or wife spending too much money, or a spouse dissatisfied with sex, it was the responsibility of disciplers to report this to leaders and/or intervene themselves depending on their status in the leadership/discipling hierarchy. Similarly, couples were asked by leaders to be open to marital counseling on any issue brought to the attention of disciplers. Ronny told me that he really "loved this about the church" and that "there is nothing that is not on the table." Members described marriage disciplers as applying constant pressure and checking to make sure that spouses followed through with the practical advice given. One wife stated of her marriage disciplers, "They keep us on top of things." Evette told me that she advised a woman who was learning to be a marriage discipler that "you made a decision for God to work in their hearts. She said, 'I'll call. I'll call.' I said,

'No, you go over and be on, keep pushing yourself, keep giving yourself [as a marriage discipler] until they tell you I don't want it.'You really have to go for it!"

Premarital counseling was also talked about in ICOC formal and informal discourse as a unique and mandatory group asset.[5] In many other churches and in secular society, couples' marriage and premarriage counseling is an individual choice; generally both partners must agree to go in order to reap the benefits. A major narrative point in stories of heroic and productive marriage discipling was that spouses and future spouses could not opt out. Had I been a single woman conducting field studies in the ICOC, chapter 2 here may have highlighted narratives of church singles as family, dating in the Kingdom, and stories of "awesome" monitored and mandatory dating and premarital counseling.

This mandatory counseling expectation, the inescapable relationship with another church couple who would name marital problems and help you build practical and productive skills for avoiding and facing conflict, was presented by members and leaders as comforting and reassuring. Like other Christian marriage counseling approaches, ICOC members stressed the individual Godly marriage triangle. As one member said to me: "Marriage is a three-way relationship—your relationship with God and your relationship with each other. And without those strands on a cord, twined together to make a strong rope, it's not near as strong, you *need* those three together to make it work." But they also made clear that you needed an adhesive to hold those ropes together: to complete and reinforce the triangle you needed to be in a discipling relationship with another ICOC couple. Discipling (marriage and one-on-one) was, in so many ways, represented as a kind of intermediary, mediating relationship with God and each other. This was a large part of the appeal, and in the end, as the unified movement failed, a large force in downfall and disillusionment. But for at least two decades, member narratives, guided by experience and formal group discourse, were able to present a somewhat convincing portrait of disciplers as exceptionally able to mediate and navigate the cultural paradoxes of gender.

Disciplers Navigate the Gender Maze

During separate interviews I asked Ronny and Julie to tell me about the couples that they felt they had helped the most as marriage disciplers. They both spoke of Adam and Mindy. Ronny described this couple as coming from families where "the woman ran the show," and having to teach Adam how to be "assertive." Julie described Mindy as "very outgoing and a take-charge person," who took advantage of her "laid-back" husband and did things like "go out and spend eighty dollars on a bottle of shampoo." They understood their efforts to help this couple as constant and demanding. Ronny said he would "challenge him on really taking responsibility for the household." Julie related that at one point they both told Adam, "We're going to buy you a pink dress, put it on you, and give her the blue jeans!" Adam and Mindy finally had the "hearts to change," but not after a great deal of intervention and counseling from Ronny, Julie, and other church members. This representation of marriage discipling signifies the constant, inescapable cultural processes of gender construction and negotiation, the particular challenges that contemporary society poses to these processes, and the presentation of management of these processes by ICOC marriage disciplers.

The rich body of literature on gender and religion produced by sociologists over the past twenty years explores the negotiated and complex character of gender and family roles and ideology in conservative Christian movements (Ammerman 1987; Bartkowski 2004, 2001; Brasher 1998; Gallagher 2003; Gallagher and Smith 1999; Griffith 1997; Ingersoll 2003; Lockhart 2000; Rose 1987; Stacey and Gerard 1990). Julie Ingersoll (2003, 16) notes that "gender is a central organizing principle and a core symbolic system" in the U.S. Christian evangelical subculture and that the "interpretation and control of that symbol is not fixed and permanent, but . . . the result of an ongoing process of construction (production), which entails a tremendous degree of negotiation." Religious institutions are historically well-known for actively negotiating, challenging, and constructing gender boundaries, even if it is only in the last few decades of the twentieth century that gender as a category of analysis in the discipline of sociology has received rigorous attention. A close look at the Oneida community, for example, a mid-nineteenth-century socialist Christian movement in New York State, offers an interesting case for the process of both challenging and upholding current cultural assumptions of gender and sexuality in religious communities.

Under a radical system of group heterosexual marriage, Oneida members were forbidden to fall prey to romantic love but were encouraged to have sexual relationships with various commune members (sexual relationships had to be approved by leader John Humphrey Noyes). Women were not expected to have babies and required permission from the community if they wanted children. Noyes taught "male continence," withdrawal before ejaculation, as a "necessary condition for the inauguration of complex marriage" (Klaw 1993, 58). Noyes's belief in "complex marriage" and his monitoring of the practice of male continence allowed Oneida women choices in sexuality and reproduction not available to them outside the community. Furthermore, if a woman had a child, she was not responsible for domestic duties for about a year after, and at a certain point was required to turn the child "over to the foster mothers in the Children's House." In a clear challenge to then current ideals of female caretaking and motherhood, one Oneida community writer noted, "We do not believe that motherhood is the chief end of a woman's life; that she was made for the children she can bear. She was made for God and for herself" (Klaw 1993, 132). Women's lives within the Oneida community also departed from then normative white Protestant assumptions of womanhood as isolated domesticity as they lived "in close association with other women," and "found long-lasting friendships with other women" in an extended domestic community (Klaw 1993, 132–133).

Spencer Klaw, in his detailed historical look at the Oneida community, *Without Sin: The Life and Death of the Oneida Community*, notes the complexity of women's position to both challenge and adhere to cultural gender expectations: "While Oneidans agreed with such militant feminists as Victoria Woodhull and Tennessee Claflin that women in America were cruelly exploited by men, they differed with these and other leaders of the women's rights movement on a fundamental point . . . they ridiculed the feminist claim that women were, or should be, the equals of men." The Oneida community provides a vivid example of the inevitable tensions and complexities in religious communities as they work to negotiate and construct gender roles and responsibilities that will appeal and make sense to their members. Religious groups, and especially high boundary religious groups, are active social sites for appropriating, rejecting, and constructing gender ideals.

Many would argue that Ingersoll's point about the centrality of gender as an organizing principle in the evangelical subculture is true for all people in all cultures. Gender, the assigning of profound cultural meaning to body and sex, is a universal social process.[6] As Judith Lorber (1994, 13) notes,

> Talking about gender for most people is the equivalent of fish talking about water. Gender is so much the routine ground of everyday activities that questioning its taken-for-granted assumptions and presuppositions is like thinking about whether the sun will come up. Gender is so pervasive that in our society we assume it is bred into our genes. Most people find it hard to believe that gender is constantly created and re-created out of human interaction, out of social life, and is the texture and order of that social life. Yet gender, like culture, is a human production that depends on everyone constantly "doing gender." (West and Zimmerman 1987)

Doing gender today, one could argue, is no more difficult than doing gender was in the mid-nineteenth century when Oneida men and women pledged commitment to Noyes's system of complex marriage in a dominant Protestant society. This was a point in history where the forces of an industrializing nation ushered in new idealized gender relationships and social spaces that saw women as Godly caretakers of home and children and men as venturing away from home into a harsh world of wage labor. Clearly, negotiating and constructing gendered selves and communities today could be no more difficult a task than it was to black men and women throughout U.S. history—individuals who have consistently developed distinct gender ideals while being held accountable by whites to dominant notions of masculinity and femininity.[7] Yet, negotiating and constructing gendered selves at the turn of the twenty-first century does present a historically particular complex social gender and family landscape to master. Connell (1995, 73) reminds us that "gender is an internally complex structure, where a number of different logics are superimposed." The logical organization of gender is based in social structure and is continually challenged by individuals and institutions, thus "masculinity, like femininity, is always liable to internal contradiction and historical disruption." The gender dilemmas, beliefs, and practices that arise in members' narratives of ICOC marriage saves demonstrate a range of historically particular structural gender beliefs about men, women, and the institution of marriage.

In stressing gender confusion and ambiguity as rampant in our society, ICOC leaders and members echoed conservative Christian and antifeminist gender discourse. For example, James C. Dobson, founder and president of the conservative organization Focus on the Family, writes: "Traditional concepts of masculinity and femininity have been battered and ridiculed for more than 20 years, creating confusion for both men and women. . . . Should a man stand when a woman enters the room? Will he please her by opening the door for her? Should he give her his seat on a crowded bus or subway? Have all the rules changed? Is there anything predictable and certain in the new order?" (Dobson 2003) ICOC members and leaders used sentences like "Men don't know whether to wear a pink dress or pants," like Ronny and Julie earlier, many times during services, small Bible studies, and interviews. This description hit a very real core of member day-to-day life experience. Many were young families, dual-earner households juggling work, family, and church responsibilities. They were also men and women who had been raised in a culture where competing notions of gender abounded: for example, promotion of egalitarian marriage and professional careers for both husbands and wives alongside images of women as the natural caretakers of children and domestic specialists; and images of fathers as engaged in child rearing and emotionally present alongside male breadwinner ideals and persistent essentialist notions of men as more logical and lacking in emotionality.[8] These late twentieth-, early twenty-first-century ideas and expectations coincided with precarious economic conditions: the widening of the gap between the rich and the poor, a rise in the contingent workforce, and the growing inevitability that for a family to survive, most parents must work for wages outside of the home. In these contemporary work and family social conditions, gender responsibilities and ideals were negotiated and contested daily: Who pays the bills? Who does the grocery shopping? Who plans family meals? Who initiates sex? Who is responsible for watching the kids when both have a major project due at work that week? Who stays home if the kids are sick? Who supervises homework? Who takes the kids to ball games? Who takes them to dance lessons? ICOC's organizational gender repertoire provided various answers and methods of reconciliation to these and other spousal dilemmas.

Most important, ICOC's gender repertoire, reflective of secular culture and the evangelical subculture,[9] seemed endless—descriptions of marriage discipling prescriptions and naming of marital problems drew from various cultural beliefs and essentialist notions about what women and men should do. My field notes, interview transcripts, and group formal literature reflected a multitude of contradictory ideas: men were to be good providers/breadwinners for their wives and family, women were to be caretakers and domestics, God outlined specific and clear-cut traditional gender roles in the Bible, Jesus called for gender equality and egalitarianism in marriage, women were to pursue an education and be respected for professional and church leadership careers, men were to be caretakers and connected emotionally to their wives and children, men were to participate in domestic chores, women were to be "strong-minded," women were to be strong leaders in the church, men were to be strong leaders in the church, men were to "lead" the family, women were to "shape the family," men were to be aggressive in bed, women were to let men lead in bed, women were to instigate and plan sexual encounters with their husbands, men were to respect their wives' sexual needs, men were to express their emotions, women were too emotional and talkative and needed to listen more, women should express their emotions and make their feelings known, men should not be too emotional, and anger was both a masculine and feminine characteristic to be controlled.

At first, I found the variety of these deeply asserted beliefs about gender in member and leader narratives of marriage discipling an overwhelming analytical challenge. I suppose I expected, given that I knew they promoted conservative gender ideals and a return to the "traditional' family," that they would offer a more cohesive ideology. But their discourse seemed a magnified mishmash of gender dos, don'ts, and inevitabilities, no more clear than any individual or organizational approach outside the group—a reflection of the gendered waters we all swim in. At times, as I reflected in my field journal, they seemed even more confusing because leaders and disciplers expected members to enact each gendered stance, position, and performance with such heightened passion and commitment. Was there a clear ICOC gender ideology, a set of beliefs about how men and women should interact in marriage relationships, a set of beliefs that articulated family roles that members and potential converts were drawn to? Was this ICOC set of ideas about gender more "traditional" than not? Why did their beliefs and statements about relationships between the sexes shift and change from narrative to narrative? How could that uncertainty and variation prove attractive to members and potential converts? Recent social theory and empirical research in conservative religious groups provided clues to these questions.

Conservative and evangelical Christians' ideas about how men and women should behave are widely misunderstood, often cast by liberal Christians and secular folks as solely an antifeminist return to traditional patriarchal family and church arrangements. This assessment is understandable; to listen to the rhetoric of Dobson, Phyllis Schlafly, Pat Robertson, Jerry Falwell and other highly visible conservative Christians, one could easily develop a picture of women in the home, stripped of professional career choice and raising the kids, and men out in the workforce as breadwinners "leading" their families. Yet, if one pries the door open to look more closely at this conservative family model, we find that it is not so simple, nor does it represent a reclaiming of a normative nuclear family. Empirical findings to date suggest that conservative religious groups and individuals are indeed involved in a project of balancing and making sense of various contradictory gender ideals and practices. Furthermore, research suggests that conservative religious folks are navigating our cultural gender maze using therapeutic tools and practical approaches that are really not so different from those of many liberal religious and secular heterosexual married couples.

The Promise Keepers, a well-known controversial interdenominational Christian men's movement that received a great deal of media attention for its reported "antifeminist" conservative gender ideology, offers a model contemporary case. First, Promise Keeper ideas about masculinity and femininity are not of a single "traditional" stance, but reflect various ideas and practices (Bartkowski 2004; Lockhart 2000), the particulars of which are worked out in smaller Promise Keeper cell groups of men who meet throughout the country. These formal Promise Keeper ideologies, Lockhart (2000, 78) argues, are indicative of those prescribed in much conservative Christian Protestant literature. Biblical "traditionalists," he notes, "argue that gender differences and roles were created by God" and that "God desires a hierarchy of order in society." These roles and hierarchy of order are to be found in the Holy Scriptures and "those placed in authority by God are husbands, parents, and pastors." In the most recent works of the traditionalists, the "authoritarian perspective is balanced by a strong stress on loving and serving one's family." This traditionalist gender approach was a prominent gender stance in the ICOC. For example, Sam Laing preached to a large group of ICOC men at a regional event: "God wanted men to be men and be strong and firm and lead the household. . . . You need to repent and become masculine." In the ICOC and other conservative religious movements, traditionalist approaches are often legitimated through an *essentialist* gender discourse: the idea that women and men behave, as a group, in particular ways because of some inherent, biological, or natural cause.

Essentialist gender discourse made sense to ICOC members and individuals in other conservative groups because it resonated with popular presentations of the importance of nature in the ways women and men behave. For example, members and leaders often referred to John Gray's popular book, *Men Are from Mars, Women Are from Venus: A Practical Guide for Improving Communication and Getting What You Want in Your Relationships*, as they attempted to make sense of communication and sex in marriage relationships. Jeremy described men as naturally more pragmatic and logical, and who should therefore be leaders in marriage and family. He and many other ICOC men talked of having to *learn* to communicate and express their feelings, constantly fighting that "male" tendency to go into a "cave." Leaders reinforced essentialist discourse. Sam Laing argues in *Friends and Lovers* (28–29), "Let's face it: It is usually men who hold back in communication. For the most part, wives need to talk, want to talk and try to talk. Most women would give anything if their husbands would stop and listen to them. But men so often do not hear." Laing casts such gendered behavior as sinful: "They [men] do not talk. They sit in silence and superficiality. Let me call this masculine trait by several names it so richly deserves: *Arrogant. Hard-headed. Ignorant. Foolish.*"

Laing's focus on the importance of male expressivity reflects a now competing model of masculinity that took shape as medical therapeutic models came to dominate in mid-twentieth-century U.S. society. During this time, social scientists and medical professionals began to argue that an instrumental male role model was potentially physically dangerous and argued that men needed to adopt expressivity and cease working long hours in an anxiety-provoking world of work. Barbara Ehrenreich (1983, 70) captures the genesis of this moral panic surrounding middle-to upper-middle-class manhood in her book *The Hearts of Men: American Dreams and the Flight from Commitment*: "In the 1950s, medical opinion began to shift from genetic to psychosocial explanations of men's biological frailty: There was something wrong with the way men lived, and the diagnosis of what was wrong came increasingly to resemble the popular (at least among some men) belief that men 'died in the harness,' destroyed by the burden of responsibility. The disease which most clearly indicted the breadwinning role, and which became emblematic of men's vulnerability in the face of bureaucratic capitalist society, was coronary heart disease." Male expressivity as representative of freedom from the bonds of deadly breadwinning took shape in the mid-1970s through Men's liberation books like Warren Farrell's *The Liberated Man* and Jack Nichols's *Men's Liberation;* these writers "argued that the male sex role was oppressive and ought to be changed or abandoned," that to be healthy a man must be able to release and express himself (Connell 1995, 23–24). Expressivity as a relational skill is now ingrained in our therapeutic culture; yet, it still exists alongside the notion that men are breadwinners, naturally more logical, and have to work harder to learn emotive habits and better communication skills. ICOC leader Gordon Ferguson (1997, 110) states: "Men in our culture have what appears to be a natural aversion to this level of communication. However, women are much more comfortable with it, and most wives deeply desire to experience this kind of communication with their husbands." Both mainstream and religio-therapeutic prescriptive approaches suggest that men develop skills of relationality to combat this inherent gender disease. In the ICOC, relationality was presented by members and leaders as the discipler's scalpel, an ideological instrument that "Dr. Gordon," Sam Laing, Kip McKean, and other skilled local and regional ICOC Christian counselors would use to cut deep into the "hearts" of Kingdom "brothers" to remove natural male attitudes that stood in the way of mutuality.

Tackling and conquering the negative manifestations of gender essentialism filled descriptions of disciplers' marriage interventions and advice for how to achieve a healthy married sex life: Sam Laing suggests: "A man needs no emotional reinforcement at all to become aroused. The mere sight of his wife's body can quickly move him . . . women, on the other hand, need a stronger emotional connection with their husbands" (Laing and Laing 1996, 97–98). "Women," he notes, "do not have to have an orgasm during every session of lovemaking to experience contentment while a man must." Laing tells us: "Men . . . [y]ou become frustrated and impatient, wondering why your cold frigid wife does not start to heavy-breathe when you try to pull her blouse off, or when she beholds you in all your unclothed masculine splendor. Wives, you wonder how this sex-beast could go from the depths of hardly speaking to you all day to the heights of passion in under ten seconds!" Laing's answer to these essential differences involve mutuality: "If husbands and wives practice the law of love and are more eager to please than to be pleased, the issue of frequency can be solved." The bottom line, "How much sex is enough? The answer is really quite simple: You are having enough sex when both people are completely satisfied. If either partner is not content, then increase your frequency until both the husband's and wife's needs are met" (Laing and Laing 1996, 86). Furthermore, with regard to quality and kind, "the goal should be to allow your wife to enjoy orgasms as often as she is capable, but without a sense of preoccupation or performance. . . . Focus instead on a loving, mutually satisfying relationship, and you will feel content and connected" (Laing and Laing 1996, 98). To feel connected, Laing stresses, couples must express themselves and listen well: "TALK! Don't make your partner be a mind reader. Develop your own special 'love language' "(Laing and Laing 1996, 100). City COC narratives of marriage discipling were full of references to disciplers teaching spouses how to talk openly about sex.

In stories of disciplers' interventions, removing selfishness from hearts leveled essentialist gender difference and promoted "open hearts" and egalitarian marriage practices and habits. "Selfish hearts" surfaced frequently in member and leader stories of marriage discipling efforts as a metaphor for undesirable essentialized gendered characteristics and cultural stereotypes. "The aggressive feminist," "the physically and/or verbally abusive husband/father," "the overbearing, talkative wife," all made an appearance in ICOC's production of relational conditions cured by disciplers teaching mutuality.

Christian movements like the ICOC and Promise Keepers, groups that promote traditional and essentialist gender notions, have to contend with another strong ideological current in secular culture and Christian subcultures: gender egalitarianism. This, which Lockhart (2000, 80) names a "Biblical feminist" perspective, "focuses on the unity of humanity" and encourages that "God created both men and women, and declared them 'very good.' " This viewpoint sees the solution to marital ills as empowering all: "God empowering the man to change his life, the husband empowering his wife as a co-leader, the father empowering his children to become equals." Biblical feminism surfaced in the ICOC as what Judith Stacey (1991) has called a kind of "postfeminism": an attachment to core tenets of first and second wave feminisms (like egalitarianism and concern for the empowerment of women) while at the same time naming feminism dangerous. One way that Christian groups resolve the contradictory stance of sustaining both traditional, essentialist ideology and biblical feminism has been through stressing, as a grounding principle, core tenets of therapeutic culture like relationality and mutuality.

Lockhart (2000, 80) argues that evangelical and conservative religious groups heavily support a third distinct approach to gender negotiation, the "Why Can't We All Get Along: The Pragmatic Counseling Approach." He notes that this is the "most prevalent" perspective in conservative Christian literature, a "more pragmatic or therapeutic" approach that concentrates on "healing hurts and finding practical solutions." Lockhart stresses that these "pragmatic counselors are not as concerned as others about the details of where masculinity and femininity come from or what gender roles are supposed to be. Instead, their concern is what best can be done in each situation to help people get along and do what needs to be done"(Lockhart 2000, 81). This Why Can't We All Get Along approach was dominant in ICOC discourse as well. I later use here a well-documented enigmatic conservative Christian doctrine, female submission, to illustrate the construction and negotiation of gender traditionalism and biblical feminism through a pragmatic counseling approach—three contemporary religious approaches to facing gender issues in conservative Christian groups.

The traditionalist perspective in conservative Christianity legitimates female submission by drawing from the book of Ephesians 5:22–24, which reads, "Wives, submit to your husbands as to the Lord. For the husband is the head of the wife as Christ is the head of the church, his body, of which he is the Savior. Now as the church submits to Christ, so also wives should submit to their husbands in everything" (NIV). However, as I, and most other ethnographers studying female submission in conservative Christian groups have found, wives are quick to follow Ephesians 5:22–24 with 5:25–31 when they talk of submission: "Husbands, love your wives, just as Christ loved the church and gave himself up for her to make her holy, cleansing her by the washing with water through the word, and to present her to himself as a radiant church, without stain or wrinkle or any other blemish, but holy and blameless. In this same way, husbands ought to love their wives as their own bodies. He who loves his wife loves himself."

It is not hard to see how verses 5:25–31 can work to support the biblical feminist position. Enacting this contradictory stance, where women are to "submit to husbands" in "everything" and the husband is the "head of the wife," while husbands are called to give themselves up for their wives, as we can imagine, can be confusing in everyday application. In fact, in the City COC, stories of marriage discipling saving couples' relationships frequently referred to female submission as a "confusing" and "funny" kind of thing. Amy, a black woman in her late thirties, told me, "When I'm marrying, I'm marrying my brother. We are sister and brother first before anything else. I'll submit to God, but there's no man made me. I won't submit to another man." She continued, "People think of submission as you have to submit, well my husband washes the dishes, my husband cleans the bathroom, and I do the same!" Amy insisted that female submission was misunderstood by most, and when actualized within the ICOC movement, under the guidance of skilled disciplers, it was a great source of relational power.

Women titled their stories as about female submission (traditionalist), their tone and defense was communicated with seemingly biblical feminist intent (as Amy's assertion above suggests), but narratives were mostly about learning to enact mutual submission and relationality (in line with Lockhart's Why Can't We All Get Along approach). I only heard a few practical descriptions of wives learning to submit to their husbands' wishes that did not entail mutuality, and these were primarily around financial issues. Several women told me that they were counseled by their marriage disciplers that they should not spend any money without first "talking it over" with their husbands. Two women told me stories of disciplers helping them "fight a selfish heart" because they wanted to buy an item that their husband felt they could not afford. These stories were performances of femininity that adhered to cultural assumptions of men as the financial heads of households. But most stories of marriage disciplers helping with communication and sex issues were primarily about learning mutual respect.

Janet, a white woman in her early twenties, began her story of female submission with a biblical feminist voice. She told me that it was extremely difficult for her to "learn submission" after having been a leader in the City COC's singles ministry for several years. She was opposed to the idea of submitting to her husband and had gained a great deal of informal organizational power and respect from her position as a singles ministry leader. She said that disciplers had to teach her how "powerful female submission" could be for a woman once she opened her heart to it. She offered as an example the following discipling session that occurred late one evening after Janet and her husband put in an emergency phone call to their marriage disciplers:

> The wife of her marriage discipling couple asked both her and her husband to read First Corinthians 13:4–7 out loud. "Everywhere it says love," her discipler instructed, "you put your name in." Janet read: "Janet is patient, Janet is kind. Janet does not envy, she does not boast, she is not proud. Janet is not rude, Janet is not self-seeking, Janet is not easily angered, Janet keeps no record of wrongs. Janet does not delight in evil but rejoices with the truth. Janet always trusts, always hopes, always perseveres." The discipler then asked Janet if she had been all those things to her husband. Janet admitted that she had not lived up to these standards of love. Her husband then read the passage aloud, substituting his name. The wife of the discipling couple then asked him if he had been all those things to Janet. He admitted not living up to these standards of love. Reading this passage aloud, Janet claimed, made them realize how silly they were being and brought her closer to her husband. They took this lesson as a tool and applied it frequently, their biblical marriage mantra given to them by marriage disciplers.

Janet's story (and those of other City COC women) of learning that female submission is really about mutual submission is not surprising. Gallagher and Smith (1999) argue that female submission, in the discourse of evangelical Christian women, manifests as a "rhetorical" submission and "practical" egalitarianism. Gallagher (2003), Brasher (1998), and Griffith (1997) offer works that suggest female submission for contemporary evangelical and fundamentalist Christian women can be an empowering stance, and that women often find power in the creation of their own social spaces and practices born of institutional religious gender segregation and hierarchy. However, the discursive attachment to the language and concept of "female submission" is also indicative of the limitations of institutions and individuals to fully embrace egalitarianism and mutuality; the insistence on adhering to female submission as part of a threefold conservative gender ideological position leaves much room for individual interpretation and power abuses.

Bartkowski (2001, 2004), Gallagher (2003), and Ingersoll (2003) offer evidence that the empirical reality of female submission is far more complex than previous research suggests. My ethnographic story here confirms their assertions. Most conservative religious efforts to perform gender in family are far from clear-cut, typically reflect individual circumstances, and depend a great deal on organizational practices that accompany a submissive female ideal. And too, as Ingersoll (2003, 1–7) makes clear, those telling us stories of female submission, especially if the research participant is still invested in the religious worldview, are likely to frame their stories in empowerment, mutuality, and egalitarianism. Research participants are aware that cultural ideals of mutuality and egalitarianism in intimate relationship are pervasive and that if they were to tell a story that centered on wives giving in to their husbands' wishes, they would be crossing normative assumptions of contemporary egalitarian marriage. So they present selves that adhere to secular gender and relationship norms. The voices of former ICOC members reflect this complexity of experience.[10]

Former ICOC female members told different stories of female submission. Some talked of being silenced and disempowered by female submission. Others spoke of female submission as empowering, a marital ethic they carried with them as they found a new home in another evangelical church. As the unified ICOC movement fell apart and female members voiced concerns on-line about the effects of submission, their stories varied as well: some saw ICOC female submission as a dangerous teaching, others found it brought them power and influence. All of these data support the assertion that female submission was a "puzzling," confusing teaching in the ICOC, and that resulting power dynamics in marriage and church relationships were highly dependent on individual circumstances. Still, the idea that "female submission" would bring mutual respect and strong marriages remained a distinguishing piece of the movement's gender discourse repertoire.[11] Female submission in the ICOC appealed to members because they were told stories framed in biblical feminist principles, stories of mutual submission and egalitarianism; and they were promised sacred marriage disciplers, personal ideological specialists who would figure out the appropriate submissive position for each marital interaction or disagreement.

Someone to Tattle To

Egalitarianism and relationality emerged as most prominent in City COC women's presentation of self. Alicia told me, "It's great because we are not alone in marriage. We have free counseling, someone to tattle to." Indeed, several women told me stories of "tattling" to their marriage disciplers, of using their marriage disciplers to get what they wanted. I heard more of these stories from women than men, most likely because I was limited in my interactions with male social groups. However, movement leaders encouraged spouses to "tell on" each other, and gave the impression that tattling went on in the marriages of top evangelists. At a large men-only event, Sam Laing used his marriage as an example: "There have been times when I've come home, ticked off, ready to give up on the Kingdom and become a Baptist. . . . Geri says, 'What are you doing? You sinner. You go and fix this up.' . . . I even give her permission, you can call anybody, call Steven Johnson, call Kip, call Randy, just tell on me. She will do that. . . . I will do the same for her and have many times."

City COC women's stories of "tattling" showcased mutual submission and relationality as the core ethic at work in their efforts; but implicit in their presentations was the idea that if the desire for something was very deep, they were able to get it through employment of disciplers. Alicia told a detailed account of using a marriage discipler to fulfill a longtime dream: a family dog. Laura told a story of how marriage disciplers helped her in a long-fought marital issue: her desire for her husband to initiate sex more often. These women had different end goals, but both stories illustrate disciplers as being used by members with status to fulfill individual and relational goals.

Recall, at the beginning of this chapter, that Alicia told a marriage discipling story stressing communication, learning to control her emotions, and developing a romantic and sexually satisfying marriage relationship with Jeremy. She also insisted that church women had taught her how to be a submissive wife. During our formal interview, Alicia told me about how much she admired the husband who had been (along with his wife) counseling (marriage discipling) Alicia and Jeremy for years: "He is one of the most kind people in the world. He is very focused. Every time we get together he asks how things are going and he helped me get my dog." "How so?" I asked.

> Well, Jeremy was like, we don't live in a barn we cannot get a dog! So I sat at the table and cried. I said Mike [the marriage discipler], I always had a dog growing up, always. And now you mean to tell me that I have to put my dream of having a dog away for the rest of my life. I'm like, I want my kids to know that feeling of man's best friend. I want that. And I was so convicted about it and Carrie [Mike's wife] was like, well she didn't like pets either, so she wasn't helping at all. She could have cared less if I got a dog or not and she told me that. And so I just looked at Mike and said, "Help me." And he said, "You know what, brother [to Jeremy], whatever makes your family run smoothly is what you should want for your family." He was like, "What is the harm in having a little dog?" And Jeremy, at that point, he wasn't really ready so he said he'd think about it.

"And so you got the dog?" I asked.

"Yeah, a little black dog. He's a mixture." She pointed to the dog sleeping in a corner. Laura, a thirty-five-year-old white woman married to a computer engineer, Charlie, a white man in his mid-thirties as well, told a story of how her marriage disciplers helped her husband initiate sex more often. Laura, who had given up a career as an accountant to stay home and raise their two children, complained to the wife of their marriage discipling team that Charlie was not initiating sex enough, and that she was always the aggressor. Her discipler advised her to "submit" and "let him lead." At the same time, Laura's husband was discipled by their marriage discipling couple on initiating sex more often. Laura explained,

"See, I was intimidating Charlie by the way I was acting [asking too often for sex]. After we got help it felt so good to be led in bed. I can be submissive then. Women crave that. Women get turned on when men lead." Laura suggested that their disciplers had enabled her to enact a more normative and desirable female sexuality: woman as receiver of sexual advances. Disciplers' solutions were described as preached in a language of essentialized femininity and masculinity, but, as Laura's description of her utilization of marriage disciplers suggests, she was taking charge of her sex life, leading (in bed) if you will, by involving marriage disciplers in the dispute. Similarly, Charlie could now feel as if he was "leading" because his behavior had been labeled such by disciplers and Laura, when, in fact, his advances were shaped by a marriage discipling process driven by his wife's concerns that he become more of a sexual leader and aggressor. Had Laura submitted, or did Charlie submit to her wishes? The answer is subjective, but clearly, the story she told achieved a purpose: marriage discipling was presented as an intimate therapeutic process able to help couples negotiate sensitive issues and to *enact mutuality*. Several women suggested that the "men, the brothers," can get through to their husbands—"The guys can get through to him where if I said the same thing it would be like I'm bugging him. If they talk to him, he can see it clearer." In their stories, marriage disciplers were presented as helping couples listen to each other—to see a spouse's position more clearly while sifting through various cultural assumptions of gender and sexuality.

Stories of successful marriage discipling interventions regarding marital sex consistently wavered back and forth from a language of female submission and male leadership and featured practical lessons of mutual submission and pleasure. Laura and Alicia described an essentialized sexuality, suggesting that women naturally "desire" men to "lead in bed," and at the same time offered lists of ways that women could seduce their husbands and "take charge." Alicia laughed as she recalled, "Jeremy takes charge and I tell him, that turns me on, I love that when you do that, even when you look at me and tell me, 'You need to be quiet.' . . . I'm like . . . it kind of makes me mad but women love that, women love to be led." Her description of another sexual encounter (encouraged by advice from her marriage discipler) involved her submitting to her husband by playing the role of servant and aggressor: dressing up in a sexy gown, disrobing her husband, and feeding him fruits and chocolates. In many ways this contradictory position of submissive sexual partner and female aggressor made sense to these women; they lived in a society that supported similar contrary positions regarding female sexuality.[12]

Members' descriptions of heroic marriage disciplers depicted these counselors teaching mutuality as easily accessible; day or night, couples claimed that they were given almost immediate attention. By entering the marital conflict "on the spot," as Pat suggested, marriage disciplers enter "real-life conflict" and can "work miracles." Laura, for example, had to phone her marriage discipler on several occasions to help control her tendency to "lead" in sexual encounters. Members suggested that they felt "confident" they could work through any problem that came up in a marriage because "disciplers are always right there." One woman described calling her marriage disciplers late one night and the counselors sitting on their couch for therapy within an hour of their request. Alicia also spoke of marriage disciplers at her fingertips in the midst of marital conflict: "I could call on them anytime with anything. . . . Once I was on the phone with this sister [her discipler] and I was crying and I was like, I need to stop crying in front of Jeremy and she was, 'No, you don't. He needs to see the real you . . . he needs to see it. When you get off the phone explain to him why you were crying.'"

Descriptions of intimate, at-your-fingertips marriage therapy intensified the sacred power of the discipling community by suggesting that a member would never be without an advisor and/or marriage counselor who would enforce mutuality. Julie told me that "even after you get married there are tons of other married people in the Kingdom that you can get different interpretations from." Assigned marriage disciplers were not always presented as having the answers—but the discipling network was talked about by members as able to compensate for this inevitability by bringing in other couples when necessary. One member related: "It hasn't always been easy, you know we have had, with the discipling, just isn't getting anywhere, other couples do come in . . . and it's always worked out . . . a third party comes in and it comes together!" Members and leaders stressed this extended network as a unique backup system—contributing to the idea that the marriage discipling system was almost foolproof.

Member descriptions of marriage disciplers emphasized that they frequently came from similar life situations. Like self-help groups, then, marriage discipling gained legitimacy and power through like-minded individuals coming together to listen to each other's stories and learn from each other's mistakes and advances. Members talked of being "matched" to marriage disciplers from similar life situations, of being given marital therapists with specialties in areas where marriages were weak (sex, communication, disagreements on child rearing). Members raved that marriage disciplers were able to offer sound advice largely because they had firsthand experience with negotiating sex, managing money, and/or breaking through "dysfunctional" communication habits. Ronny stated, "If you are not getting along in any area, be it financial bumps or I'm feeling stressed about the bills and I don't know if we can, just go and get some input from somebody who has been down that road." Jeremy said, "There's a couple we're discipling now, she has a real high emotional quotient, and he has a very low one. So in a lot of ways there are things in their lives that they are facing that we faced years ago. And so we are able to share with them how to go about getting through it and how to transform." Discipling relationships (marriage discipling and one-on-one) were presented by members and leaders as driven by relationality and grounded in authority and submission.

A Secure, Though not Invincible, Raft

Discipling was presented by members and leaders as a safety network of sacred counselors, ideological specialists equipped for survival in a pressing contemporary divorce culture. Marriage disciplers did not provide couples with a concrete and simple repertoire of gender beliefs, practices, and approaches to married life; they presented a number of proper ways to enact femininity and masculinity, various ways to be husbands and wives. The received repertoire could have been confusing, but stories about improving spousal communication and sex life showed disciplers reconciling traditionalist and essentialist gender notions with more egalitarian ideals of family and intimate relationships and grounding their efforts in therapeutic process and ideals—thereby producing a more coherent picture.

Chapters 4, 5, and 6 delve more into disciplers' gender prescriptions and interventions as they tried to make sense of gender roles in relationships with family of origin, in parenting, and as brothers and sisters in the

ICOC Kingdom. In a world where cultural presumptions and values of motherhood, fatherhood, husbandhood, and wifehood are so fraught with contradiction and ambiguity, it is virtually impossible for any religious movement to propose one clear, coherent set of gender ideals and practices. Research in conservative religious movements over the last twenty years offers strong confirmation of this inability, and the inevitability of organizational accommodation, appropriation, and challenging of various cultural gender beliefs and practices. The ICOC, however, was somewhat different in their approach to providing clarity of action and ideology. Unlike many other religious movements, they assigned mandatory, individual sacred counselors to help each member and each married couple discriminate between contradictory practices and beliefs as they arose through particular spousal issues. In our therapeutic culture, this assignment resonated deeply with members' cultural tool kits—an expert guide they should show deference to, available to help with approach and resolution of any number of personal and relational problems.

Individual member anecdotes of using the discipling network to achieve personal goals in marriage relationships, as with Alicia's dog story and Laura's sex initiation account, told with emphasis on relationality and mutual submission, may give the impression that women were, in some real sense, empowered by their experiences of "traditional" ideology and female submission in the ICOC. I want to make it clear that my analysis here is not meant to argue an empowerment or disempowerment position on female submission, or that female submission may be purely rhetorical in the ICOC. Heroic discipling stories and Alicia's and Laura's descriptions were, as noted, performances of successful discipling framed in cultural values that they knew I, and others, would respect. We went on our journeys of improving the self using the same cultural tools. I was socialized, as most of my research participants were, through media, schools, religious groups, and families that taught me to respect therapeutic values.[13] Given the obvious *performance* of moral selves and relationships I was audience to as a researcher in the ICOC, my analysis calls attention to a more complicated sociological phenomenon: the existence of multiple ways of managing cultural ambiguity, and the idiosyncratic outcomes of balancing contradictory positions. Personal history, social location, and where and among whom one attempts to assemble cultural cohesion greatly determine empowerment and disempowerment outcomes.

Alicia and Laura offered a presentation of self and relationship meant to impress. If their accounts are accurate, it is likely that their position in the congregation as longtime members gave them social resources and local knowledge that enhanced their ability to manipulate marriage disciplers. They were also respected disciples in the congregation, members who had long-established commitments to the group through proselytizing, monetary giving, and extensive family group counseling efforts. When they brought a concern to their disciples or lead evangelists on a local level, leaders listened; they were well-respected "older Christians" (time in church). Narratives of marital healing from "younger" City COC Christians did not contain this kind of direct presentation of discipler manipulation. Younger disciplers' stories were more of how disciplers actively named their problems and helped them achieve respect and mutual submission in marriage. It is also significant that Alicia and Laura were educated women who had well negotiated bureaucratic institutions and developed social skills and habits that enabled them to succeed in career and achieve a seemingly secure middle-class lifestyle. They knew how to follow rules, defer to authority, and thus achieve and maintain respect within the ICOC system. The experience of marriage discipling, and especially any statement of power relations among spouses, was clearly dependent on group status and, I would argue, on individual background, education, and socioeconomic status.

Because members I spoke with had a high investment in presenting themselves as flourishing under discipling, it is necessary to think seriously about ex-member experiences and contrary accounts in light of group status and socioeconomic position. For example, members boasted of the absence of domestic violence in group: how could domestic violence continue, Pat insisted, if we are "in each other's lives" and "not afraid to name" problems? Pat and others insisted that if a woman was being physically or verbally abused, they were going to know about it and the husband would be "harshly disciplined" by the "brothers." Given the frequent and extensive involvement I witnessed in the City COC discipling community, this assertion seems logical. Yet one former member told me of how he saw women silenced through marriage disciplers' teachings of female submission. He also argued that some women were encouraged to stay in physically abusive relationships. This ex-member, who had been part of a local nonpaid leadership staff in a southwestern state, suggested that leaders decided who should be pushed and who should not be pushed. His account again speaks to the importance of group position: a husband or wife with high group status who was integral to congregational and movement success may not be pressed as deeply in marriage discipling.[14] Other ex-members have suggested that disciples who were doctors, lawyers, and individuals with high degrees or celebrity status were not discipled as harshly because their membership was seen by leaders as legitimating for the movement.

Furthermore, Alicia and Laura were women who knew whom to approach with a particular problem. Alicia, for example, knew that Mike was more likely to be sympathetic of her desire for a family dog. Carrie (Mike's wife), she made clear, could have "cared less" whether or not she got her pet. Alicia's decision to approach Mike likely has something to do then with her church tenure: knowing whom to "tattle to" is acquired, insider knowledge. Furthermore, Carrie's and Mike's personalities and individual circumstances no doubt had much to do with how they approached marriage discipling. With no formal training, marriage disciplers pieced together relational skills and therapeutic techniques from a number of different sources: previous life knowledge, possibly professional training, pop psychology, Christian marriage self-help literature, and a cursory lesson of therapeutic techniques given by ICOC disciplers and leaders. It is no surprise, then, that marriage discipling method and therapeutic approach would have varied greatly across the nation. All of the above—group status, church tenure, socioeconomic status, education, life position, and lack of official training for ICOC marriage disciplers—suggest that experiences of marriage discipling were highly dependent on individual circumstance.

The varied experience of marriage discipling in group speaks to the power of ICOC's organizational performance. The organization was, to an extent and for a limited time, able to keep a picture alive of extraordinary healing in a tight-knit community where couples experienced varying levels of discipling effectiveness. How did the organization do this? For one, they developed a discourse repertoire with excessive ideological breadth that resonated deeply with members' and potential converts' understandings of moral ideals and approach. Second, the organization developed somewhat effective ways to confront negative labels head-on—they were able to keep damaging stories at bay by naming them as forbidden "spiritual pornography," the authors as having "closed hearts," and discrediting intent and accounts. Finally, they were able to keep powerful group hegemonic tales alive through the frequent telling of narratives and creative use of contemporary media like DPI texts, KNN video, film, and the ICOC website. Members understood these narratives of healing self and relationships as grounded in their real, day-to-day experiences of relationship within the discipling community. In each of these efforts, members and the organization worked to construct boundaries that cast all outside as lost and all inside as saved; outside as not-Christian, inside as Christian; outside as lacking divine power, inside as bursting with Godly healing energy.

Unresolved marriage disputes, breakups, and serious marriage discipling failures were curiously absent from member and leader presentations. When divorce and separation were spoke of they were used as examples of disciples who had "selfish" and "closed hearts." I had to push hard in the field to hear anything of marriage discipling failure. When life events in leaders' stories of marriage healing did not make sense to me, I would ask for clarification of circumstances, and on a few occasions I learned of members whose spouses had affairs in group and unfaithful couples who had left the ICOC community. Still, leaders argued, this did not negate their claim to no divorces in the Kingdom because those who divorced left the movement. So the movement did not have divorced couples, but they did have members who had divorced, their stories of divorce in group shadowed by their testimonies of remarriage in the Kingdom or fulfilling life as a single ICOC disciple.

The movement was successful, for a limited number of years and to a limited number of people, in presenting an ideal picture of marriage discipling as a secure raft in a foreboding divorce culture driven by gender confusion; but it was clearly not an invincible raft. Marriage discipling was, to many over twenty years, a great way to manage cultural confusion, to navigate messy gendered and relational waters, to turn all the uncertainty of intimate relationships into what they perceived as romantic, communicative, "awesome" marriages. Even as the unified movement crumbled, and former members from across the country debated discipling, the One True Church doctrine, and top leadership's intent, some still held firm to their marriage discipling success stories. Clearly, a large number of marriages were "saved" in the movement, perhaps those lucky enough to have marriage disciplers who had effective therapeutic relational skills, or those who stayed in the movement long enough to take advantage of the benefits of long-term Christian therapy. Perhaps some of those success stories were couples who may have been at a point in their relationships when they were ready and eager to change. It is possible too that many marriages were threatened and/or destroyed by the movement. In the flood of conversations between former members on-line in 2003–2004, there were many stories of marriage disciplers weakening and destroying relationships. As in secular society and any other religio-therapeutic approach, therapeutic outcomes depend largely on individual circumstances. The ICOC well performed a Kingdom full of exceptionally able Christian marriage counselors, but they could not always deliver.

NARRATIVES AND PERFORMANCES of heroic marriage discipling were only one venue for ICOC's powerful organizational performance of awesome marriage. The movement also succeeded in sustaining an image of excellent and unique sacred power through grand charismatic and theatrical collective performances of awesome family, group rituals that reaffirmed the therapeutic effectiveness of the discipling community.

CHAPTER 3

Collective Performances of Healing

THIS ETHNOGRAPHIC STORY I tell of "awesome family" is biased in particular ways. Had I been under thirty and single, I would probably have been matched with a church informant who was young and single. I would also have been invited to regional singles retreats where I would have worshiped and met other available ICOC Christian singles. Had a I been a single mother, I would have been introduced to another single mother and invited to single parent group meetings where I would likely have felt accepted and understood. Because I was a woman studying a group that separated frequently by gender, I inevitably spent more time with women in the church. In addition, the City COC congregation was composed mainly of married families with children, and so there was an abundance of these targeted events to attend. Field studies in another ICOC congregation may have presented more opportunities for events aimed at singles and college students. Had I been that under-thirty single sociologist, I would probably not have been so eagerly invited to participate in the large yearly regional event extravaganza, Marriage Enrichment.[1] With each invitation, I politely declined for my husband, telling Pat and other leaders that I preferred to keep my research separate from my marriage. Yet I was still encouraged and welcomed at these retreats, where I sat on two occasions, along with a handful of other lone women, surrounded by church married couples and potential converts anxious to learn how to spark romance and heal marriages.

Talk of "Marriage Enrichment 1999" began weeks before the retreat was to take place. "Go out there," City COC's lead evangelist said during the Sunday morning service, and find the people who are "having problems" in their marriages. Bring them in so they can "get the cancer out" of their failing unions. Leaders encouraged members to describe to friends, family, and acquaintances a church that had the power and game plan to intervene intimately in lackluster marriages and transform them into "awesome" unions. Members were given an exciting Marriage Enrichment itinerary to entice friends: a night alone with your spouse in a nice hotel room, inspiring speakers, a massage workshop, an "Evening in Paris" dance and reception on Saturday night in the hotel ballroom, and, as church rumor had it before the 1999 marriage retreat, a sermon for the men that included a serious look at Clifford and Joyce Penner's 1981 mainstream Christian prescriptive text, *The Gift of Sex: A Guide to Sexual Fulfillment*. Retreat attendees paid a twenty-five-dollar fee and the cost of a room if couples desired an overnight romantic stay in the hotel.

The lobby outside the large hotel ballroom at the start of the retreat was full of activity and excitement. A book sale area was set up where members and their guests could purchase ICOC books, videos, and tapes. Members from around the region welcomed one another with hugs. Travel bags on trolleys were piled in a corner as people arriving minutes before the event tried to check in. There was a small band (composed of City COC members) in the corner playing the wedding march. A registration table was set up outside the ballroom doors. After finding my name on the preregistration list, a young single church member (the "singles" helped run the event so that the "marrieds" could concentrate on the retreat) handed me my retreat envelope. The package contained information on restaurants and downtown attractions and the "You're Still the One Marriage Enrichment Retreat" weekend schedule:

You're Still the One Marriage Enrichment Retreat

Saturday (date)

10:00 a.m.	Registration and Check In	
1:00 p.m.	Singing and Welcome	(name of CCOC hosts)
	Ballroom— First Floor	
	From This Moment	Randy McKean
	You're Still the One	Randy and Kay McKean
3:45 p.m.	The Spice of Life . . .	
	Men: Ballroom—Third Floor	
	Women: Ballroom—First Floor	

	Communicate Your Love	(male speaker)	(female speaker)
	Dating in Marriage	"	"
	Massage	"	"
	Variety	"	"
6:00 p.m.	Dinner Break		
8:00 p.m.	Dance and Reception—"An Evening in Paris" Ballroom—First Floor		
11:00 p.m.	Worship Service		
	Communion		
	Personal Sharing—"Always and Forever" Ballroom—First Floor		

The retreat schedule was printed in a booklet with extra space for note taking. Taking notes during sermons and events was an informal group norm, which rendered my constant note taking not out of the ordinary. My Marriage Enrichment package also included a personalized invitation to the Evening in Paris Dance and Reception that read: "It pleases us to invite our friends *Mark Lerman and Kathleen Jenkins,* to a Dance and Reception at the special *Evening in Paris*." Other handouts for the retreat included an 8½ × 11 inch pink paper that read: "*Massage Class 101*—This class entitles you to think like you're a doctor—Enjoy your new role in life!" The paper offered diagrams of massage points for "headaches/neck stiffness," "sinus congestion/headaches," "mid back tightness," and "low back pain/menstrual cramps." We also received another sheet, "Variety Is the Spice of Life," that listed fifty suggestions for how to make our marriages exciting and fun:

> Variety Is The Spice Of Life
> Ideas To Keep Your Relationship Special
>
> This list was developed with the hope that each couple will add or subtract from it as they strive to keep their relationship as fun and exciting as it can be. We hope you'll find some of these ideas helpful in stretching your imagination:
>
> - Go on a date once every week.
> - Write the story of how you met. Get it printed and bound.
> - List your spouse's best qualities in alphabetical order.

- Tour a museum or an art gallery.
- Notice the little changes your spouse makes in his/her appearance.
- Float on a raft together.
- Take a stroll around the block—and hold hands as you walk.
- Stock the cupboards with food your spouse loves to eat (but only if he or she *isn't* on a diet).
- Give your spouse a back rub.
- Rent a classic love-story video and watch it while cuddling.[2]

At that point, there was no question in my mind that constructing romance and reinvigorating couples' sex lives would be a key component of the retreat. The clinical therapeutic tone and intimate nature of ICOC marriage intervention was clear.

As I walked away from the check-in station and searched for Pat in the crowded, bustling lobby, the young woman at the registration table called back to me, "Wait, you forgot your gift!" I returned to the table and she handed me a bag with a personalized candle that read *Mark Lerman and Kathleen Jenkins, Marriage Enrichment Day 1999*, a bottle of massage and bath oil, and body lotion. I read through my retreat packet and thought about how my engraved candle would look on the bookshelf in my home office beside other church event favors: the potted plant printed with "How Does Your Garden Grow" that I received on Women's Day and the chocolate mints with the saying "I will get there [heaven and the event]" printed on the wrapper. These event favors were part of ICOC material culture, religious objects that reinforced the event's message. The Marriage Enrichment Day candle, lit in the privacy of one's home or hotel room, signified that the discipling community was the only Christian church where you could be assured of having a romantic, fulfilling, and long-lasting marriage.

Pat finally found me in the crowd. She was excited about the retreat and told me again that my husband really should have come, "just for a fun time." She and Tom had arranged for baby-sitting with a younger church member and were going to spend a night in the hotel. We walked together into the ballroom of the upscale hotel. In the front of the room there was a raised stage decorated with plants and twinkle lights, two huge speakers, and to the left of the stage a large movie screen. There were rows of folding chairs (enough to hold approximately eight hundred people) that took up most of the large room. Pat had saved a seat for me a few rows from the front and introduced me to Janice, a white woman about thirty-five from a nearby congregation. I said hello and, as I did with almost everyone I met in the ICOC, mentioned that I was there because I was a sociologist interested in writing about the movement. Janice and her husband sat to my right and Pat and Tom to my left. By the start of the service approximately four hundred married church couples from across the New England region had gathered in the ballroom.

We began the service singing hymns from the movement's songbook, our arms around each other's waists and shoulders. Most ICOC services and events began this way, although the majority of members did not bring their songbooks, as they knew the songs by heart. This clearly designated me as an outsider at first; over time, I too began to sing along comfortably now and then. Following the opening songs on Marriage Enrichment 1999 we listened to a group of five men (three white, two black), dressed in black and wearing sunglasses, perform an Elvis/Motown musical comedy skit, followed by another white female member in evening attire singing a pop rock love song. After the musical introduction, the lights dimmed and all attention focused on a large screen for a slide show that featured many of the ICOC couples present at the retreat: wedding photos followed by more recent photographs. Smiling couples flashed in front of us, communicating the idea that the community was a church family composed of happy and healthy marriage relationships. The wide-screen ICOC family wedding album closed and the lights came up. The first speaker stood at the podium. I grew uneasy as I came to understand what this local male evangelist had in mind. He was going to begin his portion of the retreat with a strategy for couple closeness I had experienced for the first time during Marriage Enrichment 1995.

In 1995, the guest speaker, longtime member and church author Gordon Ferguson, was introduced to us by the City COC lead evangelist as a "doctor." "Dr. Gordon does not have an MBA, an MA, or a PhD, but he is a doctor nonetheless, and he is going to get the cancer out of your marriages." Ferguson was presented to us in 1995 as a kind of sacred surgeon, armed with the power of God and the power of therapeutic belief and practice. Church leaders frequently used the word "cancer" to describe marital disease and illness. Relational cancer was a powerful metaphor (Sontag 1979); cancer has been stigmatized and associated with imminent death, and in some cases individuals were blamed for being susceptible to cancer (through what they eat, or whether or not they keep a "healthy" lifestyle). More recently, some cancers (prostate for example), due to advanced medical screening and treatments, are thought of by many as more of a living disease. Individuals with cancer today are increasingly expected to continually appeal to doctors and medical "experts" for treatment and "surveillance" (Clark et al. 2003). Such a pursuit signals a faithful attempt at wellness and healing for physical, emotional, and relational health. ICOC's formal discourse of relational "cancers" and disciplers as sacred surgeons drew from cultural standards that a genuine pursuit of healing involves seeking the very latest therapeutic medical prevention, intervention, and treatment.

In 1995 "Dr. Gordon" asked the eight hundred or so attendees gathered in an old, beautiful, majestic theater to stand and face their spouses. I stayed seated while almost everyone in the theater stood and turned to look at their partners. Gordon told us that some of the couples had probably had a relationship "bump" earlier in the day or week but not to worry, he was going to show us how to fix that. He asked that the husbands say to their wives, "Honey, I'm wrong. I'm sorry. Please forgive me." The husbands repeated his words, and many in the audience giggled and laughed. The laughter seemed to be instigated by the unfamiliar and awkward public nature of the scene: hundreds of couples staring into each other's eyes, embarrassed perhaps at enacting what might typically be a private moment of social interaction. Gordon then asked that the women say the same to their husbands. They did. Gordon noted that some of the couples were kissing and quickly named this open display of affection a good thing. He wanted more, though. He told them that it shouldn't be like a kiss for a friend, it should be a "real kiss!" They seemed, in 1995, to eagerly follow his instructions. And I felt, my head lowered, as if I had intruded on an intimate yet clearly social moment of spousal affection.

There I was again in 1999, taken by surprise that the service was to begin with the same ritual performance that highlighted and reaffirmed members' faith in ICOC romantic marriage. I found myself suddenly wishing that I had sat alone in the back row. Like "Dr. Gordon," this leader was not satisfied with the first kiss and so asked that couples kiss again. Using Gordon Ferguson's 1995 approach, he voiced disapproval at the first passionless kiss, and members laughed and giggled at the prospect of kissing again. We were told that the next kiss needed to be a "long, hot kiss" and that it should last for ten seconds. Pat leaned over and whispered in my ear, "Poor Kay."

"That's OK. I'm all right," I assured her.

At that moment her husband, Tom, reached his arm around to hold Pat and offer her that "long, hot kiss." As he did so he accidentally bumped my shoulder. We pretended it did not happen. And then I stood, for ten very long seconds, with hundreds of church members kissing around me.

One kiss was not enough, two kisses were not enough, even three explicitly passionate kisses were not enough to achieve the kind of heightened passionate energy leaders wanted to fill the atmosphere of the large hotel convention room where "awesome" ICOC love stories would be performed throughout the Marriage Enrichment production. So, as if in a school pep rally, this leader set the stage further by calling out congregations, region by region, and assigning them "lover" names. As he spoke, each group stood, applauding, some laughing, some repeating phrases like, "Yeah, go brother!"—all responses indicated that they were pleased with their regional romantic nicknames.

> Here are the red hot lovers from the —— region!
>
> And we have the passionate lovers from the —— region!
>
> Then we have the wild and crazy lovers from the —— region!
>
> And then we have the anything goes lovers from the CCOC region!

With each assignment of a nickname, and the loud, energetic congregational responses that followed, Marriage Enrichment's formal production pumped up an image of church couples as engaged in uncommonly erotic and sexually satisfying sacred unions.

The tone and nature of ICOC's explicit brand of Christian couples therapy was further set by the Marriage Enrichment guest speaker. The Marriage Enrichment 1999 featured speakers were Randy and Kay McKean, the brother and sister-in-law of the group's founder, Kip McKean. During most regional ICOC events a speaker, usually high-status well-known ministry leaders in the movement like the 1995 Marriage Enrichment guest "Dr. Gordon," delivered a lengthy message (sometimes over an hour), followed by several shorter ten- to fifteen-minute testimonies by regional members. Guest speakers' performances were filled with humor. McKean's talk that day was no exception.

At the start of his message on Marriage Enrichment 1999, Randy began with sexual humor. He stressed the oneness of the marriage union, giving much emphasis to couples being "joined." He said he was "fired up that God also made women" and that he "likes women." Great laughter followed other heterosexist jokes like, "God created marriage with Adam and Eve, not Adam and Steve." In the ICOC, like most other conservative Christian movements, "homosexuality" is considered a sin. Randy continued with his comedic script: "Revenge of the church ladies," he reads from a magazine article, "a survey about church ladies and the men who sleep with them." "They have," he went on, "more sexual freedom and are happier." These church ladies benefit, he told us, from having husbands who believe that God created sex and who tells us in Proverbs 5:18–19 (NIV), "May your fountain be blessed, and may you rejoice in the wife of your youth. A loving doe, a graceful deer—may her breasts satisfy you always, may you ever be captivated by her love." "Christian husbands," he stressed, "are taking this passage quite literally!" The congregation laughed loudly. Some members around me in the audience had tears in their eyes from laughter.

During Marriage Enrichment 1999, McKean, visibly sweating, worked the Marriage Enrichment audience into a heightened sacred state with his sermon packed with humor and his personal romantic marriage story. He moved his arms as if conducting an orchestra, directing the palpable collective energy he and the local leader who first took the podium had worked so hard to create. As he lifted his arms in front of him he said,

> Marriage is the total commitment of the total person for the total life.
>
> It's like two rivers joining.
>
> When they meet they become turbulent.

His arms then became two rivers joining, hitting, and mixing:

> But if you look downstream, it is bigger, better, and deeper. . . .
>
> Marriage must be centered on Jesus Christ.

His arms settled calmly before him.

> Marriage needs a delicate touch and patience.

McKean then asked that the husbands and wives stand and face one another and take off their wedding rings. My heart beat rapidly as I stood again, fearing another kissing couple episode. All the couples in the convention room stood and faced one another. Couples were touching each other lovingly on the hands, the face, the shoulders. I lowered my head to avoid trespassing romantic glances. Then McKean slowly read passages from the Song of Songs, a poetic Hebrew Bible book that contains many love poems. He had the men repeat vows and biblical love poetry and women repeat vows and poetry, and then had the couples exchange wedding bands and give them to their spouses again. The room felt charged with passion. Pat again acknowledged the awkwardness of my sitting alone through these interactions. "Poor Kay, here you are again," she offered.

"It's OK. Really, I'm fine."

Marriage Enrichment's strong and detailed emphasis on sexual fulfillment as an ideal expectation in marriage is reflective of contemporary society. The availability of reliable birth control, the separation of sex from reproduction in the early twentieth century, the sexual freedom of the countercultural revolution, and the medicalization of sexuality have produced a culture that expects that individuals will work to have "healthy" sex lives. Try to imagine preindustrial family spouses traveling to the then moral authority (ministers) for a meeting intended to teach them how to ensure that they are both sexually satisfied. The minister shows them diagrams of male and female genitalia, talks of how to find the clitoris, talks of how to make sure that both couples are getting enough sex, and encourages them to go on romantic dates and write each other poems and love notes. Kay McKean stood at the pulpit in the afternoon on Marriage Enrichment Day in 1999 and told the group of

ICOC women: "I'm going to get kind of down and graphic here now. . . . There is one piece of the human anatomy, of males and females together, only one piece whose only function is pleasure and that is the clitoris—did I say that right? Oh, now I'm embarrassed." Her emphasis is a reflection of contemporary notions of sexuality, feminism, and our therapeutic focus on the importance of self-fulfillment.

To potential converts and ICOC members, the groups' heavy emphasis on sexual satisfaction, the bottle of massage oil, the engraved candle, the hotel room, diagrams, and exercises that taught them how to please themselves and their partners seemed not radical or out of place, but crucial for a healthy Christian marriage. The methods and discourse were familiar from both mainstream secular counselors and popular psychology and Christian marriage counselors (recall Clifford and Joyce Penner's [1981] book *The Gift of Sex*). Furthermore, orchestrated physical interactions during Marriage Enrichment Day (couples kissing, and advising couples to recite biblical love poetry) were powerful performances—a kind of religio-therapy that appeared to bring immediate results. McKean's and Ferguson's Marriage Enrichment performances illustrated the kind of intimate and hands-on marital coaching and advice that members and potential converts could expect to receive from mandatory ICOC marriage disciplers: disciplers who would shape unsatisfying, boring, stuck-in-a-rut marriages into heightened romantic ecstasy, who would help you understand when to submit and when to stand strong in opposition. In secular culture, couples may shop around for that perfect professional, the one who is able to provide a combination of listening, inspiration, and practical advice. The ICOC, through formal events like Marriage Enrichment, made the discipling movement seem the "right" therapeutic choice.

THE EFFECTIVENESS OF COLLECTIVE RITUAL

The life circumstances of an ethnographer influence how she perceives and experiences individuals and cultures; the stories she tells and her interpretations of events are seen through her own life concerns, race, socioeconomic status, religious upbringing, and gender. Perhaps no one understands the relevancy of life history and social location more than church disciplers, who customized their evangelical approaches and performances of awesome church family to impact potential converts in meaningful ways. Pat, my major informant, was white, like me, and was college educated. I spent the most intimate of my participant observation with female disciples who were married, had small children, and were from similar educated middle-class backgrounds. During my final year of field observation Pat and I each gave birth to our third child and so shared complaints of pregnancy and the exhilaration of new life. We were similar people in very many ways.

Pat's reaching out to me after my first informant moved to another ICOC zone in a distant state may well have been purposeful; ex-members and members confirmed that church leaders tried to "match" potential converts with like disciples. In fact, shepherding couples and ministry leaders met weekly to discuss how to "help" potential converts and church members and assign appropriate disciplers. I asked several times to attend one of these meetings, but my requests were denied. When I inquired about what exactly went on at a particular weekly meeting, Pat told me that one of the things they had talked about was how she might work with me in Bible studies to make sure I understood why being a disciple was so powerful for her. Many of the group performances I observed were ones that ICOC leaders felt would resound with my own needs, and reflect kindly on the church. Such researcher choreography on the part of leaders in new religious movements (NRMs) that have been named deviant by anti-cult groups and media are not uncommon (Rubin 2001).

In the end, my position as a researcher in the movement was primarily that of an audience member: what I saw was mostly *front-stage* action, the scenes they wanted me to see (Goffman 1959). But this front-stage action is incredibly important: they are the main-stage productions that played a large role in drawing so many people to the ICOC. These performances, combined with my attempts at pulling up the backdrop here and there—hearing ex-member narratives, speaking with members from various race/ethnic and socioeconomic status backgrounds, asking for tapes of men-only events where I would not have been welcomed, interviewing members much younger than me, and observing snippets of informal interactions in members' homes—confirmed that whether single or married, young or old, building an awesome family was a dominant group theme.

The church held large regional events like Marriage Enrichment several times a year, occasions where hundreds of members gathered in one place to address a particular point of family healing, where theatrical performances of self and organization reaffirmed discipling's unusual therapeutic powers. Individual members' stories of marriage discipling as powerful were affirmed as they came together with hundreds of other church couples and leaders to celebrate, worship, and be inspired by stories of miraculous marriage healing. Single members had their own elaborate worship events like the Valentine's Dance and Singles' Retreats where regional members and church leaders came together and told stories of how dating in the ICOC was safe, loving, and fulfilling; how disciplers guided the church dating process, monitoring dates and demanding respect, love, and sexual abstinence. Men across the region gathered yearly for a Men's Day where they told stories of becoming better husbands, fathers, and brothers in the "Kingdom of God." Women gathered at annual regional Women's Days, where they celebrated the divine power present in discipling relationships that had helped them be "awesome" wives, mothers, and sisters.

Humor was a popular and frequent method of raising the performance energy during these events and services. Religious communities often use jokes and humor as a mechanism to focus a group and "stimulate or sustain a gathering" (Heilman 1973, 194). Early on in my fieldwork I observed Randy McKean raise group energy at another regional event by telling a joke meant to emphasize the necessity of keeping relationships alive in God's Kingdom (the ICOC). He began: "A group of men go ice fishing. They cut a hole in the ice and try to fish but catch nothing. A small boy sets up beside them, he cuts a hole in the ice and starts pulling out massive amounts of fish." At that point members sitting around me responded loudly, "Ahh," and "Where are you going with this one, brother?" He continued over audience responses, "The men ask him how he does this. The boy mumbles something inaudible. They ask again, and again the boy mumbles something inaudible. They ask a third time." Randy then wiped his nose and his mouth, making a slurping sound, and said, "You've got to keep the worms warm." Most members found the underlying sexual innuendo funny and laughed. Several chose not to laugh but instead responded, "Gross!" or "Oh, no." During Marriage Enrichment 1999, after the men and women separated, Kay McKean began her message to church "sisters" with humor. She offered passages from an old "cookbook" entitled *How to Cook a Husband*. "They don't like to be pickled," she read. The women laughed as she continued,

"They take awhile to roast but are very tender and good when cooked properly. Don't prick them with a sharp instrument to see if they are done, and if he sputters and spurts and fizzles till he's done, it's OK." The women around me laughed so hard it took awhile for them to settle down. Kay then asked us, "How can we keep our marriages hot? There are lots of ways." She continued, "I'm not talking about meeting your husband at the door wrapped in Saran Wrap with a glass of wine in your hand. I've never tried that." All laughed, and one retreat attendee called out from the crowd, "They have colors now!" "Yes, that's right," Kay confirmed, "red or blue, but no, I've never tried that. Maybe I will." We all laughed again.

Jokes were often repeated from one service to the next; yet told in the collective social body where charismatic leaders had created a heightened sense of time and place, members laughed at the same stories and recollections. Perhaps many found the stories funny time and again, for others laughing may have been more of a group norm; like the joke that Dad or Grandma told every Sunday at dinner and family members laughed out of respect or habit, even when the humor and irony had long ago been spent. Ex-members claimed that their smiling during services while singing and laughing at leaders' jokes was explicitly orchestrated by the leadership, a backstage ICOC direction. One ex-member told me, "Leaders told us to smile and laugh a lot." In general, guest speakers and performers were often very entertaining, charismatic, funny, and skilled at raising the energy in an audience. During one Women's Day regional event, entitled "I Will Get There," an ICOC "comedian," Jennifer Salberg, opened the event. Hundreds of women were at this particular event, held in a large convention center in Boston, and so Jennifer's image appeared on either side of the stage on wide screens. She bemoaned and made fun of the number of illnesses women suffer from today: "PMS [premenstrual syndrome]," "IBS [irritable bowel syndrome]," and "CFS [chronic fatigue syndrome]." How, she asked, are women supposed to live in the "fast lane," "eat everything and not be tired," and at the same time have great bowel movements? The women in the audience laughed throughout her presentation. Regional and local events also frequently staged humorous theatrical skits; for example, one local Women's Day began with a comedic script that poked fun of Martha Stewart, and another regional Women's Day event began with a skit based on a popular television game show. As a participant observer, I found myself laughing at jokes and comedic performances quite frequently. Sometimes I found leaders' stories genuinely funny, other times benign, on occasion offensive; yet each time I laughed. Humor is both subjective and infectious, an incredibly powerful mechanism for bringing a group of people together and charging a ritual event.

Interestingly, humor was also one of the performance mechanisms leaders used to diffuse accusations from ex-members and anti-cult organizations. During formal group performances, main-stage events like weekly Sunday services, and large regional Marriage Enrichment retreats, leaders addressed the "cult" question by casting ex-member and critics' concerns as ridiculously funny. For example, a leader during one morning service said, "Can you believe it, we care about each other too much. We spend a lot of time together. We think Jesus meant for us to live together as disciples! We are too much like those first-century Christians!" Members of the congregation laughed at his obvious sarcasm.

Every large regional event I attended featured talented (some professional) musicians and vocalists. Most of these musical performances were orchestrated to represent the quality of intimate relationships that members experienced through discipling. During one large regional event held in a concert stadium, ICOC's pop rock group, the Radicals, sang a song celebrating the "radical" kind of church family love that disciples shared: "Now fifteen years have come and gone and see what God has done. . . . It's a radical love that we share. A love that's heard around the world, shows how much God cares." ICOC music, like the Discipleship Publications International (DPI) books, tapes, and videos for sale during church events, were mechanisms of ideological encapsulation (Greil and Rudy 1984, 267–268) that encouraged members to bring the sacred healing power of discipling with them when they were outside the physical and social boundaries of the church. During that concert, the church pop rock–style song "Radical Love" was followed by a centuries-old popular and moving hymn, "Amazing Grace." On Marriage Enrichment Day 1999, we began together with our arms around each other singing old hymns and contemporary Christian songs; we then listened to pop rock and Motown. Variety in worship can be an attractive feature of contemporary congregations, eclectic music and worship style a quality that may help congregations draw members from various age and racial/ethnic groups. While the ICOC seemed to be primarily composed of couples and singles age fifty-five and younger, they were exceptionally diverse with regard to race and ethnicity in a country where, as many have lamented, Sunday morning is the most segregated time of the week. The ICOC's worship style, especially in these large regional performances, contributed to its image of exceptional ICOC family diversity through "ritual inclusion," welcoming diversity in music, language, and ritual practice (Becker 1998, 452).

Slide shows and video presentations, many produced by ICOC's own video production company based in Los Angeles, Kingdom News Network (KNN), were a frequent form of event entertainment. These productions were powerful venues for highlighting the necessity of being engaged in active ICOC discipling relationships if one wished to be saved and experience family healing. One KNN video shown during a Wednesday evening women's service offered the story of a young bride and groom who, through the constant efforts of disciplers, had learned to care deeply for each other and respect and love one another. During one large regional Women's Day, we were shown a movie that presented a married couple who were having difficulty communicating, were anxious and depressed. In the video, after disciplers entered their lives, the husband and wife were presented as happier and better able to parent.

Another routine congregational mechanism that contributed to the collective performance energy was the frequency of standing ovations in response to individual speakers and members' testifying, singing, dancing, and performing. A standing ovation from an audience generally symbolizes that audience members have been extraordinarily affected by a performance. During regional events and local services, standing ovations were frequent and at times seemed excessive; at the end of one service during my initial year in the field my first major informant, Leslie, told me, "We get stuck in the standing." Marriage Enrichment 1999 was no exception. We stood for the McKeans, we stood for the local leader, we stood for the singers, the slide show, and for individual testimonies.

Standing ovations, applause, theatrical skits, dance, humor, high-tech movies, computerized slide shows, and charismatic jocular Christian preaching to large church audiences in what feels like a tightly choreographed and packaged performance are characteristics of what some sociologists have named a "megachurch" worship style and organization. Researchers have called attention to the rising number of megachurches in the U.S. religious marketplace (Eiesland 1997; Vaughan 1993). ICOC events like Marriage Enrichment succeeded, as megachurches do, in bringing together great numbers of people for scripted religious performances. Such ICOC "big-theater liturgy" (Eiesland 1997, 193) events like Marriage Enrichment Day were very important group rites, public rituals that continually reaffirmed, through a heightened collective emotional state, the sacred healing power of the ICOC. Bringing large numbers of members together in the same ritual space also affirmed the evangelical success and power of the movement. With hundreds of members as convincing evidence, leaders at these regional events often compared their growing movement to the "empty pews" and "dead churches" of other religious movements.

Marriage Enrichment's controlled erotic displays of spousal affection, musical performance, slide shows, humor, applause, standing ovations, and charismatic speaking were performance mechanisms that renewed church healing potential and produced a palpable collective power. Leaders and members talked of this power as instigated by a divine external force. Sociologists recognize this kind of ritually induced presence as very real social force: a sweeping collective emotion with the power to lift up the beliefs of participants. In Emile Durkheim's (1912, 216–230) conceptual framework, this represents a kind of collective effervescence. Both members and ex-members have talked about how they were moved by the high level of energy and emotion experienced during ICOC services. One ex-member recalled this group energy as seductive and intoxicating: "Members took me to highly energetic and emotional functions and to put it mildly, that energy got me hooked" (REVEAL; www.reveal.org 1998). Stories of family healing through discipling relationships told and retold in these energetic ritual performances stressed that marriages and families outside the movement were seriously threatened and unhappy.

A Time and Setting for Marital Healing

Regional performances like Marriage Enrichment Day, through a ritually produced sense of collective effervescence, set the church's approach to marriage and family apart from other religious groups and secular society. They were organizational attempts to create high boundaries around the world of ICOC disciples, to achieve a high level of social and ideological encapsulation (Greil and Rudy 1984). The ICOC appeared a religious community where, as Kanter (1972, 52) suggests, members "have a clear sense of their own boundaries" and construct a "strong distinction between the inside and the outside." This was a large part of the ritual work of Marriage Enrichment Days, Women's Days, Men's Days, and Singles' Retreats: setting apart, making the discipling community distinct and sacred, and casting relationships inside the group as safe and superior.

Painting divorce as an ever-present evil was a large part of individual performances of heroic discipling, as seen in chapter 2. Formal group rhetoric and large regional performances of exceptional in-group healing shaped and reaffirmed members' stories of escaping divorce. During Marriage Enrichment 1999, Randy McKean slowed down his peripatetic sermon, ending his performance with a slow-paced reading of lyrics to a well-known song:

> What's the glory in living?
> Doesn't anybody ever stay together anymore?
> And if love never,
> lasts forever,
> tell me,
> what's forever for?

The audience voiced a soft but audible "Mmm," as if we had all heard these lyrics before from our car radios, reminding us of lost romances, and understood *exactly* that fear and pessimism that McKean was emphasizing. With charismatic steam and theatrical skill, he repeated the lyrics, moaning the loss of forever after in a culture of divorce:

> What's the glory in living?
> Doesn't anybody ever stay together anymore?
> And if love never,
> lasts forever,
> tell me,
> what's forever for?

He then challenged members and guests: "From this moment on . . . what will your marriage be?" His dim mood then lightened as he contrasted what marriages in the Kingdom could be: the "hottest, most romantic, most sensitive, greatest marriage!"

Church leaders' presentations of dating and intimate relationships outside the church were of empty and dehumanizing experiences. During one local special event for women, a female speaker from another congregation stressed that we lived in a "wild, desperate time." She held up the shooting at Columbine as evidence and repeated a section from "something" she had read recently that addressed the question of what people say they are willing to do for $10 million. She read, "abortions, killing a stranger, giving up your kids, lying, prostitution for a week." The women attending this special brunch responded verbally, with "ahs" and "oh nos," a chorus of disbelief as backdrop. She continued by criticizing our computerized world, emphasizing how dating on-line had become a dangerous and often disappointing method for finding a life partner. She told a story of a woman who had a relationship on e-mail with a man in England and that this woman traveled overseas to meet him and had sex with him. Soon after, she told us, he told her to leave because sex was all he had wanted. Like many leaders' media anecdotes told in regional performances, the source of the story was not always completely clear. "I read in a magazine" or "heard on the news" was a common beginning to many tales of disturbing and abusive relationships in secular society. This leader ended, however, with an example of our "wild, desperate time" from her own observations of emptiness, human disconnectedness, and family tragedy in society at the end of the century:

> She told a story of moving to a new neighborhood several years earlier: they tried to meet their new neighbors but this proved a difficult project. They would invite families over but no one ever came. In the end, they did have the couple behind them over for dinner, but only after a tragic experience. She was washing her dishes one day and looked out her kitchen window to see the teenage son of the couple that lived behind them hanging by a rope in his backyard. She told us that she hoped we would never have to see such a sight, how "sad" and "sobering" this experience had been.

During special church events and large regional gatherings, individual members also related their stories of discipling as sacred and the world outside as dangerous and uncaring. Individual members frequently told stories or "testified," a common performance in many religious communities and identity transformation organizations (like Alcoholics Anonymous). Their testimonies related individual experiences of the healing power found in ICOC discipling relationships. Members' stories told to me and during regional events painted dating and marriage outside the group as frightening, disappointing, and traumatic. During one local special event for women, a woman told the following story:

> When she was just out of high school she met and fell madly in love with a man named "Mohamed." She spent a lot of time with him, had sex with him, talked with him about everything in her life and "gave everything over to him." One day, she called Mohamed's house and a woman answered the phone. "Hello, may I speak with Mohamed?" she asked. The woman challenged her, "Who is this?" "This is Mohamed's girlfriend," she replied. The woman on the other end of the phone stated, "This is Mohamed's wife."

The woman testifying began to cry and had a hard time getting through her story, which ended with her conversion to the ICOC and how disciples had helped her heal. As she cried, the women around me offered her soft verbal encouragement, a soothing background of "Mmm sister," "You're OK, sister," and "Tell it, sister" that consoled her tale of deception and heartbreak and constructed life within the discipling community as incapable of such desolation.

Choosing a spouse without the help of church disciples was presented as a risky business. During one large regional event for men entitled "Real God/Real Men," movement author and speaker Sam Laing told an all-male audience:

> The Kingdom is trying to help you to put together a really Godly and spiritual relationship. Amen?! I mean because we don't want you to go through the mess we had to go through because we got married maybe before we were discipling and the scars are so deep. . . . So, you have a chance, single brothers, to put it together, but instead you [might] say no. I really want to marry this girl, you people are slowing me down. . . . We don't listen and we end up doing something, having sex or run off to get married or we make a decision to

> buy a house or move in the middle of Podunk somewhere where there are no other disciples. And really [we think] this is gonna work, it's gonna be great and we end up paying a horrible price. You need to learn to make good decisions, to listen to God's word and to listen to the people God's put in your life. (audiotape of all-male event)

Not listening to disciplers' advice about who and when to marry, where to live, and what type of house a married couple should live in were portrayed by Laing as dangerous.

Members and leaders acknowledged that other churches tried to counsel individuals before marriage, but stressed that the ICOC's discipling method was more foolproof. Like many other tight-knit religious communities, members and leaders presented the discipling community as a "safe dating haven" in a society where dating had become evil, dangerous, and misguided (Kanter 1972; Davidman 1991). Group performances included many presentations of disciples meeting "awesome" spouses in the church: the woman who whispered to me on Marriage Enrichment 1999, "I met my husband here," the leaders who included ICOC dating in their sermons, and members like Ronny and Julie (chapter 2) who praised ICOC dating and premarriage discipling. They presented their potential mating pool as exceptional, better than what you might find in another church or in the secular dating world—better because disciplers were teaching "respect." Some members and ex-members even suggested that the ICOC dating pool was exceptional because there were lots of physically "beautiful" and "handsome" brothers and sisters to choose from in the movement. In the words of one young City COC male member, the Kingdom was full of "awesome, powerful, and beautiful women of God."

Sam Laing and his wife, Geri, coauthors of DPI's marriage advice text, *Friends and Lovers*, and highly respected ICOC marriage experts and regional speakers, described secular society as full of ill-fated marriages: "The headlines are full of marriages that began with high promise and ended in disaster. From the storybook marriages of royalty to the glamour of Hollywood to the neighbors next door, more couples are not making it to the finish" (Laing and Laing 1996, 145). In the introduction to their marriage book they offer an ICOC alternative:

> Even if we have the most serious of problems, we still do not have reason to quit! *Even in the case of adultery, divorce is permitted, but not*

> *necessarily required or encouraged.* I have seen many marriages salvaged gloriously [in the ICOC] from the wreckage of adultery.
>
> Therefore, I would urge you to ban all talk of divorce. Even in moments of frustration and anger, never utter the word. Always assume and believe you are going to stay together and work things out. Marriage is for life!

In general, marriages outside the group were depicted as contingent and lacking the exciting romance and friendship in ICOC unions: "Friendship and romantic love are the two essential ingredients of a great marriage. . . . Although this should be the norm, few of us grew up seeing such marriages, and perhaps even fewer of us believed that we could experience such a relationship ourselves" (Laing and Laing 1996, 21).

All church leaders depicted outside relationships in a culture of divorce as lacking communication, openness, mutual spousal submission, love, and forgiveness—missing characteristics that threatened to "kill a marriage." During many Sunday morning services leaders quoted the popular misleading U.S. divorce statistic "50 percent of marriages end in divorce." One Sunday morning a leader added, "If you find your wife here, you have a 99 percent chance of your marriage lasting forever!" This is a figure with great appeal, yet one that grossly misrepresented the possibility of spousal defection from such a high-boundary, controversial new religious movement. During another large event years earlier, I heard Randy McKean tell approximately eight thousand members from around the region: "The divorce rate is high and experts say it's hard to stay in love but we [church members] will never leave that commitment of marriage." In fact, during the course of my fieldwork I heard whispered accounts (literally) of high-ranking leaders having an extramarital affair and leaving a woman leader alone in the church. The rumor had an "awesome" ending, of course, as the wife left behind found a more suitable and dedicated husband "in the Kingdom." Kip McKean, in his 1992 newsletter to the Kingdom, criticized not just secular marriage, but any marriage outside the boundaries of his movement—pointing a finger directly at the Mainline Church of Christ and naming its "spiritual condition" as ranging from "lukewarm to disgusting." He stated, "After almost 200 years since the inception of the Churches of Christ movement in the United States . . . the divorce rate was around 33%" (McKean 1992). ICOC's aggressive missionary teams were characterized in group literature as bringing the power of ICOC marriage disciplers to diseased marriage relationships across the globe. The 1995 *New England Mission Report* church letter given to us during one large regional event read: "On a continent (Milan church) where marriage has long been a dying institution with the family crumbling around it, the light of the Laing family (as ICOC missionaries) was a beacon." ICOC formal discourse was replete with images of doomed and unhappy marriages outside the group. One longtime white male leader stated during a Sunday morning sermon that "you may know people out there who look like they have a good marriage, but if you put a microscope up to it, you're going to see problems." ICOC marriage discipling, leaders and members insisted, was the only answer.

KINGDOM NEWS NETWORK PRODUCTIONS OF ICOC HEALING

Large regional events held across the country often featured Kingdom News Network (KNN) films. KNN worked hard to set the ICOC community apart as safe and powerfully charged, as a family oasis in a "wild, desperate time." For example, on New England Women's Day 1999, after we were entertained by comedian Jennifer Salberg, eclectic music, and a series of testimonies, our attention was directed to the two large movie screens on either side of the stage. The KNN film that day, *The Prodigal Daughter*, was based on Jesus' parable (Luke 15:11–32) of a younger son who squanders his inheritance. He is forgiven by his father, while his obeisant older brother challenges the father's actions. In KNN's version of the story, the son is a daughter, a young woman from a white upper-middle-class family who wastes her college fund on a number of societal ills: drugs, abortion, and living with a boyfriend who physically and mentally abused her. She, like the prodigal son, was reunited in the end with her parent(s). In this modern-day Los Angeles KNN version, the family was reunited specifically because they learned to love and communicate with one another as disciples in the ICOC family of God:

> Two young girls are on pottery wheel making a mug together for their mother's birthday. We watch the girls give the mug to their mother. Film then cuts to several years later when the girls are teenagers. The older daughter is having an argument with her parents.

> We watch this prodigal daughter as she berates her mother and father and finally leaves her parents' home. She is dressed in black with heavy makeup, and her boyfriend is at her side. Before she leaves, the mother gives her the money that they had saved for her college education. The daughter and boyfriend walk away from the family home on a beautiful California beach. The "good" sister dutifully attends college, staying at home in the family beach house with her parents who are depressed about the younger daughter's behavior and unhappy in their marriage.
>
> The film follows the prodigal daughter's destructive ways. She gets pregnant by her abusive boyfriend and has an abortion. The boyfriend is enraged when he finds out about the abortion and threatens to kill her if she does not leave immediately. In a subsequent graphic scene she is with a "friend" from the drug and prostitution world who is shooting up.

The women sitting in the audience around me gasped as a needle pierced skin and the prodigal daughter's friend vomited and then died of an overdose. Through graphic visual imagery, KNN succeeded in painting the outside world as dangerous and deadly. A dramatic script and skilled actors illustrated how a multiracial ICOC family of disciplers could radically heal wounded families.

> The prodigal daughter becomes increasingly more lost and distraught. At the same time we watch her mother transform from depressed over the loss of her daughter and a stressful marriage, to contented as she develops an intimate relationship with a young black ICOC woman who responds to an advertisement the mother puts in the paper for pottery students. The mother teaches the young woman to throw pottery and the young woman, an ICOC Christian, studies the Bible with the mother. The young woman and the mother work together on a project for a local soup kitchen: they make a series of mugs (that resemble the mug her two daughters made as young children for her birthday). The prodigal daughter, hungry and confused, finds a broken mug in the alley behind the soup kitchen. She is startled by how close in likeness it is to the one she and her sister crafted years ago. She wanders into the soup

> kitchen and talks to the young ICOC woman who had been studying the Bible with her mother. The ICOC disciple, recognizing that this is the woman's daughter, tells her how much her mother misses her.
>
> The film cuts back to the family in the beach house. The mother, after studying the Bible for a considerable time, has changed demeanor; she is now smiling, laughing, and happy with her husband. The husband too begins to study the Bible. The now happily married couple rejoice as they see their prodigal daughter (having been influenced by the young ICOC discipler in the soup kitchen) walking toward them on the beach.

The women around me clapped as the mother, father, and prodigal daughter were baptized into the movement in the ocean waters in front of their home. Their baptisms depicted on the large screens in front of us, and the standing and clapping throughout the convention center, lifted the energy in the large convention hall. A feeling of collective relief that this film family had survived the evils of the outside world through the intervention of ICOC disciples filled the room. When the lights came up, I saw that several women were crying, pulling tissues from their pocketbooks and hugging the women who sat next to them. I wanted to cry too, but I did not. I thought that perhaps the women crying around me were remembering (as the film had caused me to do) difficult relationships—husbands with whom they could not communicate, daughters or sons who were involved in drugs or estranged from parents. I thought of my oldest child, my son, and how our relationship had suffered through high-conflict divorce. I felt, for a brief moment, the hope that there existed such a sacred therapeutic cure for family conflict and trauma. The moment quickly passed as ethnographic objectivity and my interviews with ex-members reminded me of the numerous failed discipler attempts at healing family relationships.

KNN films were not home videos; they were professionally crafted theatrical projects. In a culture where many individuals are entertained daily by television and film, KNN's Hollywood medium produced effective performances of awesome ICOC family pushing away the trauma of dating, divorce, and drugs and resolving a number of family ills. The ICOC, like other religious groups today, employed various contemporary media venues like film, publishing, music, and video to a high degree. From the early nineteenth-century printing presses to late twentieth-century construction of religious websites, evangelical Protestants have been quick to employ media in the expression of sacred symbols, images, and worldview. As David Morgan (2002, 37) notes, from the beginnings of modern mass culture, two hundred years ago, "evangelical Protestants . . . were in no doubt about the rhetorical effectiveness of images." Furthermore, he argues, "American Protestants manifest a persistent inclination to experience media as an untrammeled representation of 'the truth.' " We should not be surprised then at the financial success of Mel Gibson's recent celluloid Passion play, nor the many audience members who left theaters weeping and proclaiming a renewal of faith. Jesús Martín-Barbero (1997), has suggested that media in collective, religious identity making is a kind of "re-enchantment" of our "rationalized" (Weber) world. In the ICOC, KNN films were dramatic, magical depictions of disciples in the ICOC successfully healing family wounds and resolving cultural contradictions for members.

Regional events as a whole were carefully crafted ritual productions that reinforced discipling relationships as exceptional: counseling others and submitting to disciplers' advice and intervention as a shield against family dysfunction and the most effective salve for relational injuries. These carefully orchestrated productions served the organization well, reinforcing members' commitment and providing a powerful forum for evangelical outreach. For individual members, such well-attended "big-liturgy theater" confirmed that the costs of ICOC membership, the daily work of discipling, submission to disciplers, and the constant pursuit of converts, was a sound family investment in a dangerous society. Events like Marriage Enrichment also gave members a language and stories through which they could construct and reaffirm their own presentations of awesome church family healing.

The Prodigal Daughter set the stage that day for members' evangelical outreach to their biological families and/or families of origin as they experienced, through the power of film, a hopeful, happy ICOC ending to strained and contentious family relationships. Regional performances and formal group rhetoric created a strong desire on the part of members to convert their mothers, fathers, brothers, sisters, aunts, cousins, and grandparents. Formal performances of domino conversion—the idea that if you were to convert just one kin, this could potentially result in multiple conversions of extended family—was a prominent and persistent theme in formal group discourse. These formal constructions of domino family conversion ignited much hope and disappointment, revealed through the stories individual members told of trying to save family members from the outside dangerous, diseased, and deadly world—stories of mostly failed attempts to turn fathers and mothers into Kingdom brothers and sisters.

Chapter 4

In with the Old and the New

The fictional account of family healing and reconciliation in KNN's *Prodigal Daughter* was representative of a very real dream. ICOC folklore was full of sons baptizing fathers, daughters baptizing mothers, family of origin sisters and brothers baptizing one another. Late one night, as I sat on the basement floor of a leadership couple's home for an "all night women's Bible study" that began at 7:00 P.M. and lasted till only 10:30 (Pat said they used to go late into the evening until most of them starting having children), Ann asked that the twelve women present join hands to connect our circle. I clasped one hand around Pat's hand and the other around Jill's. Ann began with the following prayer: "I'm so thankful for my mom, God. For my mom who, I can't even believe it when I say it. It's a miracle. My mom is a disciple now. She has been a disciple for a year. I can't believe it. It is so miraculous, thank you, God. She is coming to see me next week. I ask you to help me, God. Father, help me to love the rest of my biological family. God, help me not to close the door. With my sister especially, God. Even though it is so hard." She paused, fought back tears, and took a deep breath to continue: "When I see her she slams the door in my face. Help me, God, not to give up, to love her." She continued her prayer through gentle crying: "Thank you, God, for bringing my father back into my life. I have some kind of a relationship with him now and I'm thankful for that. When I want to keep far away from them, to hide from my biological family, please help me to love them, Father. I thank you, Father, for my brothers and sisters in the Kingdom who teach me what love is, who help me learn to love."

When I first entered the basement that evening, I found it stuffy and wondered if (three months pregnant, tired, and nauseous) I would make it through the evening. By the end of the night, the basement was no longer a stifling room, but a sacred and active space transformed by stories of healing and reconciliation with kin: a room charged by tears, physical comforting, prayer, confession, and testimony of how church membership had enabled members to become close and loving with fathers who had abused them, mothers who were neglectful, and siblings with whom they had fought. There was a palpable collective spirit of community in prayer, an energy named by believers of many faiths as the "obvious presence of the Holy Spirit" (Searl 1997, 99). Members spoke of God as there with us, in the basement space, as active in their marriages, and as radically present on their journeys to heal relationships with families of origin.

The women took turns expressing how disciples had helped heal their marriages, relationships with biological/families of origin, their own children, preteens and teenagers. I was invited to speak, but quietly declined. Pat placed a psalm in front of me to read instead. I thought of speaking; after three years of fieldwork, I wanted to be a part of the physical circle, to talk of my own family and how I had learned to forgive. Even though I could have framed my prayer as thanking a disciple, Pat, for our conversations about forgiveness, I could not speak of her as my "sister," nor talk of a "miraculous" discipling relationship, nor credit her with my ability to make peace with family wounds. My reticence is important because it speaks to the social pressure of telling a particular version of successful family healing in the ICOC. I knew that my words would have seemed out of place; I knew that I would have weakened the sacred energy that made its way through the bodies around me and disturbed the master narrative of miraculous family healing and conversion.

Narratives of Domino Healing

Telling stories about how the discipling community was able to bring about multiple family of origin conversion was a common group narrative theme. Such stories of converting kin were full of contradiction: they promoted ultimate loyalty to both church family and family of origin; they promoted forgiveness of past familial abuses alongside individualism and the ultimate importance of the self; and they cast biological mothers and fathers as sisters and brothers. At the same time, these narratives described a discipling approach and practice that appeared to resolve numerous ideals and expectations of family. Members prayed that they too would one day be able to stand at the lectern in front of their church family and proclaim, as Judy did during one women's gospel night, "God has worked miracles in our family's [biological] life!" Stories of extended biological families joining en masse, learning to respect one another, and protected from "evil" divisive outside influences were prominent during formal services and special events, in DPI literature, and in KNN video/film productions.

Testimonies

Fighting back tears, Jan Dealy looked out among the four hundred women on Women's Day finishing coffee and cheesecake, having just been entertained by a sketch featuring "Judge Judy" as host of the game show, *Who Wants to Be a Millionaire.* A local member had dressed as Judge Judy and quizzed contestants about their commitment to God. Jan motioned to her twenty-five-year-old daughter sitting nearby. She proudly announced that her daughter had led her to God, and that now, both her son and daughter were disciples. Jan told a story of her daughter calling home from college one day extremely excited, informing her she had met "really great friends and was going to church and studying the Bible and finally, that she was to be baptized." Jan said that she remembered feeling proud of her daughter, yet disheartened by her own life circumstances. She had been married thirty years to an abusive man who drank too much. One day she and her daughter were shopping in New York City when a man handed them a pamphlet that read: "The end of the world is coming." She said she looked at her daughter and vocalized how frightened she was about her present life situation. Her daughter said to her, "Mom, you should be sure where you stand before God." Jan was shocked by her daughter's suggestion: "What is this girl saying to me? I'm her mom!" The congregation laughed at this reversal of parental role. Jan then explained that it was through her daughter's bold efforts that she began to attend ICOC services. Her daughter was also presented as instrumental in leading Jan to attend a Marriage Enrichment Day with her husband. Jan completed the First Principles study and was baptized and became a disciple. She ended her testimony praising the bold and heroic efforts of her daughter: "I stand before you today with confidence, that same confidence my daughter confronted me with years ago."

During another local City COC Women's Day event in 1997, three women—a mother, daughter, and stepdaughter—narrated a kin conversion chain reaction, a story of family of origin made awesome through disciplers' efforts. The mother, Bobbie Kemp, testified first. She described being so impressed by the people in the congregation that she asked her daughter to come back with her: "I shared the Bible with my daughter [older teen at the time]. . . . When I was baptized, she was baptized along with me, and it was such an exciting time because God gave me my daughter. My stepdaughter was baptized too." Bobbie's daughter, Erin, testified after her mom. Erin told of attending an ICOC service and learning "more in that one service than I had ever learned in my life!" She converted soon after. Bobbie's stepdaughter, Tracy, was the third to testify. Tracy offered an image of God's power working through her biological father's family: "Using Bobbie, Erin, and Mark, God worked it out so that I could have a second chance, I could have an opportunity for Hope, Love, and Salvation. On May 16, 1994, my dad baptized me."

Such narratives of domino healing gave collective assurance that family of origin conversion was sacred work, in God's hands, unexplainable coincidences leading to kin conversions filled formal discourse. For example, during Wednesday night services, members would sometimes stand up and offer brief descriptions of recent healing and conversion successes. During one such service, members gasped out loud as a female member explained that her biological mother, with whom she had been studying the Bible over the phone, was "out of the blue" offered a job and an apartment nearby the City COC congregation. During another service, members gasped and praised God out loud and in unison as one woman told of going to an ICOC congregation in Florida while on a business trip and discovering that her cousin had been invited to the same service by a Florida disciple. "Awesome," "unbelievable," and "what are the odds?" were some of the comments whispered among congregants. Divine intervention was the implicit message behind these brief, yet powerfully legitimating stories.

Kingdom News Network

KNN produced films that enhanced a portrait of domino family healing and family of origin conversion. During one special Wednesday evening service in a hotel conference room, Dana, the women's ministry leader, told us that we were going to have a special "treat," a movie that the church had just released called *Secrets of the Heart.* She told us she would follow the film with a lesson on forgiveness. The lights dimmed as we anticipated our "treat," but the video was not working properly. Dana's husband, Ron, the congregation's lead evangelist, rushed to the video equipment to determine what was wrong. Working with audio and video equipment was gendered in group as in outside society, men were often talked about as naturally better with electronics and were almost always assigned these tasks at mixed gender and segregated events to help with such backstage responsibilities. Dana quickly reversed the evening's plan and said she would begin with her lesson on forgiveness. The women around me cheered her on, "Go, Dana! Come on, Dana!" Dana held up her hands in a forceful display of biblical feminism and exclaimed, "Women power!" The women applauded and I noted, for a brief moment, that it might have appeared to a passerby in the halls of the hotel that we were a group of radical feminists.

Like most messages delivered by ICOC leaders, Dana divided her sermon into sections, numbered them, and gave each a catchy title: "I am going to lay out three simple points: one, acknowledge the problem; two, accept his plan; three, activate the power of forgiveness." She bemoaned a "growing awareness of blame and not forgiveness" in our society. We must "accept his [God's] plan of forgiveness." She recited a list she had composed earlier in the week entitled "Things That Come from an Unforgiving Heart." Included in her long list were "hurtfulness, anger, vengeance, hatred, hardness, scornfulness, rage, violence, ugliness, meanness, bitterness, murder, and divorce." Dana, the woman who had just declared "women power," then told us that her parents' divorce had caused her to be raised by a single mother in a "feminist household" where she grew up developing a "man-hating" attitude. Her denouncement of feminism alongside a celebration of women power offers a strong example of what Judith Stacey (1991) names postfeminist rhetoric: an explicit disdain for the label feminist yet a rhetorical and practical application of core feminist principles—here namely the assertion of female power. Before she could fully review her three points, Ron signaled that he had mastered the video's audio problem (we had been listening to a local radio station instead of the film's audio track). Improvising, Dana quickly wrapped up her talk and let *Secrets of the Heart* demonstrate discipling's power to activate family of origin conversion and healing.

SECRETS OF THE HEART. The film began with a white woman (in her thirties) standing in a line of bridesmaids with a big smile on her face. Music played as we watched this woman miss catching a bridal bouquet. We saw a repeat of the same woman at several different weddings, missing various bridal bouquets. Her attempts grew more comedic as she began diving and falling to the ground in pursuit of bouquets through slow motion clips.

Film cut to this same woman sitting with her boyfriend at an upscale restaurant. Her boyfriend repeatedly tried to ask her a question but kept stumbling, "Will you mmm . . . will you mmm . . . will you mmm." The woman daydreamed as he struggled and we briefly saw an image of her in a wedding dress. Boyfriend finally got the words out, "Will you move in with me?"

Film cut to the woman sitting on her couch eating ice cream. Her roommate came in and gave her a hard time about agreeing to move in with the boyfriend rather than insisting on marriage. The roommate argued, "Two and half years of dating isn't enough to know!" As she nervously ate the ice cream the phone rang. It was her younger sister calling from a pay phone. The younger sister announced that she was getting married and that she wanted her older sister to come to the wedding and be a bridesmaid. The older sister had a pained expression on her face at the prospect of wearing yet another bridesmaid dress and missing yet another flower bouquet.

The older sister and her boyfriend arrived in Los Angeles the night before the wedding. She found her younger sister surrounded by her Christian friends (ICOC disciples). Her sister was trying on her wedding veil. We learned that the bride was blind and that her blindness was caused years ago in an automobile accident when their father, an alcoholic, was driving while intoxicated. We also learned that the groom, who arrived at the church with his family, is black. I heard women around me in the conference room whispering, "Ahh, he's black," seeming to anticipate that the parents might have an issue with interracial marriage. The family conflict that ensued, however, had nothing to do with the racial makeup of the couple.

That evening at the rehearsal dinner, disciples toasted the couple and talked about how much the future bride and groom loved each another. During the rehearsal dinner, the older sister began talking to the bride about how terrible their father was. A disciple intervened and asked her to stop. The disciple told her that it was a bad time to bring up the father because the father had called the younger sister that day and asked if he could attend the wedding. We saw the father appear in the hallway. The biological mother asked the father to leave as tomorrow was a big day for their daughter and she did not want him to ruin it. The father stated that he was there to "make amends."

The song "What the World Needs Now Is Love" played softly. The older sister became very upset about the alcoholic father's presence and ended up on the chapel floor late on the evening of the rehearsal dinner, sobbing about how much she hated her father. The younger sister followed her into the chapel and knelt beside her. In the balcony above, the groom and the bride's discipler were listening. The younger sister admitted that she too felt anger and resentment toward their father, but that God was leading her to do the right thing—she wanted to forgive her father for causing her blindness and let him participate in the wedding ceremony and celebration. The older sister was taken by her younger sister's efforts to forgive their father; she told her that if she was able to forgive him for his alcoholism and taking away her sight, she would listen to what her little sister had to tell her about a relationship with God. Late that night, the bride sat in a car with her fiancé and her discipler who both encouraged her to do the "right thing," to lead her family into forgiveness: "You have what your family needs," they told her.

The next day, right before the wedding ceremony, the older sister gave the younger sister a kiss and then left the bride alone with her discipler in an anteroom. The discipler looked into the bride's eyes and told her that her eyes were "so beautiful." The bride replied, "My dad used to say that to me."

Film cut to the foyer of the church where the bride's biological father was signing the guest register. The father told his blind daughter, who was to walk down the aisle momentarily, that he had stopped drinking. The daughter gave her father a flower to wear on his suit and asked him to walk her down the aisle. He told her that he was not dressed properly. She responded that he looked fine to her.

Father and daughter walked down the aisle. Biological mother appeared shocked, as did the older sister. The disciplers in the congregation were smiling and pleased at the reunion. A young man played the guitar and sang the lyrics "In your eyes I've found my place."

During the wedding reception, the older sister gave the keys to the apartment back to her "live-in" boyfriend and said, "I made my little sister a promise." The women around me in the conference room clapped. The older sister finally, having made a promise to study the Bible if her sister forgave their father, caught the bridal bouquet. The song "What the World Needs Now Is Love" played throughout the credits. A clip at the end of the film read, from book of John: "Perfect love casts out fear."

LIKE OTHER KNN video events, when the lights came up, I noticed many women in the congregation were crying. I looked to my left and Pat had tears in her eyes. I looked to my right and noticed another woman crying. I thought of the stories that these three women had told me during formal interviews over the past few years; each had fathers they were estranged from, none had been able to grow close to their fathers or make them into Kingdom brothers. One of these women had a father who was sexually abusive, another had a father who had abandoned her as a child; both women struggled to "forgive." The KNN film caused me, as I tried to sit back and observe, to work to push back emotions regarding my own family relationships.

Ann stood and spoke to us from the lectern in the front of the room as they wiped their tears. She gave us a context for individual interpretation of *Secrets of the Heart*. "The woman in the film was me," she said. She told us of her stressful relationship with her father, and how a disciple had persuaded her to call him. During the first call her father had asked curtly, "What do you want?" "That hurt," she said, but tried a second time, to which her father responded that he "couldn't take the time" to come and see her and his grandchildren. How does she get through the pain, she asked. It is only through the help of church members who have taught her how to "continually forgive" that she is able to love her father despite his resistance and cold responses. Recall that Ann had affirmed her commitment to mending fences with her father during the "all night" basement Bible study, thanking God for bringing her father back into her life and for her brothers and sisters in the Kingdom who had taught "what love is."

Pat gave me a ride home that night and told me more about how her time in the church had helped her come to terms with her own father's distance and inability to express love. Earlier that evening, feeling the fatigue that often comes with the first months of pregnancy, she had struggled with not wanting to come to church on a Wednesday night. "What would be new [about the service] after fifteen years?" she had asked herself. "Just that day," she told me, she and her husband, Tom, had struggled with the task of how she could go on forgiving and loving a father who had so little involvement in his child's and grandchildren's lives. She had been "amazed" by the ability of the church to provide a new tool (the KNN film) to help her face again the old, yet open, wounds caused by her father's harsh emotional distance. Watching the estranged and wounded family in the film come together gave her hope and patience to keep loving and trying to communicate with her father, and to pursue these efforts through a community of caring church disciples.

ICOC production efforts like *Secrets of the Heart* gave Pat and others renewed hope that their church family was the very best community to help them heal relationships with parents and siblings. KNN also fortified group boundaries: vividly reminding members of a conflicted and helpless picture of family relationships outside the church and of the strong potential for healing within.

KNN features like *The Prodigal Daughter* and *Secrets of the Heart* speak to the power of film as a mechanism of group commitment and conversion. *Secrets of the Heart* emphasized, through a familiar and effective medium, that the ICOC community had the power to heal the worst of family history tragedy. The film's production values were good: the sound design (rich with classic tunes) had dramatic effect and the acting was convincing. It is no wonder that members described KNN's video and film products as seeming "so real": they passed as professional films for many members.

The plots also magnified the dangers threatening contemporary families and intimate relationships. In *The Prodigal Daughter*, abortion and drugs threatened young daughters; in *Secrets of the Heart*, alcoholism destroys children and tears a family apart. As in narratives of heroic ICOC marriage saves, families then experience healing, transformation, and reconciliation through the interventions of disciplers: this radically deviant father transforms into a symbol of the good father, the protective father who walks his daughter down the aisle of the church at her wedding. The sister, swimming in disappointment in a dating culture that offered little security, is now living among a community where she is likely to find a willing and caring church brother to marry. The title of the film, *Secrets of the Heart*, calls to mind ICOC rhetorical images of open, submissive, and "teachable" hearts. Hearts that hold nasty biological family secrets and destructive relational habits, but through disciplers' interventions become catalysts for the opening of successive biological family members' hearts.

Notable was that throughout the entire film, the bride was surrounded by her own discipler and other disciples in the church. When she and her sister were in the chapel, disciples were listening to their intimate conversation on the balcony above. When she was in the car late at night trying to decide whether or not to forgive her father and let him participate in the wedding celebration, the discipler was there. When she was in the chapel before the wedding ceremony, it was her discipler who helped her see that she had the power to forgive. Not only did her conviction as a church member allow her to forgive her father and lead to her father walking her down the aisle, it was the impetus for her biological sister's conversion to the ICOC, the action that led her sister to leave a sinful relationship with her boyfriend.

This young bride became the biological family heroine, the daughter who, through membership in the ICOC, was able to heal and reconcile her family. Her sister was now a "real sister," a sister for eternity, sure to develop a loving marriage with a dedicated ICOC brother. We were given no solid clues of the father's motivation—left to wonder that, perhaps, as in other narrative instances, his willingness to make amends was divine intervention. Given the scenario that unfolded in front of the mom and dad, we were left with the impression that the parents may be well on the way to becoming brothers and sisters in the Kingdom and perhaps even remarried.

The potential for the discipling community to bring about family of origin change was performed in the ritual participants viewing of the film: we sat in a room surrounded by City COC disciplers. Immediately after the film, Ann, a discipling group and family group leader, demonstrated application of the film to life experience by beginning, "The woman in the film was me," and then applying the message to her own situation. Immediately after viewing *The Prodigal Daughter* we had a share time, a break in the service where members and potential converts and disciples and disciplers began talking together spontaneously in small groups about how the film had touched them and how they had similar family troubles. The social environment where media messages are received is essential to audience impact. The showing of KNN films and video newsreels, in my observations, were primarily viewed during services or in homes where disciples gathered; they were not routinely given to potential converts for home viewing. Viewed alone, *Secrets of the Heart* would no doubt lack the collective energy that sitting among disciples brought; viewed alone, members and potential converts would be left on their own to interpret and apply to their own life circumstances.

> *Discipleship Publications International*
> One of the special treasures that God gives to people on this earth is the family. . . . [O]f course, many families experience divorce, adultery, lack of forgiveness and other painful scars. . . . [T]he true disciple sees these needs as an opportunity to introduce his or her family to the healing power of Christ. . . . As Christians, we are commanded to love and care for our families. (Kim 1998, 56)

The previous excerpt from Frank and Erica Kim's DPI text, *How to Share Your Faith*, stresses the dangers social disease poses to biological/families of origin. This text is replete with success stories that named and illustrated the domino effect: "Let us not hold back one day longer with the people we should love the most on this earth—our families! . . . [W]e baptized nine mother and fathers of disciples in six months! . . . The domino effect of parents being baptized also allowed many siblings, children and even grandparents to be baptized into Christ! Families in Tokyo were reunited and also united in Christ like never before" (Kim 1998, 58–59).

In fact, an entire chapter, "Love Your Family," is devoted to domino conversion stories. The following narrative is indicative of the organization's domino effect script, successful conversion through bold disciple efforts producing a conversion chain reaction:

> About five summers ago, my nephew, Jeremy, came from Colorado to stay with my family and me for six weeks. At fifteen years old he had begun to drift away from his mother, from a good conscience and into sin and rebelliousness. . . . As he lived with us and participated in the church activities, he changed immediately.
>
> Then we went to our summer Christian youth camp. While there, Jeremy decided to become a disciple of Jesus. He started studying the Bible that week while at camp. We continued studying, and ten days after camp I baptized my nephew into Christ!
>
> The change in his life was so radical that my sister and my mother (his mother and grandmother), though three states away, perceived his transformation merely in their phone conversations. They were so impressed that they decided to attend the church in Denver and began studying the Bible with the women's ministry leader there and with my wife, Debbie, over the phone. . . . Five days later I drove Jeremy, along with our two children, John and Amy, to Colorado and baptized my mother and sister into Christ as disciples. It was a glorious time for our family!
>
> A few months later they all moved to Dallas to be near us and to be a part of the Dallas church. Jeremy now is in the third year of a football scholarship at the University of Central Oklahoma. My sister lives across the street from us and leads a group of disciples. My mom, a Bible discussion group leader, works for me as my personal executive assistant. All three are very fruitful in their ministry for the Lord. Because of Jesus and the church, our family has been redeemed, and our relationships are better than ever before. Praise God for these blessings! (Kim 1998; 62)

This text, as with other DPI publications, were read alone, discussed in Bible study groups, featured during larger services and events, and carried with members as constant reminders of the potential for domino conversion.

Ex-Member Narratives of Bio Conversion

The extreme movement focus on converting family of origin that I documented in group was also a subject of ex-member and media attention.

For example, the ABC News program *20/20* did a spot on the ICOC on October 15, 1993, entitled "Believe It or Else." This exchange is typical of media cult accounts that stress ex-member horror stories—this one, in particular, depicting a child, a girl of fourteen at the mercy of relentless "cult" leaders.

JOHN STOSSEL [*20/20* journalist] [*voice-over*]: When Nancy could not persuade other children to come to her church, leaders told her—

MS. CONE [former church member]: "You have something wrong with you. You're not close to God." And they said, "You need to beg them. Tell them this is a life-and-death matter. Even if they say no, beg them until they say yes."

STOSSEL [*voice-over*]: She tried, but when she couldn't recruit anyone else, church leaders told her that she and her family would burn in hell.

MS. CONE: I couldn't go to sleep at night, wondering if I woke up the next morning if my mother would be dead or my father would be dead and they'd be in hell. You know, that's what they told me. "Your parents are going to hell and you're responsible for their souls." And that was a real big responsibility for someone who was only 14 years old, and I couldn't take it anymore. I felt like I was going to crack. (ABC News *20/20* transcript #1344, October 15, 1993, pp. 2–3)

Nancy said she told the church she was leaving and that they warned her not to go. Ms. Cone details more of leaders' threats and how she thought of suicide and scratched her wrists till they bled. Stossel tells us that Ms. Cone "was hospitalized for a month. She says being in the hospital and not being allowed to take church leaders' phone calls is the only thing that allowed her to escape the church."

Ms. Cone's story may have been dramatized; however, her media account taken together with my ex-member interviews, and my member interviews and field observations, suggest that members did feel great pressure in group to convert family—not just for bringing them together as brothers and sisters in their new church family, but to save them from eternal hell and damnation.

FAMILY OF ORIGIN DILEMMA

As members formed intimate new relationships within church boundaries that demanded extensive loyalty, emotional attachment, intimacy, and frequent association, the time they spent with their family of origin naturally diminished (unless those members had converted as well). New religious movements that have demanded strong in-group bonds, consistent and/or constant physical association, and submission to group norms of behavior have historically carried a mark or stigma of biological/family of origin destruction (e.g., Children of God or "The Family," and the Unification Church, labeled the "Moonies"). Members of such groups naturally experience role conflict as normative family responsibilities and expected ideals of caring and concern clash with their current position as sister, brother, mother, or father in the new group. The anticult movement that arose in the 1960s and 1970s was sustained by parents convinced that their young adult children were being "brainwashed" and taken away from their families in "cults." After the mass suicide of nine hundred people in the 1970s in Jim Jones's movement, the People's Temple, family panic grew over youth membership in "cults." The social impact of this historical anti-cult moral panic left many ICOC members' biological families nervous and in serious fear of being abandoned.

Like many parents of young adults who joined new religious movements in the sixties and seventies, contemporary parents of young adults in the ICOC nationwide have voiced serious opposition to the movement. Media coverage and anti-cult literature are replete with heightened rhetoric fueling cult accusations. ICOC campus activities were in fact banned from several college campuses (Paulson 2001; Rodgers-Melnick 1996). Criticisms echo the concerns of original anti-cult, biological family instigated organizations that responded to new religious movements of the 1960s.[1] For example, the AFF (American Family Foundation) published a book in 1996 entitled *The Boston Movement: Critical Perspectives on the International Churches of Christ*, edited by Carol Giambalvo and Herbert Rosedale. The editors state as their mission: "to study manipulation and cultic groups, to educate the public and professionals, and to assist those who have been adversely affected by a cult experience." The majority of contributors to this volume view the ICOC as a destructive group, and as especially detrimental to family. Speaking from a place of medical therapeutic authority, Lorna Goldberg and William Goldberg's piece (in Giambalvo and Rosedale 1996, 47), "A Mental Health Approach," begins, "We are clinical social workers who have been working with families of current and former members of cults and destructive groups since the 1970s. Typically, membership in these groups has hurt both the member and his or her family." Another contributor, long outspoken critic of the movement, Robert Watts Thornburg at Boston University, writes, "The Boston Church of Christ discourages new prospects from associating with nonmembers, systematically cutting out any contact with family, friends, or outside sources of reality checks" (Giambalvo and Rosedale 1996, 21).

Such anti-cult literature, often authored by former members and members' family of origin, posed a serious threat to the ICOC organizational performance. Stories of losing young family members to the ICOC are grave images. In these narratives, members are not heroines or heroes, but victims, and their disciplers evil representatives of an organized effort to "steal" children. Imagine how the following narrative, written by the parents of an ex-member, might drain symbolic renditions of the discipling community as exceptionally able to heal biological families through the teaching of forgiveness and relationality.

> *The Stranger in My House: A Parent's Story*
>
> Karen [daughter] was outraged when I said her new friends reminded me of Moonies and it seemed like the church was a cult. . . . Karen said that there was "spiritual warfare" going on in our household and that Satan was using her parents to try to keep her out of the church. . . . I still remember the words of a pastor from a mainline Church of Christ. . . . "I'm sorry I have to tell you this, but your daughter is in a religious cult." . . . The harmful effect is that the person becomes totally dependent on his or her discipler for all decisions . . . the church member must imitate his or her discipler in every way. This causes complete loss of identity and autonomy. . . . With Karen's recruitment came "the invasion of the body snatchers," or, more accurately, the invasion of the mind snatchers! . . . For five months, from March until August, we didn't see Karen. She lived with a family who had been asked to help out in the San Francisco Church of Christ. . . . Karen slept on the sofa in the living room of the couple's rented home. . . . It has been almost four years since Karen was recruited into the International Churches of Christ, and I have found ways to cope. . . . It is puzzling to me that my daughter

> no longer shows any signs of emotion. She has no laughter, no tears, and no anger. Her temperament remains the same, except during those rare times when the old Karen slips out. It is a great loss to me that the two of us can no longer be close. Before her recruitment Karen was very open and honest, but now she seems to have many secrets and hidden thoughts. (Giambalvo and Rosedale, 172–180)

What we don't hear in these cult war stories (ABC News and Karen's mom, above) is the emphasis that the group also put on, as I witnessed, forgiveness and interaction with kin. On the other hand, what we don't hear in the ICOC discourse is recognition that church family commitment to organizational therapeutic and evangelical goals necessarily meant less time and commitment to family of origin members. I did find that if a family was engaged in trying to "deprogram," or get their family member out of the group by offering them "spiritual pornography" at every turn, leaders and disciplers suggested that members spend limited time with these parents and kin. ICOC leader and author Sam Laing offered biblical justification for keeping distance from biological family during one large regional event: "Abraham did not do all that he should have done. . . . God called him to leave his father and move. . . . I remember another famous guy in the Bible who wanted to have his relative along with him and it messed him up. I'm not saying your relatives can't be beside you in the Lord or in the Kingdom, but there are times when we are compromising to do that." If parents and kin did not pressure members to leave the church, it seemed that disciples were encouraged, in their limited "free time," to be with families of origin.

What is most interesting in narratives of ICOC critics, especially regarding our understanding of the cultural implications of this group and other religio-therapeutic organizations, is how anti-group discourse drew from the very same well of cultural beliefs and practices that the ICOC organization did. As sociologists studying deviance and the framing of social problems have noted, labeling an act, group, or organization as deviant takes place through moral battles where organizational actors draw from deeply resonating symbols and stories as they frame their arguments (Becker 1963; Snow and Benford 1992; Loseke 2003). Children, for example, are a particularly powerful and much used symbol in social problems' battles: a child as the ultimate helpless/innocent victim. The ABC transcript, Karen's mother, and other family of origin ICOC relatives present their children as victimized, losing individuality, becoming like robots, lacking emotion and expressive feeling. Karen's mom ends with the statement: "I plan to do my part to make people aware of this evil plot to snag our bright young people and take away years of their productive lives."

Group and anti-group discursive repertoires were similar, based on normative therapeutic and family values: biological family as normative, families as providing unconditional caring, and families as teaching appropriate gendered roles and behavior. Karen's mother ends her narrative by noting she reminds her daughter that "our love is unconditional—that we love her no matter what" and that "the group members' love is conditional" (Giambalvo and Rosedale 1996, 172–182). ICOC and anti-group spokespersons as "moral entrepreneurs" (Becker 1963) drew heavily from therapeutic cultural discourse, assembling those cultural beliefs, strategies, and practices that they knew would best resonate with individuals socialized to respect therapeutic values and practice. As we have seen thus far, formal group discourse stressed relationality and expressivity as core practices of the discipling church family. Critics claimed the opposite, that the group took away true emotions and "snatched" minds away. Critics also cast discipling as a manifestation of major "diseases" in therapeutic culture: for example, discipling as "codependency," a contemporary relational "dysfunction" defined by some therapeutic "experts" as individuals who become too wrapped up and dependent on one another.[2] Given the extreme accountability and dependence on disciplers for day-to day negotiation of self and sifting through cultural expectations, it is not surprising that critics and ex-members leveled this therapeutic indictment. A former member posted on the Delphi Forum chat room in early April of 2004: "The ICOC is extremely codependent. . . . It's prevented a lot of people from growing. . . . The church will not get healthy by remaining inclusive, looking inside of itself for answers. . . . The only way to get healthy is to separate one self from sick people and look for a healthy environment." The debate that ensued between ICOC members, families of origin, and critics of the movement operated through ideals like expressivity, emotionality, and concepts like dysfunctional family and codependency. This emphasis speaks to the cultural weight afforded therapeutic ethos in contemporary U.S. society.

CULTURAL TOOLS: THERAPEUTIC STANCE AND STRATEGY

It is possible that the heavy emphasis I documented in ICOC family productions on converting, forgiving, and reconciling with biological kin in the late 1990s was partly a response to over a decade of harsh "cult" accusations and former members' labeling of church family "dysfunction." The Kims' book was published in 1998 and KNN films *The Prodigal Daughter* and *Secrets of the Heart* were produced in the mid- to late 1990s, both well after the flood of harsh criticisms in the early 1990s that made much of how the ICOC took members away from biological family/family of origin. Without question, these narratives were performances meant to cast the movement as healing and bringing together biological/families of origin.

Some researchers warn that staged events inhibit understanding what is really going on in controversial new religious movements. They are "tricks" of cults eager to fool and craft researcher presentations of group to the outside world.[3] The benefit of listening carefully to former members and movement critics as you conduct intensive fieldwork over time in the community is that you come to understand the function of formal performances and individual presentations in both individual group experience and movement construction. Even if the stories I heard from individuals and in formal group performances were staged and selected events meant to shape my interpretations and counter negative "cult" accusations, there is still much to be learned. These intentional performances were meant to shape not only my opinion but also potential convert and member conceptions of the group as therapeutically sound. The disciples that joined hands in the basement prayer circle I describe at the beginning of this chapter were bolstered by a promise: a new family who would help you care for the old; a new family that would teach familiar therapeutic and religious healing strategies; and a new family that would help you resolve contradictory familial expectations. These performances suggest that religious communities today understand the power and appeal of offering new and familiar cultural skills and approaches to helping people mend fences with biological/families of origin, and that a religious promise of such healing ends must incorporate core therapeutic values, skills, and approach.

Forgiveness

Forgiveness as a strategy for improving self and relationship is culturally ubiquitous. As Swidler (2001) stresses of such beliefs, practices, and models of making sense of social experiences, they are deeply embedded—they are familiar and seem right, and this is why they make sense to us. Forgiveness is one such cultural habit: a rhetorical interaction of weighted ambiguity. We are taught through major social institutions (e.g., family, religion, medical therapeutic) to say, "I forgive you," to accept apology, but what does that mean—how does it manifest as a practical strategy for improving self and relationships? Members were told that discipling would clarify forgiveness.

For those who converted to the ICOC from other religious groups, forgiveness was already a familiar aspect of their faith. Christianity, Judaism, Islam, and many other faiths stress a need to make amends with those who have hurt us or those we may have wronged. In fact, the teaching and enabling of forgiveness is a driving commodity in today's religious marketplace.[4] For members who converted to the ICOC from other Christian faiths, they recognized forgiveness as a key aspect of Christology: Jesus died on the cross to forgive the sins of humankind. Jesus taught in the Lord's Prayer (Matthew 6: 9–13) forgiveness as key to individual salvation: "For if you forgive others their trespasses, your heavenly Father will also forgive you; but if you do not forgive others, neither will your Father forgive your trespasses" (verse 14, NRSV). A large part of the Christian "tool kit" for mending relationships with others and God is the ability to enact forgiveness. Griffith (1997, 189) found, for example, a "vast energy" among the women in Aglow (an international, interdenominational evangelical women's group) "given to teaching each other to pray for and forgive parents for their shortcomings and to work through the anger caused by their mistakes." That ICOC disciplers would teach forgiveness one-on-one, take you by the hand day or night and help you figure out when to forgive, when to name sin, that they were supposedly offering you a new, effective, and seemingly coherent approach to practicing forgiveness, was no doubt extremely appealing.

ICOC author and lead evangelist Sam Laing told a group of men at a regional event: "A lot of us, it's the old sin of bitterness that's wrecking up our heart right now. . . . It may be toward your dad. It may be toward the person who sexually abused you, it may be toward the wife who's committed adultery." He continued, stressing that forgiveness took away the pain of estrangement from biological family: "It is the most liberating thing you will ever do in your life when you finally stamp that bill of sale you've been holding over their head—paid in full. I forgive you. . . . You must forgive or your life will be a living hell." The best way to walk in the path of forgiveness was with ICOC disciples who could teach you how to forgive, who could "activate the power of forgiveness." Clearly, a strong message of *Secrets of the Heart* was that disciplers could help a member sift through the pain and questions surrounding when and how to forgive: disciplers would be there to help you approach and overcome physical and mental scars.

An expectation of forgiveness is pervasive; it extends beyond explicitly therapeutic and religious endeavors, yet its meaning is so often vague. Forgiveness is grounded in therapeutic culture and core U.S. values: individualism, humanitarianism, and unconditional familial love. Forgiveness, like apology, is expected: when Richard Clark, a top former counterterrorism advisor to the Clinton and Bush administrations, stood in front of the September 11th commission in 2004 and apologized for failing the people, there was some expectation on the part of the public that families of those killed in the terrorist attacks should accept the apology and "forgive." Despite our national tendency to see forgiveness as a therapeutic and social good, practical implications and actions of forgiveness remain vague and are often primarily rhetorical.[5]

Contemporary theologians have wrestled with the meaning and practice of forgiveness in our therapeutic culture.[6] To forgive is to let go of past abuses, to love those who have hurt you. Yet in contemporary culture, we are also encouraged to embrace and understand these abuses and express our own pain and desires. Forgiveness exists alongside therapeutic ideals that demand individuals to not be "taken advantage of," "enable," promote "codependence," or inhibit growth of the "self." Demands of therapeutic culture then render the process of forgiveness, and "letting go" of past abuses ambiguous. Forgiveness in ICOC discourse still embraced these contradictory elements, but claimed a new approach in overcoming the confusion. Disciplers would teach you when and where to embrace a particular therapeutic or Christian ideal or practice, just as disciplers would help you figure out, as a disciple, when to submit to church leaders/disciplers and when to speak your mind. As the KNN film *Secrets of the Heart* and the one-on-one discipling efforts that took place directly after its viewing indicate, discipling was promised as practical assistance for enacting the indefinite cultural expectation of forgiveness.

Biological and Family of Origin Bonds and Responsibilities

> I love this church, it's a family. We don't give up on each other.
>
> —Alicia

The popular phrase "You can't divorce your family" reflects a profound sense of the permanency and high expectations of kin care and interaction in our society. Even though many people are estranged from family of origin, and you can, in effect, sever ties with parents and children through various legal and informal means, such actions are perceived as deviant, as departures from how people *should be* doing family and kin. Normative family ideals call us to love and care for our families through "thick and thin," and, in contemporary culture, we have an added responsibility to appeal to therapeutic experts when serious problems arise that threaten family health.

Biological family is the normative family construction: for the most part, we think of "real" family as those connected by blood. Our legal and medical institutions legitimate this model: for example, biological family members often have rights to visit and make decisions in medical emergencies (if spouses as next of kin are no longer available), and family courts persist in primarily viewing biological family as true family. Despite the rising acceptance of a number of alternative family structures of "choice" such as adoption, gay/lesbian marriages and civil unions, and stepfamilies, the "molecular connection still implies a sense of belonging, continuity, and care that makes families—and society—possible" (Wegar 1998, 41). Our new popular genetics discourse makes this connection seem even stronger; a discourse of genetic essentialism in media presentations warning us of inherited genes responsible for a wide range of disease and illness. Genetic essentialism and legal, religious, and medical institutions continue to legitimate biological family as normative. If we undergo a serious socialization process that involves naming new kin, we become beholden to that old set of expectations demanding care, love, and unconditional support for family members—they are transferred to our newly constructed kin ties.

Family is for life. We don't give up on families. Families are there for each other, forgiving, caring, taking care of each other, sacrificing for each other. This is not unique to U.S. society, or a new social expectation. Other cultures may have different ideals and practices of family/kin caretaking, but core expectations are often similar: you don't abandon family, especially biological family. In the Christian and Jewish traditions family responsibilities are front and center. ICOC members who saw, like other evangelical Christians, the Bible as a guidebook for life, found scriptural affirmation for high kin care expectations. In the Hebrew Bible God speaks to Moses the now familiar commandment, "You shall each revere your mother and father," and later, "You shall not hate in your heart anyone of your kin." Leviticus 21:1–3 notes that only for "his mother, his father, his son, his daughter, his brother [nearest kin]" was a man expected to perform mourning rituals like shaving the head and mutilating the body (Leviticus 19: 3, 17, NRSV). Caring, revering, and sacrificing for family is a cross-cultural, long expected social action, legitimated by religious texts and reinforced by various social structures.

We have high expectations for family and kin care, yet family has always been the site of massive contradiction: namely, domestic violence and physical and emotional abuse. While the local news would have us believe that our cities and neighborhoods are dangerous streets to walk today, we are more likely to be hurt by our families than a stranger. Our biological/families of origin are the people in whom we place our faith, who are supposed to always be there with gentle and loving hands and "heart," yet they are the very people who deal the deepest blows. This social contradiction is painful and difficult to resolve on individual and structural levels. In contemporary U.S. society, we are often expected to turn to therapeutic professionals for assistance in making some sense of this disturbing contradiction.

There has been a significant rise in family therapy options and investment in the last half of the twentieth century (Herman 1995; Irvine 1999, 37). Despite our notion that families are autonomous and parents should decide what is best for their own children, we harbor a great moral responsibility to turn to these "experts" (Lasch 1977). This responsibility to seek secular therapeutic expertise is sometimes formally enforced, as in family court when a judge may order parents in high-conflict divorce to seek family therapy, or in educational institutions, where educators and courts may work together to encourage parents and children to receive counseling. It is also informally enforced: for example, when religious leaders refer families to outside counselors, or family members themselves put pressure on children, siblings, or parents to enter into family counseling. In the ICOC, and other religious movements, a search for outside therapeutic help is replaced (or enhanced) by in-group religio-therapeutic efforts.[7] Christian marriage and family counselors provide options to secular psychologists and counselors. The ICOC discipling system was presented by members and leaders as the ultimate family therapy choice. Given our high cultural expectations for seeking family counseling and "expert" assistance, ICOC's performance of disciplers as exceptional family counselors made an impact.

Expectations of family care and engagement in therapeutic guidance naturally presented ICOC members and potential converts with a deeply felt contradiction: they maintained a responsibility to both their family of origin and their new church "real" family to engage in a therapeutic family process. Resolving this contradiction, for members whose families engaged in anti-cult therapeutic efforts like "deprogramming" (using former members and other religious or therapeutic experts to counsel members out), was extremely difficult as they were encouraged by the group to keep a distance from these kin members. However, for those whose parents/family of origin were not actively engaged in an effort to get them out of the church, the discipling system was presented as a therapeutic community that would help them not give up on their family of origin. In fact, in the evangelical mission of the church, the pledge to save your family of origin came to life through aggressive action. By proselytizing and converting family members you would be saving them from hell while healing old wounds. Even more, domino conversion narratives suggested that your mother, father, sister, and brother of origin could be with you as sisters and brothers in the Kingdom on Earth, and for an eternity in heaven. In these efforts, ICOC discipling was presented as truly "awesome" family therapy, with exceptional power to heal and reconcile the old family by making them new ICOC family, a Christian family driven by unconditional love and dedication.

Yet, the reality was that many members were not able to convert family of origin. How did the movement keep this common experience from debilitating the organizational performance of the group as exceptionally able to achieve these ends? One way they managed this inconsistency was by maintaining that disciplers would help members stay strong in their commitment to love resistant family of origin members; they promised that disciplers would help them to continue to forgive fathers and mothers as they closed the door again and again; and they continually reminded disciples that God may choose to open the door to family members' hearts at any point in the future. So, even if family of origin members never converted, you were still engaged in a valuable process and therapeutic strategy. Members, even if domino healing was far from the story they were able to tell, still presented themselves as genuinely working to open lines of communication and forgive families of origin.

As members and leaders talked about negotiating, working to heal, convert, and forgive family of origin, they made clear that disciplers would be available to manage this painful and confusing process. Not surprisingly, in their narratives and descriptions, they, and their biological/family of origin members, were often cast as victims of social disease.

Victimization

ICOC's plan for family reconciliation sustained another familiar cultural contradiction: individual as both victim and responsible agent. Victims are important characters in the social drama of therapeutic culture. We understand, through the powerful social construction and performance of institutions like the media, the judicial system, and our educational system, that people can be victims of corporations (Enron, coal miners), crime (robbery, identity theft, rape), and schools (lack of qualified teachers, curriculum, and funds). We believe too that individuals can be victims of family: for example, through "dysfunctional" families, "codependent" families, and divorced families. To self-identify or identify others as a victim of family experience is a popular and well-understood stance in therapeutic culture, a popular talk show subject (Lowney 1999), and a perfectly acceptable position that can bring much sympathy from others. ICOC's discourse repertoire was deeply grounded in the language and moral construction of victimization, primarily victims of family disease and dysfunction, often the damaging results of the gender sins of parents and society.

To sympathize with victims seems "natural," especially sympathy for children and youth. Those who abuse children are afforded little sympathy from the public, while those who abuse adult spouses may be more easily forgiven. The social debate around victimization, from both lay and medical therapeutic "experts," centers around the acceptance of the validity of victim status and individuals using the label to gain sympathy and escape responsibility. For example, one can be perceived as a victim of the socially constructed "disease" of alcoholism and at the same time seen by many as responsible for his or her behavior, perhaps even as morally bereft, or as a criminal (Ries 1977). Furthermore, we have social methods of assessing who deserves sympathy, who does not, and how much: "Receiving sympathy has its patterns and rules," it is "part of our moral code" (Clark 1997, 11, x). To self-identify then as a victim of domestic dysfunction is to enter into a world of cultural confusion, an often ambiguous position that must be defended according to "moral codes." Most often, this self-identification comes along with an expectation to heal from victimization and to turn to the appropriate medical therapeutic experts. Here again, disciplers would hold your hand, they would help you figure out and navigate victimhood: when to claim victimization, when to name parents as victimized, and how to engage in a process of healing from abuse. Disciplers were presented as able to produce a coherent approach to victim identification, responsibility, and action.

The ICOC was one of many contemporary religio-therapeutic spaces committed to making sense of how to negotiate this contradictory therapeutic stance. Griffith (1997, 190) found that "Aglow fosters a kind of victimology that attributes women's suffering to their family—often construed today as 'dysfunctional.' . . . Aglow offers women the chance to reinterpret family crises in ways that replace the burden of guilt and shame with redemption and hope for healing." Griffith's work in Aglow highlights the core contradiction in identifying with a Christian and therapeutic victim stance: "Although the notion of victimization and the conviction that one's 'sickness' is one's own burden of sin apparently contradict one another, these beliefs are held together through an avowal of the need for prayer and surrender" (1997, 190). In the ICOC, prayer and surrender to God were important individual responsibilities, but only third-party Christian counselors, disciplers, could provide the keys to the process of balancing and negotiating the contradictions of victimhood. One must first surrender or "submit" to the wisdom of older Christians. Disciplers were there to monitor your precarious identification as victim—to tell you when to perform victim, when to stop, when to begin to enact change, and what strategies for change made sense.

What were the crimes in group discourse that justified ICOC members' victimhood? A range of abuses and social diseases, but most prominent in the data I gathered were *gender sins:* not enacting and/or embracing inherent and biblically grounded gender roles and responsibilities. Gender sins were presented by members and leaders as the root of much family of origin "dysfunction." The discipling community was presented by many members and leaders as helping you figure out what exactly Mom and Dad did wrong, how your parents may have been the victims of social and individual gender sin. Disciplers would help you sift through cultural expectations and circumstances of fatherhood and motherhood to determine how you became a victim of parental gender sin. And disciplers would, after holding your hand through the puzzling process of interpretation, tell you when you should stop "whining" about the abuse, how to come up with an approach for healing and forgiveness, and how to convince your mother and father that they too should live in righteous gender relationships within in the ICOC Kingdom of God.

GENDER SINS

In the forefront of victim talk was a divorce culture where mothers and fathers had made grave mistakes in raising their children. As with group and individual discourse that presented marriage disciplers and individual spouses as successfully balancing varied and often contradictory gender stances (like female submission/mutual submission), presentation of disciples' biological/family of origin parental gender sins embraced and challenged multiple and contradictory ideas. Disciples' biological fathers were often described as distant and uncommunicative. Many times fathers' characters were further diminished by stories of alcoholism and/or sexual abuse. Fathers were often depicted as too caught up in their work lives and as harsh disciplinarians; yet they were also sometimes praised for teaching disciples the value of discipline and hard work. Some fathers were indicted for their lack of leadership in the family and for letting strong mothers walk all over them, and at the same time praised for their ability to listen and be open and communicative with family members. Biological mothers were frequently portrayed as not teaching female disciples how to be good caretakers and nurturers, and as setting bad wifely role models because of their participation in the workforce. Some mothers were depicted as weak because they allowed overbearing patriarchs to dominate. In one of the greatest gender sins named by disciples, mothers became "feminists," who taught daughters that they should "hate men," yet these same mothers were often praised by female disciples for teaching their daughters how to be strong. This wide range of parental gender sin was depicted as causing family disease, instigating divorce, and in some cases, producing homosexual relationships (a prominent gender sin articulated in most conservative Christian communities). Members' stories and formal discourse presented disciplers as helping members interpret and learn from family of origin gender sins.

Distant Patriarchs, Absent Fathers, and Feminist Moms

The dream of converting and healing biological fathers gave rise to multiple reflections on distant and unemotional fathers, images of a traditional patriarch, a father who holds ultimate economic and relational power in the home but was never in the home and emotionally bereft. Disciples' narratives were full of childhood and adult memories depicting fathers who took breadwinning masculinity to the extreme, failing to incorporate contemporary ideals of paternal presence and emotional attachment. Casting a lack of emotionality and physical presence as the gender sins of modern fathers reflects historical constructions of what we have come to expect fathers to do for their children.

Post–World War II U.S. society brought rising cultural expectations of greater paternal involvement from men—a call to be breadwinners and establish a strong presence in the home as disciplinarians and male role models. Voices from prominent mid-twentieth-century psychologists, social researchers, and popular child rearing "experts" linked absent fathers to a number of social ills that would befall their children, from juvenile delinquency to "homosexuality" (Pleck 1981, 1983). Today fathers are held to similar incompatible ideals, the contradictions therein magnified as therapeutic culture and gender egalitarianism rise in ideological dominance. We expect fathers to be breadwinners, to protect, provide for, and endow their children with the tools to succeed in life, while at the same time we demand that they are present in the home, involved in children's activities, actively disciplining, and emotionally present for their kids (Townsend 2002). These contradictory ideals of fatherhood are made even more difficult to live up to in a contemporary economic climate that offers lower salaries, a substantial contingent workforce, and a workplace climate that informally demands an over-forty-hour full-time workweek (Fried 1998; Hochschild 2001; Jacobs and Gerson 2004; Schor 1981). ICOC member and leader accusations of distant and absent fathers mirrored these long-standing historical tensions and gender expectations of fatherhood.

When ICOC men and women spoke of trying to forgive fathers, it was almost always in the context of fathers who were harsh disciplinarians and excessively uncommunicative. Stories of biological reconciliation for women often entailed teaching their fathers, with the help of the discipling community, how to "open their hearts" and be "real"—how to embody relationality, how to become that new father that embraced therapeutic ideals. Only some could cast these efforts as successful. Pat remembered her father as an "angry" and "distant disciplinarian." Learning to forgive him, she told me, was the hardest thing she had ever done. Forgiving her father was "never ending"; she was "constantly having to forgive him and love him" despite the fact that he didn't "know how to love." Pat laid blame on her father's resistance by describing his "heart" as "closed." She sadly admitted, "Some people just can't get their hearts to move and sometimes we have to accept that." Some male members remembered distant fathers whose absence in the home, in the words of one twenty-year-old member, left them knowing "nothing about how to be a dad and good husband."

Disciplers were presented in many members' anecdotes as key in bringing sons and fathers out of their silent masculine worlds and facilitating a healing *male expressivity*. One member told me that his involvement in other religions did not help him see that he had to make an effort to become closer to his biological father; it was not until he studied the Bible with a City COC discipler that he was forced to learn to communicate with his father:

> My dad, we've never had a great relationship . . . we hadn't talked in, uh, four years. . . . I didn't want to talk to him because I was doing my own thing and it was not until I studied the Bible [with City COC discipler], . . . they would not baptize me until I made peace with my dad. . . . Finally we did talk and I shared with him how I felt and it was amazing because he had basically felt the same way and we just really didn't know how to communicate. I kind of learned about his own past. I didn't really know I was angry at the wrong things because he was always there, I was always fed. . . . What I was looking for was that he never told me he loved me. He did love me, but to me he wasn't there for me when it was important. In my mind. But he was, you know.

In this member's recounting of his relationship with his father, we can hear the confusion in the memory of his father's presence and purpose in his life. He was "there" and made sure his son was "fed," but it didn't feel like he was there "when it was important." This member's confusion over the exact nature of his father's gender sin is cured by disciplers' insistence that he listen to his father, make peace, and learn to communicate with him.

Absent and distant fathers were prominent characters in stories of naming parental gender sins. These absent fathers were sometimes the result of mothers' gender sins. ICOC discourse was full of stories of fathers who cowered in the paths of women who had picked up the "feminist sword." Feminist moms pushed dads away, produced daughters who were too forceful, and led children into sinful "homosexual" relationships.

Members' narratives and formal discourse of dangerous feminist moms echoed a long-standing social phenomenon of mother-blame: in the later half of the twentieth century, mothers have been blamed for raising children to be autistic, homosexual, schizophrenic, and juvenile delinquents (McDonnell 1998; Terry 1998). "Feminist" mother-blame (speaking primarily of second wave feminism) is one of our most recent chapters in this historical legacy of maternal deviance: feminist mothers work and so leave their children unsupervised or spoil them to overcompensate; feminist mothers teach their daughters to hate motherhood and men; feminist mothers, in their man-hating fervor, drive sons away.

ICOC formal discourse cast homosexuality as a result of gender sins and bad socialization process as well. Mothers who were too strong took up space on a list in formal discourse of sins that led to a rejection of heterosexuality. Mothers were also blamed for "sissifying" sons and failing to expose them to proper masculine activities. Sam Laing told a group of men that "homosexuality is a learned behavior," and offered examples for how they came to engage in homosexual relationships: it was usually the fault of somebody, he argued, whose father did not treat them well, or an "adult who confused them early on in development." Casting homosexual behavior as learned behavior allowed the ICOC, as it has other conservative Christian groups and medical professionals at mid-twentieth century, the opportunity to resocialize and offer institutionalized "cures" for the affliction.[8] In the ICOC, this was discipling; I heard several stories about disciplers who had helped members involved in homosexuality return to fulfilling heterosexual relationships. The ICOC heavily monitored sexuality through marriage discipling, premarriage discipling, and controlled dating—each of these therapeutic relationships was committed to the continual reinforcement of heterosexuality. One former member I interviewed spoke of being a "target" of female leaders who were convinced that she and her single roommate were lesbians. She was constantly lectured about the dangers of lesbian relationships, not allowed to be alone for long periods with single women (a difficult task in a group that often separated by gender!), and eventually left the group.

In naming the gender sins of parents, discourse wavered, as does our popular cultural debate, between recognition of the power of biology and genetic destiny and the power of socialization. Often the chosen emphasis is one that legitimates a particular organizational or individual goal (as was the case with stressing that homosexual behavior was a result of social, not biological, forces). Disciplers were characterized as able to help you figure out biological "tendencies," what they were and how to overcome those that would lead to gender sins. Genetic gender flaws (i.e., in group discourse of body types that did not adhere to social ideals of masculine and feminine forms) were often credited to genetics. Men whose bodies were not "muscular" or women whose bodies were not "feminine" were talked about as inheriting these conditions from biological mothers and fathers. These genetic gender body flaws were seen as fixable through therapeutic discipling relationships, disciplers who would encourage men and women to work out, lose weight, gain muscle, and monitor the shaping of masculine and feminine bodies. ICOC leaders recognized the power of genetics discourse to resonate with individuals' understanding of themselves as victims of genetic destiny.[9] The appropriation of genetic discourse was sometimes metaphorical. For example, Sam Laing stated to an all-male audience at a large regional event: "God disciplines every one of us. And he does it custom-made. . . . He knows how to get 'cha and flush your sins right outta your genetic code and get them out of there, baby. He'll do it!" Laing referred to God's discipline (ICOC discipling) as capable of "flushing" out bad genes, a powerful image in today's world where media representations of genetic essentialism often provide quick explanations for a host of undesirable conditions such as alcoholism, obesity, and bipolar disorder, to name just a few.

On Marriage Enrichment Day 1995, one female leader stated that "for most of us our moms were not role models for how to be a Godly woman." During an interview in her home, Heidi, a white married woman in her early thirties, echoed the same sentiment about her biological mother: "She raised two children after divorcing my dad, which was very hard, and she didn't give me much of a role model for being a wife and mom." It was only after she became a member of the ICOC in a congregation "down South" that she felt she had "good role models" that taught her that she did not always need to solve every problem herself. Heidi felt that her mother's independence as a single working mom taught her to be "too strong," and had set her up for feeling that she could tackle the world on her own. Yet at the same time, Heidi praised her mother's strength, stating that her strength and power as a "woman of God" and as a "strong wife" comes from her mother's influence (her mother is an evangelical Christian in a conservative denomination). Like women who balance and negotiate ideals of Christian female submission and mutuality in marriage power dynamics, Heidi vacillated as she tried to come to terms with exactly what gender attitudes and behaviors her mother had instilled in her. Several City COC women expressed the same struggle in their stories of biological family and efforts to forgive parents: how to come to terms with the independence and power their mothers (many of whom were young adults during the countercultural revolution of the 1960s and 1970s and had entered the workforce) represented, and traditionalist conservative Christian doctrine and practice that rhetorically and discursively prescribes normative gender roles and behaviors. Heather, who was raised by her mom after father "deserted" the family, offers an example of how members presented the ambiguity:

> She wasn't consistent enough a lot of times because she wasn't there [had to work], but she was always very loving when she was home and very focused on me. She couldn't provide a lot of material things, but we never wanted for anything. She taught me to be not just independent but, well, very independent. I guess as a woman that I can do things on my own and I don't need a man to take care of me and be successful and happy. . . . My first serious boyfriend, I was the boss you know. That's how I'd seen my mom while she took care of the family, so that's how I was going to be. Alan, her husband, wasn't afraid to tell me no, and as I've studied the Bible and learned what I should be, her example becomes even more clear. But I'm glad that she taught me her example, because I am strong-willed.

Heather's appreciation of her mother in the wake of divorce was one way members faithfully reconciled memories of biological family with the naming of parental gender sins. Heather fulfilled group demands by recognizing her mother's sins, yet remained loyal to family of origin by expressing appreciation for her mother teaching her valuable life skills. In doing so she was walking that familiar evangelical discursive path: back and forth from traditionalism to biblical feminism. Another City COC member stated that even though his father was not a "good" role model because he had been "sexually impure," he felt his father had instilled other admirable expressive qualities: "My father, in particular, was very much always kissing you. I found myself being very much that way. I love to touch. I love to hug." We hear a loyalty and respect for this man's biological father, alongside a condemnation of his ability to serve as a good role model. Members rarely leveled gender sin without adding a caveat of parental love and worth.

Whatever the gender sins of parents, member and formal discourse presentations of parents' mistakes worked to affirm the power of discipling. Disciplers were there to help you forgive and overcome any inclination you may have to repeat the mistakes your parents had made, to provide you with strong masculine and feminine role models and a seemingly coherent ideological approach for achieving various gender ideals and practices.

The Dream Falters

When members could not tell stories of themselves as heroes and heroines able to heal biological relationships and produce a cascade of biological kin converts, their recounting of attempts to convert still reinforced the power of discipling as an exceptional therapeutic approach. Like member and leader presentations of marriage discipling failures, failed attempts were attributed to the "closed hearts" of relatives and members who were not trying hard enough. For example, Heidi told me that her initial efforts to convert her mother "really frustrated" her. She laid blame on her own eagerness and evangelical style: "She wouldn't go to church with me because I'd always turn it into these big three-hour discussions afterwards." Still, she did not give up hope that her mother would eventually convert to the ICOC: "I've toned things down a little bit. . . . I'm not discouraged [about mom converting] because I feel like there's hope."

Depictions of family of origin who had come to "respect" the church over time were another way members and the organization dealt with failure. Progressive acceptance and respect promoted the idea that, given adequate time, all family of origin members with "closed hearts" would at least come to recognize the good disciples had found in the ICOC community. Many parents of origin became grandparents while sons and daughters were in the church and so came to see their children living "normal" lives, not swept away to a foreign country to drink poison with loyal McKean followers or giving away all their life possessions to the church, as they may have initially feared. Several City COC members who had joined the church during their college years, or soon after, were in their thirties during my fieldwork. These members frequently talked about parent of origin resistance and fear of the movement as a "dangerous cult" when they were first in the church and how parents had come to respect their church community. One man described a Catholic father who was extremely disturbed by his son's initial "change" fifteen years ago when he joined the ICOC movement. His son's membership in a group that the newspapers were calling a cult made the father suspicious and vocal about his doubts. In time his father came around: "Over the years they [parents] have gained a great respect. I know my dad is very proud. There is a lot he still doesn't understand. . . . Over the past fifteen years I have really won their respect." One woman in her mid-thirties who had been in the church for twelve years told me of a brother and sister-in-law who were at first against her membership in the ICOC, but in later years came to greatly "respect" the way they raised their children. To stress her point, she told a story of this brother turning to her for help with a teenage daughter who was "out of control," and the niece coming into her home to live with her so that she could try to help the niece with school and discipline problems.

To the many members for whom the dream of ICOC family of origin conversion never materialized, telling stories of continual efforts to communicate and enact forgiveness, coming to understand the source of parents' mistakes, and ultimately earning the respect of their parents and other family of origin members justified their choices to commit to the demanding family therapeutic strategies of the discipling community. Their narratives were of self-actively mending family of origin wounds and effecting, however small, some positive change in core kin relationships.

As I listened to the exit narratives of former members, spoke with members, and monitored websites as the unified movement dissolved, it became clear that efforts to earn family of origin respect and open lines of communication were often in the shadow of persistent fears and disapproval of discipling's authoritative and exclusive character. Even though disciples were aggressive in their assertions that one should reconcile, forgive, and come to understand the sins of their parents, the attention they had to give to the discipling community and its therapeutic and evangelical goals left limited time for such actions. Telling *stories* about learning to forgive and understand the sins of parents was a large part then of the process of understanding oneself as actively working to heal relationships and balance contradictory expectations of family life.

When the unified movement dissolved and the demands of discipling diminished, the door opened again for spending more time and effort on family of origin relationships. Those families who had converted en masse were also freed from movement goals. One former member, who converted along with her children and husband in the mid-1990s, made a point of telling me in 2004 that when her family exited, in domino fashion, they found family occasions more relaxed; they were freed, she sighed in relief, from the pressure of talking about Kingdom successes and their heavy duties as brothers and sisters in the movement, and able to enjoy being together again as just "a family."

PAT AND I listened, during New England Women's Day 2000, to a grandmother and longtime church member talk about the fate of her four married children and six grandchildren. She asked us all to pray that one of her daughters, who was trying to conceive that weekend, get pregnant. Another daughter, she proudly asserted, had become an ICOC leader in a nearby city, another was the talented young performer who had just finished performing a ballad on Women's Day. She told us that years ago her son left her and the ICOC and chose to live with his father in a faraway city—but then, "five years later he came back to Mom and church." In her "brief time on this earth," this grandmother proclaimed as her goal: "My passion is to get my children and grandchildren to heaven." She exclaimed in front of thousands of women present that day: "I will not go through the pearly gates without all of my children!" This woman, and thousands of other members, spoke with passion about converting and keeping their children in the Kingdom of God (ICOC). In the City COC congregation, where most members were families with young children, and for many other leaders and members across the country who were now at a stage where having children and raising children was a major focus of everyday life, narratives of "awesome" church family concentrated on how the Kingdom provided assurance that their children would be safe, disciplined, well-prepared, and ICOC Christians for life.

CHAPTER 5

Awesome Kids

> We should pray for our children daily. Beyond all of the wisdom, expertise, methods and words, God must move! Before my children were born (or conceived!), I prayed that they would one day give their lives to Jesus. I still pray for them now, and I will continue to do so until I die. Their names will always be held in my prayers before the throne of God wherever they are and whatever their spiritual condition.
>
> —Laing and Laing (1994, 216)

I HAVE a photo of my youngest child sitting next to Pat's youngest on her living room couch. Pat sends me a Christmas card every holiday season with a picture of her children. I had conversations with Pat and other City COC parents about the demands and joys of child rearing. It was clear in the moral world of the City COC, even though no one ever told me directly, that I was not doing all that I could to protect my children from the evil influences of secular society. Nor was I was making a serious effort to ensure my children would live on Earth and forever after in the Kingdom of God. The pressure to offer children the Kingdom of God (ICOC) was strong in group. I too live in a society where, as a parent, I am expected to do everything I possibly can to endow my children with a proper education and keep them safe from harm. I could feel the social control in their tacit judgment, even though I did not believe in their assessment or methods. With a look of calm and genuine relief, all parents I spoke with emphatically stated that they were sure that they would stay "close" with their children and that their children would be Christians throughout their lives. Pat and other members strongly believed that they had, in the discipling community, the best insurance policy available for keeping their children safe and on a Christian (ICOC) life path. This understanding was communicated against a backdrop of contemporary fears and cultural expectations of parenthood and child rearing.

As members of God's modern-day movement, members believed that their children would shed consumer identities, abstain from sex and drugs, engage in peacemaking among their peers, and develop lifelong positive and communicative relationships with their parents. ICOC youth ministry leaders talked a great deal about how children and teens in the "outside" world were bombarded with "sex talk," "drugs," "violence," and "consumerism," and that kids today don't communicate with their parents on a regular basis. Like parents in many other new religious movements, ICOC leaders and members understood their biblically grounded ideas and practices of child development and religious education as extremely important for the moral development of their children and as protecting them from dangerous outside social ills. They saw their methods as crucial for the continuance of their new religious tradition. However, like other parents in high boundary religious movements over the decades, the demands of their new church community threatened group promises of maintaining "awesome" relationships with their children.[1]

Danger

Narratives of raising children in a dangerous social climate were prominent in formal discourse and private interviews. Horror stories, like the one told by the guest speaker on Women's Day of washing her dishes one day and looking out her kitchen window to see the teenage son of the couple that lived behind them hanging by a rope in his backyard, confirmed parents' worst fears. DPI literature painted an equally dismal picture bolstered by media reports of rising rates of teen suicide and childhood depression—assertions that render our world a potentially frightening and disastrous place to raise children.

The foreword of Sam and Geri Laing's DPI parental guidebook, *Raising Awesome Kids in Troubled Times*, is written by their daughter, Elizabeth Laing. Elizabeth, age seventeen, speaking from the trenches of evangelical high school battles, writes:

> God has given me so many incredible gifts that I could never name them all! I have salvation and a perpetually clean slate before God, a

> close, spiritual family, numerous "best friends" scattered across the country, and an overall fun, fulfilling life! I realize with absolute clarity that every one of these blessings can be attributed solely to the fact that I have Christian parents.
>
> This year more than ever I have come to understand just how crucial it is for teens to know God. Only four months ago, three students from my school committed suicide within two weeks of one another. I felt as if God himself was sending me a wake-up call. For years, I had naively entertained the belief that teens are not *too* bad off spiritually and that most of them will not even think about or comprehend spiritual subjects for a few more years. I could not have been further from the truth. (Laing and Laing 1994, 10)

Young Laing makes it clear that the ICOC Kingdom is responsible for why she is protected from, and other teens susceptible to, disastrous ends: "My friends at school urgently need the guidance of parents who are disciples—not just *good* parents or even *great* parents but disciple parents. All the students who committed suicide came from well-to-do families that appeared to have it all together. However, for all the love, material things, and even worldly wisdom they provided their children, they could not give them the purpose and ultimate peace they so desperately desired" (Laing and Laing 1994, 11). Sam and Geri Laing write that they do not "presume to be perfect parents or to have a perfect family," nor do they long to put their children "on a pedestal." However, despite the Laings' stated intent, much formal ICOC discourse did put Kingdom kids on a pedestal, and some members' informal stories about their children implied that their children, indeed, were more likely to succeed and had developed a higher moral sensitivity than other kids.

Achievement and Excellence

Kip and Elena McKean's children, and those of other prominent leaders, were held up as models of excellence: good grades, athletic ability and achievement, and evangelical successes. They were "beautiful" and "healthy" children in the forefront of group discourse. Formal discourse painted a Kingdom of healthy, well-adjusted, and high-achieving kids. Recall Kip McKean's proclamation of excellence in my introduction to this ethnography: "Eric . . . led the league in scoring. Sean played point guard and was selected in his league for the all-star basketball team the only fifth-grader among sixth-graders. Also, he was just elected president of his elementary school student council for next year. Olivia, student council president of her elementary school last year, went on to break the mile record at her junior high and tied the record for the 440-yard run. She also recently qualified for the national Miss Pre-Teen Pageant. All three have made straight A's this year" (McKean RR). A local leader told us one Sunday morning that Randy and Kay McKean's children had been signed by a modeling agency. Members and other leaders echoed the McKeans' presentation of awesome Kingdom Kids by testifying during regional and local events about children's successes, kind actions, and the uncommonly close relationships children and parents in the Kingdom were able to sustain.

During formal and informal interviews and social gatherings, some City COC members talked with me about how their children were different from other children. They described them as having advanced moral centers and security in their relationship with God. During one interview, a white woman ministry leader in her late thirties encouraged her two-year-old son to perform for me: "Where's your booboo? Where did it go?" The child showed me the Band-Aid on his arm and softly murmured, "God took it away." His mother proudly stated, "Yes, that's right. God healed you." She looked at me, "You see what I'm telling you, I've got a two-year-old who is conscious that God is going to help him." Alicia proudly stated during her interview, "I just love how my daughter's life is going to be completely different. . . . She [a nine-year-old] has a mature perspective on life. . . . I'm confident that she will convert. Because the Bible says that if you train your child the way it says, they will not depart from it and I just hold on to that and I don't have to wonder and hope . . . oh, maybe, maybe it will, but I just know it's going to, just a faith, a confidence." Formal and informal performances of superior child rearing were efforts to convince me, and themselves, that living as a disciple in the ICOC worldwide community was the very best child-rearing environment available to them.

Kids Kingdom and Teen Ministries

City COC's emphasis on children, teen, and preteen ministries seemed to grow over the four years as I conducted field studies. This emphasis is not surprising; when the congregation was established in the 1980s, membership was composed primarily of "young marrieds" and college-age disciples. These members had married in the church, had children, and were now concerned about how their church membership would help them raise Godly children. This shift over the years meant that a congregation made up of mostly singles and young "marrieds" transformed into a congregation with approximately 75 percent of households with children. Like most religious congregations, the City COC had to adapt and evolve in specific ways to address these changing demographics (Ammerman 1997). It is likely that similar changes in family structure took place across the unified movement as formal discourse and publications, in the mid-1990s, began to emphasize that part of the evangelical mission was ensuring that biological and adopted children stayed in the Kingdom—an organizational evangelical goal that well matched rising parental concerns.

That members turned to a religious community in efforts to instill children with moral confidence is not uncommon in U.S. society. In addition to providing for and meeting a child's physical and emotional needs, cultural expectations dictate that parents should foster a child's moral compass. Historically, religious communities have been active participants in the moral education of children. This continues today as we see many parents, even when they themselves have not been an active member of a religious community as young adults, begin taking their school-age children to Sunday schools and attending services again themselves. Sociologist Nancy Ammerman (1997, 368) reminds us that "the tie between congregational membership and family formation remains strong in US culture," and that "those who sow wild oats as young adults often return to the fold when their children reach school age." Furthermore, "many adults see religious training for their children as part of their obligation to the world. They would not be doing good or making the world a better place if their children were denied the training provided by the church." City COC parents were no different from many other parents in our society then, those who return to childhood religions or secure new religious affiliations in an effort to fulfill their "obligation" of raising morally sound citizens. However, like some other high boundary new religious movements, the ICOC presented their worldwide community as the *only* religious environment with the skill, knowledge, and sacred power to keep children faithful and living Godly lives.

City COC members, like most parents who identify with a particular faith institution, understood that a religious upbringing within a strong religious community could be a powerful predictor of personal success and a shield against social ills. Social researchers have suggested a similar relationship.[2] Fundamentalist and evangelical Christians may build their own Christian schools or homeschool in order to avoid having their children interact with those who are not of like Christian mind, who are of other faiths—or worse, secular humanists or atheists. But this was not a viable option for an evangelical movement with such zealous conversion goals as the ICOC, a group that needed teens out there actively working to convert young folks. Therefore, the discipling system, in particular the teen ministries, was the proposed answer for countering outside influences by creating tight in-group bonds and peer groups. These close ICOC bonds enabled children and teens to interact with peers in secular society without becoming *of* secular society. Leaders like Sam Laing preached that parents need to make sure their kids were committed to the Kingdom teen ministries so that they would be protected from "worldly stuff": "A lot of you guys have made decisions that are hurting your children. You want them to be real close to the world, you think they can handle this and so you let your kids get involved in worldly stuff and amen . . . kids need to be out there in the world, but we can't let them be of the world and we can't let them be surrounded by worldly people and become sucked down into the world's mess. . . . You've got to keep them in the Kingdom of God in a strong teen ministry."

ICOC congregations also had "Kingdom Kids" ministries for small children, which included Sunday school programs and child social activities. Youths in the movement were baptized (became official church members and disciples) at approximately age twelve or thirteen. At that time each teen was assigned a discipler and teen youth group. While preteens and teens did interact with nondisciples in public and private schools and other secular activities (oftentimes in explicitly evangelical efforts), members described the majority of children's day-to-day lives as spent in discipling relationships with older members, family group activities, and events geared exclusively for children their age. Leaders made clear to members that children must remain in discipling relationships and be active in "teen ministries" to counteract outside influences. The church youth group, while optional in many other Christian denominations, was mandatory in the ICOC. If parents did not keep their teens involved in teen ministries, they were often informally sanctioned by disciplers and church leaders. Parents' presentation of their children as exceptional evangelists further strengthened the idea that the discipling community was uncommonly able to keep children faithful—they painted portraits of teens as active Christians out in the world working to "change hearts" for the Kingdom.

Parents talked with pride about children who had converted (baptized) and gone on to be "productive disciples in the Kingdom." One mother stood at the lectern on Women's Day and stated, "God, you gave me the desire of my heart—for my children to *want* to go and study the Bible with their friends." Geri Laing brags in her child-rearing text of her daughter's skill at bringing teen friends into the church family: "Another of her [daughter's] New Jersey pals . . . began to study to become a disciple, but became prideful and stubborn and backed away. . . . She got him on the phone and laid out what he was doing wrong and where he was going to end up if he did not change. By the end of the phone conversation, he was shedding tears of repentance and soon afterwards made his decision to become a disciple. Such is the power of teen friendship!" (Laing and Laing 1994, 214). Teens also heard other teens boasting of evangelizing efforts. During City COC services, I heard several testimonials and prayers from teens who recounted successful conversion attempts with high school friends. These teens boasted of suffering persecution from school friends for their "radical" commitment to Jesus. During testimonies, the congregation verbally cheered them on with "go sister," "go brother," and "praise God."

Members talked about their children's conversion as different from youths who pledged a Christian lifestyle in other denominations. Such efforts worked again to set the movement apart as exceptional and unique. Other Christian denominational conversions were described by members as profane, perfunctory, and meaningless. For example, the classes that Catholic youths attended and their first communion ceremonies were presented as "rituals" with little meaning, occasions mostly for wearing a pretty dress or handsome suit and having a party. In contrast, members who discipled teens in the City COC preteen (age twelve) and teen (thirteen and up) ministries described ICOC young people's conversion as a genuine "life commitment to disciple." Furthermore, members and leaders promoted the idea that a child's conversion in the ICOC was so powerful that it often instigated a restorative process for the entire nuclear family—narratives reminiscent of the domino family healing script outlined in chapter 4. City COC teen conversions were sometimes framed as a therapeutic family process that led to strengthening communication between parents and children and reaffirming the entire family's commitment to the ICOC mission. One female leader told me:

> When the teens are becoming Christians it converts the family all over again. A lot of these families, they became Christians as young marrieds and their children grew up in the church and now for their children to become Christians it's so great. Some automatically want to . . . most do and then some don't and it reveals a lot about what is going on behind closed doors [in the family]. They need help and the teens need help to know that it's OK to communicate what they are feeling. And the parents need to be willing to come on in and talk, so it's like a second conversion for a parent. It's not just the teen.

Once teens converted and pledged discipleship, they were talked about as spending a great deal of time with their teen group. As the numbers of children reaching the teenage years increased in the City COC congregation, leaders had to bring on "new teen workers" and spend extra time themselves working with the teens. One discipleship group leader told me, "We want to make sure that we are doing everything possible to make it [conversion of children] happen because so many of these families have given their lives [to the church]. They have been volunteers to help other people's kids. It would greatly discourage them and their faith if their children didn't become disciples." Parental adherence to the discipling structure was talked about in ICOC formal discourse as allowing your brothers and sisters in the Kingdom to disciple and train your children. Ferguson (1997, 238–239) states: "As good as things may be at home, there is still great value in these relationships in the teen ministry. Trust me here: Teen ministry leaders will often see things you as a parent are overlooking. Furthermore, even if your teen seems to be quite open with you, discussing some things, like sexual temptations, is much easier with peers or teen leaders." Adults discipling in the teen ministry presented themselves as spending considerable time and energy on these efforts.

I went to Lisa's house to conduct a follow-up formal interview. During this time together, she provided much detail about her leadership in the teen ministry. She and her husband had been in charge of the City COC teen ministry for a year. As she poured me a cup of coffee and I set out the pastries I brought, I heard two young women laughing and giggling in another room of the house. Lisa told me that what I heard were two of "my teens" who had "slept over." The young women came out of the back room, still giggling, and timidly announced, "We were dancing." Lisa introduced me to the young women and then sent them on a long prayer walk into the woods behind her house. She told them to go to the "prayer spot" that she and her husband frequented and that they should have their daily time alone with God. Lisa went on to describe her "volunteer ministry position" as taking care of, and offering parental guidance and assistance to, members' children. She told me that she and her husband "oversee about thirty to fifty kids and have eight adults helping" as disciplers. She described her interactions with the teenage girls, like the two who had slept over, as close, as intimate and time-consuming: "I take them to do activities together. I study at the library one night a week with a couple of the girls. . . . We have a teen night once a week." She continued, "They look to us as role models. The parents like it that way. They want to know that their kids will do well."

Drawing from group discourse that presents discipling relationships as facilitating greater communication skills among family members, Lisa painted an image of herself as helping parents and children become more expressive and communicative. Her discipling these teens involved teaching communication skills so that children and parents could have better relationships: "I see a great turnover in my job. Teens grow up, they come and go. . . . I'm their advocate while they're here. I help with their parents and can get the teens to represent their feelings in a way that their parents will listen to and understand." Lisa described her role as alleviating parental responsibilities, taking care of others' children, and teaching family communication.

Having no children of her own "yet," Lisa said that she had the additional time to help the teens in ways that the parents, who worked full-time and were "super busy," did not. Note that Lisa was not paid for her leadership in the teen ministries and that her own weekly schedule (detailed in chapter 1 here) was jam-packed with church- and work-related responsibilities. Still, she saw her day-to-day life as less demanding than that of many parents in the City COC congregation. Lisa presented her church community as a place where these super busy working mothers and fathers need not worry about their children receiving adequate care, discipline, and guidance, a church community that made balancing work and family much easier. Descriptions of such intense and committed involvement in the future of other members' children fueled the image of the ICOC community worldwide as one big caring family that took exceptionally good care of its youth. Church youth programs did appear to provide answers to the cultural dilemmas facing mothers and fathers today; however, a commitment to the discipling community introduced new parental challenges as well.

Cultural Dilemmas

In our society, we often place unrealistic expectations of motherhood and fatherhood on parents who must make ends meet in an economic climate that forces many households to have two wage earners, demands long work hours, and offers inadequate child care options (Garey 1999; Jacobs and Gerson 2004; Schor 1981; Townsend 2002). How are women to fulfill their roles as caretakers and domestics, being present for school field trips, doctor's visits, and after-school snacks while working full- or part-time? How are men to embody the new, engaged father, supervising and attending sports and other after-school activities and nurturing infants and toddlers while working full- or part-time? The difficulty of meeting these gendered parental responsibilities is often magnified for divorced and single parents. Teen ministries, Kingdom Kids programs, and the extended community network offered in the discipling structure appeared, at first look, to work toward alleviating many of the dilemmas faced by parents today. The discipling network provided child care options and after-school activities, monitored peer group pressure, and produced a network of church kin ready to help when a crisis arose.

Recent studies of masculinity in marriage and family clearly demonstrate that most men in our society are caught in competing ideals of fatherhood. Nicholas Townsend (2002, 78–80) argues that there are "four facets of fatherhood," cultural expectations of fatherhood that dominate in the United States: fatherhood, marriage, employment, and home ownership. Within each of these facets are powerful elements of culture that connect and often collide with one another. These elements of the "package deal" of fatherhood have to be constantly negotiated. "The continuing cultural primacy of providing for children," Townsend notes, "means that men's time and energy are devoted to, and consumed by, their paid work" (Townsend 2002, 78). They are consumed by paid work yet feel pressure to be emotionally present for their children. The resulting contradiction is one that, essentially, results from a clash of traditional breadwinner normative ideology and the "new father" ideals that have gained prominence over the past twenty-five years or so. Joseph Pleck (1987, 83–97) notes that the new father image departs from older pictures of fatherhood: the father is present at his child's birth, continues throughout the child's life to be involved, and does not just play with children but helps in caretaking. This new father is also engaged in a similar way with daughters and sons. Encouraging fathers to be affectionate and emotionally present has been a rising focus of the contemporary evangelical subculture as well (Bartkowski 1995; Wilcox 1998). This new father ideal, a gentle and loving participant in family life, was strong in the ICOC, as was the call for men to financially support their families.

The ideal of the breadwinner father exists today alongside a serious critique of this normative role as "distant," lacking in emotion, unable to fulfill therapeutic ideals of expressivity. The critique is a powerful one, and the "new father" has clearly taken root in social and individual interpretations of good fathering. Townsend's (2002, 30) ethnography paints a powerful picture of cultural circumstances where "to be a father is to reconcile competing ideals, demands, and responsibilities: time spent with children against money earned, the kind of house you live in against the length of your commute, your responsibility as a husband against your responsibility as a father." Furthermore, he argues, "None of the sources of tension are fully resolved by the cultural work men perform" (Townsend 2002, 80). Clearly the tensions that Townsend illustrates are almost inescapable in our culture; economic and social conditions, for men from varying socioeconomic positions, frame and sustain gendered expectations in marriage and family that cannot always be met. The ICOC, through its marriage and family discipling system, presented members and potential converts with a tangible and supposedly lifelong working solution: counselors who were available almost all the time and who would help guide men through the tensions that inevitably resulted when trying to perform the "four facets of fatherhood," and a network of disciplers who would serve as mediators, guiding, caring for, and endowing children with a belief system and relational skills. They would be there when you could not; in your absence, the "brothers" in the Kingdom would serve as father figures to your children. Group discourse was full of references to the Kingdom of God as composed of a family of brothers ready to serve as father figures— an image of a Kingdom full of fathers that was especially appealing to ICOC single mothers.

Brothers and sisters in the "Kingdom family" were talked about as offering a complete family structure (normative nuclear) for single parent members. The City COC congregation was composed mainly of married folks with children, but there were a small number of single moms and dads spread among the "married" family groups, so that single parents were frequently in contact with nuclear family units. Within the church, "single sisters" and "single brothers" with children described a family of disciples that welcomed single parenthood, even as the movement clearly held a nuclear family model as superior.[3] Some single parents told stories of meeting new spouses within the church family, but others praised their new "real" church family for making them finally feel "whole" and "complete," and for providing gender role models for their children.

One longtime white single sister with high church status in her midthirties was helped by the movement to adopt a baby girl from China. The ICOC's adoption ministry was not out of the ordinary for conservative Christian groups; however, helping a single working mother adopt a two-year-old child was. During the adoption ceremony I asked Natalie if the husband of the woman standing alone on stage could not attend that day. "No," she explained, "she's doing it by herself." I listened further as one of the regional lead evangelists stated, "Although she is adopting without a father, she has all the brothers in the Kingdom to set a male example." Two months later, with her arms extended wide to thank her entire "Kingdom family," she proclaimed: "God has allowed me to take a little girl and give her a great start. She doesn't have a physical father right now, but she does have God as a father and all the brothers in the Kingdom." The discipling community was presented as there to guide and assist women through whatever individual set of cultural tensions and contradictions of parenthood challenged them.

Women in contemporary U.S. culture are faced with a historically particular set of contradictory expectations surrounding motherhood that produces its own set of tensions and challenges. Normative and nascent ideals of motherhood and womanhood coexist: women are supposed to be the caretakers of children, women are supposed to be mothers, mothers are supposed to always "be there" for their children, women are supposed to embrace and perform domesticity, women are supposed to pursue a career or profession or provide "additional income" for their families, women are supposed to keep up with family celebrations, birthdays, holiday events, and gifts, women are supposed to feed their families, keep clean homes, and dress their children in clean clothes.[4] One of the most profound and demanding conditions in which married women find themselves is what Arlie Hochshield (1989) named the "second shift." When both women and men work, domestic chores remain gendered female and women end up, after a long shift at paid work, coming home to do most of the cooking, cleaning, and domestic chores—a second shift. More recently, Scott Coltrane and Michelle Adams (2001, 72), in looking at the particular child-rearing and domestic behaviors of fathers and mothers in a national sample, suggest that "most Americans now assume that mothers need to be employed to help support their families," but that we are "less certain about how much family work men should do."

Research shows that while more men, from various class and racial/ethnic positions, do become involved in domestic labor and child care than years ago, women (even when employed) still do the majority of child care, and housework remains gendered (Coltrane and Adams 2001; Demos and Acock 1993). For example, taking out the trash, mowing the lawn, and repairing and washing the car remain primarily male activities, while cleaning the bathroom, doing the laundry, shopping, planning, and cooking for meals (activities that have to be completed on a more daily basis) are primarily female activities. More men are becoming involved in "child-centered" activities like "helping with homework, driving to activities and having private talks," and thus may take on more of the housework. However, "adult-centered" child care activities, like "playing together, watching television together, spending leisure time away from home," and "community-centered" child care activities like "attending school activities, attending community youth groups," and "coaching a child's sports team," remain more acceptable for males (Coltrane and Adams 2001). These parental activities are more public, and the domestic work and child care of most mothers tends to be less visible and consume more time and effort with less public and family recognition.[5]

Furthermore, as Townsend (2002) emphasizes, despite the public attention given to the rising number of fathers involved in primary child care, men continue to see such involvement as a "choice," a choice that helps them perform the new father ideal, but a choice nonetheless. Most women do not see primary child care, especially in those early years of child development, as an option; the image of the biological mother/child bond is a powerful social force and the choice to not mother or be there during those early years a deviant one. The persistence of a gendered division of labor in households, combined with economic necessity and a desire on the part of many women to pursue professional careers and be mothers, leaves many women caught in a state of sheer exhaustion, tension, and guilt (Ehrensaft 2001). The difficulty of juggling work and family, of living up to cultural expectations of motherhood, womanhood, and good citizenry (i.e., one who works for a living), for single mothers, can be even more grave. Many single mothers parent alone and, as a group, they are disadvantaged in the labor market and so find it even more difficult to locate and afford adequate child care. The discipling network was attractive to women because it appeared to give them particular strategies for resolving the demands of single and married motherhood.

Although the church extolled women's domestic and child care efforts, leaders and members understood that dual-earning families were on the rise and that many wives and mothers wanted to pursue professional careers. Church leaders also understood that many of the parents in their religious community worked over forty hours a week and experienced serious work/family conflicts. Formal group discourse tried to address these familial concerns with the promise of therapeutic counseling, community networks, and a host of DPI self-help advice literature. Like the wider evangelical subculture, where a recognition of the necessity of dual-wage-earning couples shapes prescriptive advice, the ICOC organization worked to "redefine the appropriate conditions for women's employment and its implications for family life" (Gallagher 2003, 130). As Gallagher (2003, 127–151) notes in her study of evangelicals, gender, and family life in the United States, the question of women's employment in our contemporary setting becomes not "whether" women should work but "why" and in what conditions should they seek employment. We hear a similar focus in the DPI text, *Life and Godliness for Everywoman: A Handbook for Joyful Living* (Jones 2000), which has two entries by prominent members under the category "Mom" dedicated to resolving work and family: "Deciding Whether to Work Full Time," by Sheila Jones, and "Business at Home," by Loretta Berndt. Jones describes the difficulties when mothers of small children decide to work and encourages women to make well-thought-out choices about why they are working. She advises against working solely for the pursuit of wealth, or to live up to that image in the "popular media" of women who "go after it all. . . . The typical stereotype features a well-dressed woman with a briefcase, calling home on a cellular phone to check on her independent, yet happy, children" (Jones 2000, 71). Jones also makes it clear that some women simply have to work: "Certainly single moms have no choice in the matter," she tells us. Jones tries to ease the fears of professional women who fear they will "lose step in the workplace" if they are out of the workforce for a period of time and the feeling that staying at home to raise children is accomplishing very little. Loretta Berndt (in Jones 2000, 78) follows up with a chapter full of advice about working from the home, how to get started, for example, in direct sales or telecommuting: "If it is your dream to work from home, then picture yourself doing something you enjoy while earning an income. Picture yourself being flexible and available for your family. (As I write today, my fifteen-year-old has strep throat. I am so thankful to be home and meet her needs.)"

ICOC leaders were acutely aware of the challenges and contradictory positions of mothers in contemporary society; they fully acknowledged the contradictions and presented the discipling community and disciplers as exceptionally able to help members make sure the work/family bind did not get in the way of raising "awesome kids." Mothers and fathers in the ICOC found sympathy and were promised assistance for the contradictory demands of parenthood.

Leaders and members rhetorically took pressure off fathers and mothers by acknowledging that they could not be expected to be parents alone. They quoted the popular phrase "It takes a village to raise a child" as they suggested the discipling community was even better than a normative nuclear home. In many ways, the community was involved in group parenting—especially through the routine intervention of disciplers in the family life of members (even as they promoted nuclear family autonomy). The church community also seemed to serve, at times, as an informal and formal child care network; several of the homes where I interviewed members and spent time seemed to have *an open home* feel: women dropped by from time to time utilizing what appeared as an informal baby-sitting co-op. Some women in the local church held professional jobs, some described themselves as stay-at-home moms, a few were in paid ministry positions with the church, some worked part-time, and others managed in-home day cares that allowed them to follow Loretta Berndt's lead and "do motherhood" (Garey 1999) even as they earned a significant portion of the family income. In this way, working mothers were leaving their children with church family members, an adoptive kin caregiving choice where they had intimate knowledge about the caregiver, her values, and child-rearing mores. This is not to say that there were never discrepancies, but members talked about child care as another social relationship that was monitored by the discipling structure to ensure that differences would be resolved. Alicia told a story about her anger when a church sister who was baby-sitting spanked her daughter; spanking, Alicia stated sternly, was reserved for parents and not the day care worker. The sister who had spanked the child insisted that since they were all members of the same family of God, parenting together, the punishment was appropriate. Alicia's position, she argued, was later supported by church leadership and most other disciples, and so the church sister had to eventually apologize for the action.

Most of the members I spoke with talked about their church community as free from prejudice, a place where multiracialism was accepted, encouraged, and nurtured in a most sacred institution, marriage, and where biracial children would be welcomed and loved. Members saw the multiracial character of the international ICOC movement as resolving their desire to be involved in racially and ethnically diverse social relationships in a society where individuals tend to separate by race/ethnicity, especially in religious congregations. As a member of the ICOC, they believed they were actively teaching their children to embrace pervasive U.S. social ideals of multiracialism and multiculturalism.[6]

Members with biracial children understood the City COC and international ICOC community as "color-blind" and "not prejudiced." Social researchers have called attention to the ways in which minority parents are concerned for the "racial safety" of children in a society where educational institutions are sometimes overtly prejudiced and implicitly biased toward white culture (McAdoo 2002; Uttal 1996). For example, choosing a child care environment or school for minority parents often includes an added concern about how their children will be treated, the level of racial sensitivity teachers and child care workers possess, and the extent to which race/ethnic, cultural beliefs, and history of minority groups are embraced. The validation of racial/ethnic diversity in close, intimate family relationships in the ICOC was likely appealing to members from a growing U.S. population of biracial/ethnic individuals and interracial/ethnic couples and families.[7] Many of these individuals came to believe that ICOC's therapeutic discipling networks would provide them with tangible emotional supports—a built-in biracial, interracial, and interethnic support group. One black woman told me: "Jim is white and I'm black. My discipler, her father is white and her mother is black. . . . She [the discipler] was helpful for us. . . . We want our kids to be very comfortable with who they are going to be in a society that does have issues [with biracial children]. . . . So they [the discipling couple] were very encouraging and helpful and said if we are doing it God's way [as CCOC members] things will turn out right." Minority church members and members with biracial children saw the ICOC community as resolving various cultural issues that involved their children and social attitudes and practices regarding race/ethnicity.

The ICOC movement, in attempting to attract converts and satisfy the needs of its maturing and diverse congregations, entered our long-historical cultural dilemma and debate over discipline in child rearing. Over the last century, our society has been host to a number of pediatricians, psychologists, religious, and secular authorities who claim to have the answers to raising children. From early twentieth-century G. Stanley Hall to later twentieth-century "experts" like Benjamin Spock, Berry Brazelton, Penelope Leach, and conservative Christian James Dobson, we have experienced a barrage of child-rearing publications and approaches. These voices run on a continuum of parental authority and corporeal punishment, versus child rights and spanking as abuse. The ICOC mirrored most closely the approach of James Dobson, founder of *Focus on the Family*, a man with a background in psychology, and author of the popular 1970 evangelical child-rearing text, *Dare to Discipline*, and 2000 text, *Complete Marriage and Family Home Reference Guide*.

Dobson and others, like Gary Bauer of the Family Research Council, in the last few decades of the twentieth century placed child rearing in a "culture wars" (Hunter 1991) discursive frame. On one side we have those (conservatives) interested in giving back the family to the parents, protecting them from dangerous secular forces (e.g., media, consumerism, sexual promiscuity) and instilling a traditionalist interpretation of child discipline. On the other side are those liberal anti-spanking crusade organizations and secular humanists who are "soft" on discipline at home and prefer to place ultimate charge in the hands of the state and medical therapeutic experts. To enhance the image of parents losing their children to liberalism and secular sin, Dobson, in his 1970 best-seller, *Dare to Discipline*, begins the text with an effort to alarm: "We have ignored the turmoil that is spreading systematically through the younger generations of Americans. We have passively accepted a slowly deteriorating 'youth scene' without offering a croak of protest. Suppose the parents of yesterday could make a brief visit to our world to observe the conditions that prevail among our children; certainly, they would be dismayed and appalled by the juvenile problems which have been permitted to become widespread (and are spreading wider) in urban America." Dobson, over several pages, then details some of these urban dangers: "Narcotic and drug usage by America's juveniles is an indescribable shame. . . . Many young people are now playing another dangerous game, packaged neatly under the title of sexual freedom. . . . Another symptom of the adolescent unrest is seen in the frequent display of aggression and hostility. Young people today are more violent today than at any period in American history. . . . There are many related phenomena. . . . Emotional maladjustment, gang warfare, teenage suicide, school failure, shoplifting, and grand larceny are symptoms of a deeper illness that plague vast numbers of America's young" (Dobson 1970, 6–8). Dobson was writing in the wake of great attention by psychologists and social scientists to "juvenile delinquency" as a pervasive social problem. ICOC formal discourse on child rearing set up an equally grim background with a late twentieth-century emphasis on the dangers of a media-driven society.

DPI's *Life and Godliness for Everywoman* painted outside society as full of confusion (Jones 2000, 54): "What can we, as disciples, do to teach our children to respect authority in their lives? How can we withstand the onslaught of strongwilled children who are determined to have their own way? How can we teach respect in a society that no longer demands or even expects it from their children?" In our society, ICOC leaders stressed that media influences were strong and were at work to reverse the child/parent relationship: "Commercials and sitcoms do their part to demean the role of parents and to exalt the role of the child. In this computer age, this age of entitlement, children feel they are the parent of their parents. And they will continue to think that until they are proven wrong by loving but firm parents who respect God and who call their children to respect them" (Jones 2000, 57).

One clear threat that James Dobson, ICOC leaders, and other evangelicals bemoaned, especially in the last few decades of the twentieth century, was that psychological experts and the state were usurping parental roles and responsibilities. Some secular child-rearing experts also promoted this seemingly "traditionalist" perspective that works to give power back to parents; for example John Rosemond (1981, 1989), family therapist and author of *Parent Power!* and *John Rosemond's Six-Point Plan for Raising Happy, Healthy Children.* One of the ways that this taking back of *Dare to Discipline* is manifested is through the assertion that reasonable corporeal punishment is for the parents to decide and use if they see fit. This practical advice of Dobson and other evangelical child-raising experts in many ways echoed late nineteenth-century medical and religious approaches aimed at molding a child's will. But conservative religious folks of the later twentieth century who maintain that spanking or swatting a child is integral to instilling obedience highlight as well the loving, caring, and relational side of such discipline—in this way they creatively marry our culture's therapeutic expectations with physical punishment.

Researchers who have studied child rearing in the conservative Protestant subculture have noted that it is indeed "characterized by both strict discipline and an unusually warm and expressive style of parent child interaction" (Wilcox 1998, 796). In many ways, ICOC leaders and members were already adept at walking this discursive line: the discipling system itself had to be constantly reaffirmed as both a loving, caring, and relational structure in the midst of discipline, control, and authority.

"Awesome" ICOC parenting was modeled on discipleship. In fact, leaders explicitly called for ICOC parents to engage in "discipling relationships" with their younger children on a regular basis. Gordon Ferguson (1997, 236–238), in his DPI discipling text, states:

> Ideally, each parent should have a weekly discipling time with each child. . . . [A]s much as nightly prayer times and weekly discipling times with the children are vital, let me add that spiritual relationships are a twenty-four-hours-a-day, seven-days-a-week affair. You cannot regulate spirituality to a schedule, as important as those scheduled times are. . . . [I]f you value the discipleship times with your children, and show it by protecting your schedule with them as diligently as with others, then they will absolutely relish discipleship.

Presenting discipling as a practice that guarantees children will want to spend close and intimate time with their parents was no doubt appealing to many parents. In a society where fathers and mothers are expected to spend "quality time" with children, presenting discipling as a practice that ensured parents and children would have extended and consistent intimate and enjoyable interactions further legitimated parent/child relationships within ICOC boundaries as healthy. The practice of discipling was also cast by leaders as an assurance of parents' ability to successfully instill a conscience in their children. If you followed Ferguson's previous advice and demonstrated to your children that you were committed to a regularly scheduled discipling practice, "what you do and what you value will be transferred to your children's value system. Such attitudes and values are 'caught' as much as 'taught.' "

When I talked with members about how they disciplined their children, several hesitated before speaking and said, "You're not going to like what I say," an indication that they were aware of much mainstream disapproval for any kind of corporeal punishment.[8] They would tell me stories about when and how one should spank a child. Their justifications and descriptions of circumstance mirrored almost exactly advice rendered in DPI's book, *Raising Awesome Kids in Troubled Times*. Obedience and respect for authority through loving discipline was presented as a must for raising children. Here again, the outside world, reflected in popular child-rearing debates, had for the most part gotten it wrong: "When it comes to discipline many parents fall into one of two extremes. They either practice something much more akin to child abuse, or they go to the opposite end and neglect discipline altogether" (Laing and Laing 1994, 118). To help moms and dads find a balance, Laing suggests they "reread this section ["Winning Obedience from Children"] several times and study carefully the scriptures that have been referenced." Laing outlines the different approaches parents may take in disciplining their children, beginning with the "simplest and most common of all corrective disciplines," the "verbal correction or reprimand," followed by time-outs, loss of privileges, and spanking. The biblical message is clear, Laing argues: "Spanking is a valid, recommended and healthy form of discipline":

> What does the Bible say? Is it right or wrong? Consider these verses:
>
> He who spares the rod hates his son, but he who loves him is careful to discipline him. (Proverbs 13:24)
>
> Folly is bound up in the heart of a child, but the rod of discipline will drive it far from him (Proverbs 22:15)
>
> Do not withhold discipline from a child; if you punish him with the rod, he will not die. Punish him with the rod and save his soul from death. (Proverbs 23:13–14) (Laing 1994, 114)

But there are conditions: spanking is "valid" and "healthy" only "when employed with wisdom and love," when it "works powerfully." Laing gives guidelines on pages 115–117 for spanking that ICOC parents were expected to study and learn well:

1. A Spanking should be an event. We should draw children aside to a private location before spanking them. A spanking is not a "pop" or "whop" out of the blue as we pass by a child we see doing something wrong. . . .
2. Explain beforehand the reason for the spanking. . . . How can something be effective when the reasons are unstated or unclear? . . .
3. Cool off before spanking a child. When we are overly emotional or in a rage, we *must* wait until we have complete self control before administering a spanking. . . . Screaming, cursing and terrorizing a child is sinful!
4. Use a designated paddle or some flat object as the "rod." The "rod" gives the whole event a judicial air rather than a feeling of personal attack. It is best to decide in advance what to use . . . some people believe it must be a flexible "switch," others feel the term is not so specific. (Geri and I use a small, flat paddle.) The primary issue is that whatever you use must be weighty enough to get the job done and light enough to inflict no damage or injury. We should never use our hand to spank with the exception of the light slap on the wrist given to the very young children in the earliest days of discipline. The hand is ineffective with older children and too personal.
5. Spank on the "safe" backside or thigh. Spankings delivered to these places sting, but do not injure. A spanking should be firm enough to bring tears, but not so hard as to cause bruises or welts. *Never* strike a child on the face—this is simply too degrading and humiliating. Never strike them on any part of the body where they could be injured. Never should we strike a child with our fists or kick them, push them, slam them into a wall, or throw them to the ground. This is abuse, not discipline. Jerking a child around by the hand or arm is disrespectful and dangerous.
6. Spankings must result in a changed, contrite heart. . . . Spankings must be strong enough, and applied wisely enough, to change the attitude.
7. Bring things to a resolution. . . . The air should be clear and our relationship completely restored when everything is over.

8. Do not spank for every offense. . . .
9. Start as soon as a child begins to understand the word "No." At approximately 14 months or so, our little ones begin to understand us. As soon as they do, they begin to assert their wills against ours!

The potency of the ICOC child-rearing message was strengthened by a convincing depiction of discipling as balancing and promoting both relationality in parent/child relationships and a respect for parental authority and position. Elizabeth Laing's foreword to her parents' DPI child-rearing manual concludes: "The things I most appreciate always will be their [her parents'] unashamed effort to put God first in our family, their firm discipline, their complete, ungrudging forgiveness, and their compassion and understanding" (Laing and Laing 1994, 11).

Parents were to decide their discipline plan of action together, and both were equally responsible for punishing and loving children. At the same time, ICOC formal discourse supported the notion, reminiscent of earlier patriarchal family discipline models, that men, as fathers, were responsible for keeping children (and wives) obedient and ultimately responsible for family discipling. Sally Gallagher (2003, 123–126) reports similar gender dynamics for evangelical families nationwide. Sam Laing, during a regional all-male ICOC event argued, "I don't care how strong she is . . . she may be dominating this guy because he's a vacuum, he's too weak . . . the woman is begging for family devos [devotionals], please disciple the children . . . wimp, wimp, you cowardly dog, you need to repent and become masculine." During formal interviews, mothers supported this position on masculinity, praising their husbands' character for disciplining the children and leading the family in discipleship; however, as the parent who spent the most time with their children, they, as "good" Christian mothers, were called to discipline their children as well.

Formal DPI literature and group discourse with regard to sustaining a balance between authority, love, and caring in child reprimands were in line with much advice available in the conservative Protestant evangelical Christian literature. However, the ICOC's approach and strategies differed in the level of fellow Christians' involvement in the raising of your children. When the circumstances surrounding discipline did not seem clear-cut, members and leaders talked about turning to disciplers and other leaders in the community to get immediate and hands-on counseling. Pat's husband, Tom, noted that "day-to-day counseling" from church members and attending church parenting seminars had helped to build his parenting confidence and skill. With the help of the church, he felt sure he would "be best friends and completely vulnerable and open" with his daughters when they were grown. Parents were not only formally instructed to have regular and consistent discipling times with their children, but to let other members disciple their children as they turned to their disciplers regularly for child-rearing help and advice. Sam and Geri Laing (1994, 213) advise: "The best approach is to look at our children's conversions as a team effort. Our parental insight and influence is absolutely essential. We must not take a passive, detached role. But the involvement of others is *critical* [my emphasis] also. As parents we may be too hard or too soft, overly suspicious or completely naive. Involving a team of people ensures that our children get the benefit of the best counsel and help we can provide them during this all-important time."

Sam Laing reinforced this view at a local event: "You must have a unified approach in raising your children. If you're continually arguing about how to raise kids, the kids will pick up on it and it's going to ruin them. . . . You better get good, strong discipling from wiser people than both of you because if you continue in a divided household, you will destroy your family and destroy your children." The idea that ICOC parents must go to disciplers for advice advanced the image of the church as a family (in that all members cared about and were involved in raising "Kingdom Kids"), but more important, it contributed to the idea that raising awesome kids was dependent on full and loyal participation in the discipling structure.

Evangelical Handicap

I heard only a few stories and brief mentions of failures to get children to commit to the teen ministries and participate in serious discipling relationships. The absence of stories about children who turned away from discipling is partly because most of the City COC members I interviewed had children who were under twelve. And too, as was true with the rest of my data collection, as a researcher, I was an audience member hearing primarily the narratives they wanted me to hear. On two occasions I asked to interview members who were having troubles with their teenage children, but was told by Pat and other leaders that they were going through a hard time and that it might be upsetting for me to interview them. What I heard in group were mostly stories filtered through the organization, narratives that stressed how families who were having difficulty with teenagers needed to get more discipling as a family—that the parents needed to find out what was wrong with them and what they had done to lead their children astray. Regardless of whether members' children were committed disciples, active in teen ministries, and discipled regularly by an "older" ICOC discipler, the stories parents told of trying to keep their children in the Kingdom and of the inevitable success they would have in converting children (if they fully followed ICOC advice) accomplished a great deal. Telling these stories of working toward child conversion was part of an important process of self-identification as a parent hard at work, on-task with biblical mandates and therapeutic culture. Through telling these stories they constructed selves as actively pursuing a sound approach to saving and training their children. The ICOC organization provided them with a language, a narrative frame, and a discourse repertoire that made such stories of self in action possible. In truth, there were many ICOC organizational forces at work against the utopian picture of raising "awesome kids" in a troubled social world.

The ICOC movement, as in other areas of family life, through formal proclamation, narrative, and members' recounting of family discipling, gave the impression that the Kingdom was able to offer a great deal of clarity, but a strong commitment to the ICOC discipling system undermined parental ideals and bred confusion. The message in the ICOC was clear: leave the therapeutic system of discipling and you will endanger the loving and forgiving relationships you had learned to manage inside the community—to leave the group would put relationships between mothers, fathers, and children at serious risk. Yet, to stay within the discipling community meant that parents had to counsel other parents; and, if you were an "older" Christian parent with some leadership and missionary status, you were responsible for the care and upbringing of many children in your "village." There were no real group mechanisms for ensuring reciprocity in child care assistance and counseling. For many who worked full- or part-time jobs and were also trying to "do motherhood" and "do fatherhood" in culturally acceptable ways, the added responsibility of managing others' family child crises took away precious few hours and energy they had for their own children. One way parents tried to resolve these responsibilities was to talk about church activities and evangelical outreach during social gatherings as quality time with their children. To the dismay of leadership that wanted the ICOC to continue to show awesome growth, some parents began to count the hours spent discipling their children as points toward their ICOC evangelical efforts.

How well reciprocity in child-rearing efforts and family counseling worked for individual members was idiosyncratic. While group status seemed to benefit members' ability to work the discipling structure to their advantage (as discussed in chapter 2 re: marriage discipling), group status often presented a negative effect with regard to child rearing. The organization demanded intense time and effort from leaders and long-time members and so, for these members, family counseling and discipling imperatives often encroached on time spent with children.

ICOC guidance and intervention made it seem as if the ICOC had the most efficient and productive method of child care. DPI guidebooks, parent workshops, and a community ready with family counselors who would intervene and help you determine how to discipline in a particular situation, teach your teenagers how to communicate, and help manage feelings of anger or guilt in parenting promoted this image of exceptional therapeutic ability. Leaders preached a similar conservative evangelical Dobson, *Focus on the Family* message: give power back to the parents, keep the state and therapeutic "experts" out of the home. However, commitment to the discipling structure introduced an equally, if not more intrusive, moral authority over parents. Parents were presented with a familiar, yet magnified ambiguous position: you have authority over your child, but the discipling community has authority over how you parent. Resolving this contradiction resulted in constant discursive movement from group control to ultimate parental autonomy, a discursive dance not unfamiliar to members who were forced to constantly balance individualism with an authoritative system.

It is not surprising that members saw the availability of a committed church "village" to help raise their children as a major benefit of ICOC membership. They understood that having positive role models, parents with strong marriages, providing peer groups for their teen and preteens, and parenting with a firm, yet gentle hand, was crucial if their children were to stay Christians and succeed in this world and the next. They had heard media reports of correlations between positive home environments and child success. Members truly believed that their religious community would bring them better relationships with their children and that children would admire the communication and "awesome" relationships they witnessed in their family of origin so much that they would surely stay in the movement as adults. But all was not harmonious in disciples' nuclear families—many members were under great evangelical pressure.

It is true that in the ICOC, teenagers had intimate social networks and peer groups, but membership in these groups and networks demanded that the youths themselves evangelize, aggressively. Whether or not we agree with placing such evangelical responsibility on children's shoulders, it is clear from the voices of former members and those teens I heard testify that they were pushed to proselytize to a point where they received serious informal sanctions (positive and negative) from classmates and peers. They were treated like evangelical heroes by members and leaders when they converted others and reprimanded if they did not put much effort into proselytizing. As the unified movement fell, it became clear that the evangelical and counseling pressures both parents and teens felt from the ICOC organization drained the perceived positive benefits of the Kingdom approach to *Raising Awesome Kids in Troubled Times*. The movement claimed to offer strategies and a discipling approach that would allow you to give your child the very best, that put children first; but the organizational family demands on "brothers" and "sisters" in the Kingdom were also promoted, in formal discourse, as the number one concern of parents and teens.

CHAPTER 6

Brothers and Sisters for the Kingdom of God

> I think more of the church than I do my own family. Not that my family, when I say my family I'm talking about my brothers and sisters, not my own kids and we are part of the church so we are family. The people who are in our lives at the church, that's our family. My siblings and their families, we have a good relationship, but it doesn't compare to the depth of involvement we have with one another [in the church].
>
> —Jeremy

TO SAY, "I am a Protestant, Jew, Muslim, Catholic, etc.," can mean that you are a member of a particular church or congregation you attend once a week, once a month, only during religious holidays, or perhaps not at all. In this respect, individual identification as a Protestant is probably one among other significant social groups in which a person claims membership. But when religious affiliation involves adoption of new kin, the religious community takes on a different character, possibly becoming an individual's primary group. Religious/spiritual organizations like the ICOC, groups that resemble what some researchers have named "identity transformation organizations," organizations that teach members to rethink everyday behavior through seemingly clearly defined social roles, values, and new images of self, often present a more consuming primary social transformation of kin. Some researchers have called such processes "radical conversion" (Bankston, Forsyth, and Floyd 1981) and "self-role transformation" (Sarbin and Adler 1970; Sarbin and Nucci 1973). When ICOC members took on new roles and images of self as sisters and brothers in the ICOC, they came under great pressure in their new roles as powerful warrior sisters and brothers to develop self, body, and relationships that would lead to great personal and ICOC evangelical ends.

The ICOC community worked hard to become each member's primary group, setting relationships in the church apart from relationships in outside society by constantly renaming church family as "real family." As we have seen, this "real family," in all its therapeutic potency, was often compared to members' family of origin. As Tom told me: "When things were going bad, especially with my family [biological], I was like, let go of all that. . . . God gave you this family [City COC family]." Religious communities that involve radical identity transformation often use familial language, metaphor, and symbol to invigorate group commitment; new spiritual family bonds are constructed to represent a higher kinship status than members' families of origin (Bromley and Oliver 1982).

To identify as part of a family is a long social and psychological process: day after day, year after year of naming, interacting, and negotiating who and what our family is and does, and who we are and what we do in relation to them. To join a new family is a weighted task, an intensive secondary socialization process where the newcomer assumes fresh familial roles and a new identity. Such symbolic naming reinforces the preeminent status of the *new* religious community in an individual's life.

There are many historical and contemporary examples of high boundary religious communities that have engaged in such naming and kin construction. The Oneida community, the Shakers, the Bruderhof "Society of Brothers," "sisters" in Catholic convents, and new religious movements founded during the countercultural revolution like the Family, Hare Krishna, and the People's Temple offer just a few examples from hundreds of religious groups where members were constructed as "real" family. Religious leaders, in these groups and others, often asserted parental status: for example, "Mother" Ann Lee, founder of the nineteenth-century New England Shaker community and "Father" Humphrey Noyes, nineteenth-century founder of the Oneida community in upstate New York; also "Father" Moon of the Unification Church and Sri Mataji, who was referred to as the "Mother" of child followers in the 1970s London-born group Sahaja Yoga. In the ICOC, some leaders and longtime members were named "spiritual parents," others "moms and pops" of congregations. Use of such family language and symbols strengthens intergroup boundaries and commitments.

Constructing and naming family relationships in newly acquired social groups is a cultural strategy that we see all around us; it is perceived by many individuals as a noble and effective action in the development of intimate social bonds. In addition to religious communities, many other social groups and organizations use family language and metaphor to represent group ties, roles, and responsibilities. In the military, for example, small groups of soldiers may develop intense familial-like bonds whose importance rises above military goals (Dunphy 1972). Michael Messner (1992, 86–89), in his study of sports and masculinity, demonstrates the contradictions of experiencing intimate relationships and naming of family through sports teams in a competitive environment that often pits players against one another. Businesses and corporations often speak of their employees as a family.[1] "Quasi-religious corporations," like Amway and other direct sales organizations, are especially active in creating in-group fictive kin (Bromley 1998). Naming and constructing new family in tightly bound primary groups is a common, familiar, and respected social process. In naming City COC Kingdom family as "real family," members were involved in a culturally acceptable action for constructing and sustaining valuable social relationships.

As Christians, ICOC members and leaders also drew from a longstanding tradition of finding biblical legitimation for naming church as family. ICOC members and leaders frequently quoted Ephesians 2:19 to legitimate church as family: "You are no longer foreigners and aliens, but fellow citizens with God's people, and members of God's household, built on the foundation of the apostles and prophets." ICOC members also drew from Luke 8:20, where Jesus calls to his "brothers" who hear the word of God, and Matthew 12:50, where Jesus' followers are called "brother, sister and mother."

Talking about church members as family was not just part of the formal institutional discourse; members were constantly naming church family in informal interactions and daily experience. They often addressed each other during services, Bible studies, and other social events as "sister" and "brother." Bill, a longtime member, described one church relationship as brotherly and fatherly: "I've been close to him for fifteen years, extremely. He's been like a father figure and a big brother figure and so, when I think brothers, that's who I think of [church members]." Most of the young women (early twenties) I spoke with who had at some time lived with a City COC married couple referred to the couple as "like a father and mother." Jackie stated that one woman whom she frequently discipled in the church was "like my baby." When I interviewed Jackie, a church "sister," Linda, dropped by. This is my "sister" I was told, while Linda opened the refrigerator and poured herself a glass of orange juice as if she were at home. Linda sat at the kitchen table and joined in answering questions and offering comments. Speaking of her relationship with Jackie she argued: "I don't mean like church sisters, I mean we are sisters in the Lord but we are like real sisters. Best friends like sisters."

The construction of all church members as "brothers" and "sisters" implied equal community status, but assigning family names often worked to establish and clarify hierarchy and status in the City COC church family and discipling structure. To say she is "my baby in the faith," implied a discipler's position as a parent and the new convert's as the child. This was true of the title "younger sister" or "younger brother," which was given to members who had been in the ICOC for a short period of time. Beth described the man who baptized her as her "big brother in the faith." To call a church member one's "spiritual parent" meant that the "parent" had been in the ICOC for a number of years and that the speaker was most likely either a "baby Christian" or a "young sister or brother." For the most part, when members gave parental status to others by naming them as a "spiritual parent," it was because that person had, at some point, served as the member's official "discipler," or tended to them in some informal discipling fashion. Generally those named as spiritual parents were "older disciples" (not in age but in church tenure), and had held some position of authority (as discipler or church leader) over the member. Some seasoned disciples were identified as the "moms and pops" of their congregations. One leader said he felt like he was the "daddy" of the congregation. The meaning of in-group family naming became clear to me over time. When Lisa, the teen ministries leader, said to me, "This is my mother, she's a baby Christian," I knew that by "mother" she meant family of origin, and that by "baby Christian" she meant new disciple. While attending one Bible study in a member's home, I met an eighty-eight-year-old woman whose discipling family group members (children and adults) called her "Gramma

Kara." Gramma Kara pulled me aside and whispered in my ear, "All the children call me that. They are all my little grandchildren." As she spoke, I imaged how, just a few years earlier, Gramma Kara was herself a "baby Christian."

Formal and informal assigning of family names to church members constructed power and status in the discipling community, but it also balanced this authority by suggesting a more relational therapeutic ethic: all church family members talked about learning from one another. Talking about Kingdom family members as "brothers" and "sisters" was a primary form of naming that worked to level power and authority. Even if one was a "spiritual parent" and discipler to a member, he or she was also that member's brother or sister, and so owed them equal respect and the obligation to offer advice if they felt it necessary. In many ways, this dual status as both sibling and parent supported the ethic of relationality that was rhetorically dominant in my interviews with City COC members. Still, even as brothers and sisters, the titles of discipler and spiritual parent carried much weight in group status and hierarchy. ICOC leader Gordon Ferguson describes the discipling counseling structure as a family where older relatives carry great responsibility: "In a physical family, the older brothers and sisters teach the younger ones many valuable things. God never intended for the parents to be the sole trainers of the children. Older siblings and extended family members were all to have a part in the task. . . . God is the one with the greatest expertise, but we can and must learn much from others in the kingdom."

Individual members constructed church as family through visual representations, photographs, and slides that showcased Kingdom kin. Most interviews took place in kitchens. Even those few where we finally settled on the living room couch to talk originated in the kitchen waiting for the kettle to boil for tea or coffee. Almost every City COC home I visited had a refrigerator covered with photographs of church members at events and nuclear family photos. Refrigerators could display dozens of photographs at once; some were neatly arranged and fitted together as a collage, some haphazardly placed about the door. They were also easily altered, additions made when new City COC family arrived and family groups shifted. Because I spent a lot of my field time in Pat's home, I watched as new leaders and new family group members claimed space on her refrigerator door. When I approached the refrigerator at Jackie's home, Jackie and her "sister" Linda pointed to individuals in tiny plastic magnetic frames, putting faces to the stories they had just told me of their church "brothers" and "sisters." Members also displayed photos of church family on mantels, bookshelves, side tables, and shelves. The character of these photos resembled the family albums shown during local services through slide/video service presentations that pictured members with their arms around each other, enjoying meals and outings together. During the twentieth anniversary service for the City COC congregation, we saw a lengthy slide show of disciples sharing momentous occasions (e.g., weddings and births), disciples moving into new homes, socializing, and proselytizing at local restaurants and city landmarks. The visual presentation made it seem as if members had a long and intimate church family history.

Constructing church members as family by comparing them to family of origin members was another way individuals worked to legitimate disciples as kin. Members and leaders used a variety of adjectives to describe and distinguish biological family from their church community family: "biological," "physical," "family of origin," and "earthly" family members were contrasted to "real," "spiritual," "church" family members. Tom opened a family group gathering with a prayer in which he thanked God for his "spiritual family." Members often described church family as more "real" than members' biological/families of origin because they were "closer" to church members and church members truly "cared" about one another. Jackie's gesture, in describing her church family, symbolically cast City COC relationships as more significant than her biological/family of origin relationships: "I feel like I have a physical family (*Jackie gestures with both hands to the left as if she is setting her 'physical family' beside her*). And then I have the church (*Jackie draws a larger circle in front of her, both arms extended*). Do you know what I mean? When I say my family a lot of times it's the church (*repeats drawing of large circle*) and by that I mean everyone in the church."

I asked Jackie, "By the physical family you mean . . .?" She responded, "The family that I was born into. Even if they were members of the church they would be, you know, my family (*draws large circle again*). My church family, these are people that I am extremely, extremely close to." Jackie painted an image, through gesture and language, of her church family as bigger and as encompassing a much larger portion of her life than her biological family, whom she neatly pushed to the side for the smaller role she saw them playing in her life.

What were the individual and group consequences of naming this new religious group as family? For the community, as it has for tightly bound religious movements over time and across cultures, this naming built strong boundaries around the group, ideological walls that cast inside as most important and sacred, and outside as profane and often dangerous. For individuals, as in many other social relationships where people name new kin, this was a purposeful naming that established "fictive kin,"[2] a strategic social practice that may bring about reciprocity in emotional and practical resources. What kinds of emotional and practical resources did naming church family accomplish? We have already seen how naming church sisters, brothers, mothers, and fathers served therapeutic functions in marriage and family life, and how discipling provided a network and community for child care and teen intervention. But naming brothers and sisters in the Kingdom of God accomplished another very significant measure in the development of moral Christian selves: brothers and sisters were there to teach you how to be powerful and productive Christian men and women through upholding the movement's evangelical mission. Members believed, as many other Christians do as well, that God had called them to share their faith, to spread the Word and convert nonbelievers; becoming an ICOC sister or brother meant receiving constant encouragement, pressure, and strategies for achieving this goal.

A major subject of discourse in naming church as family was that disciples, as Kingdom kin, were supposed to be, above all, a family *for* God (*for* the movement), a family whose ultimate goal, above all else, was spreading the Word and gaining converts to the Kingdom (ICOC). "We have to take care of God," one female speaker suggested forcefully at a local Women's Day event, "and not let life get us distracted from the Word." To achieve these goals, members and leaders argued, disciples had to be fulfilling appropriate ICOC gender roles and ideals: embodying ideal masculinity and femininity would shape productive evangelists. In shaping the bodies and personalities of these brothers and sisters, the movement sustained familiar contradictory gendered expectations, and introduced a few new dilemmas as well. In institutional efforts to form muscular men and muscular women for the Kingdom's advancement, we see again that the movement's expectations and prescriptions for evangelical masculinity and femininity were anything but clear. They were, like most cultural pursuits that attempt to clarify gender, awash in ambiguity. Nevertheless, disciples marched on, trying to present a coherent vision of brotherhood and sisterhood in the movement through passionate assertions of what Kingdom warriors should be: forceful displays of wavering between traditional masculinity, femininity, and egalitarian, expressive ideals. It was an ideological wavering, as I have asserted throughout this ethnography, that made sense to members and potential converts. It was meaningful because these were the very contradictory expectations that, through various institutional venues, had already deeply affected their journeys as gendered selves.

Muscular Ambassadors/ Sensitive Brothers

> There is in the Bible an upholding of masculine strength and power. I'm not talking about arrogance and cockiness, I'm talking about a man's man . . . Moses the man. You don't want to mess with Moses. He could just burn a hole right through you.
>
> —Sam Laing, from audiotape *Real God/Real Men*

To be a true brother in the ICOC Kingdom was to be engaged in a constant effort to become a physically and spiritually strong and sensitive Kingdom man. ICOC brothers were taught to embody hegemonic masculinity: to be strong, aggressive, muscular, instrumental bodies in control of emotions (Connell 1995). Yet they were also taught to be sensitive, caring, therapeutic brothers, not afraid to express emotion and to embrace and understand the emotions of their church siblings. ICOC leaders and members searched and appropriated particular cultural tools and approaches to use on their conscious journeys to develop muscular, aggressive bodies and sensitive souls working for the Kingdom of God.

The effort to build muscular/sensitive ICOC brothers was in many ways not so different from the pursuit of masculinities imposed on men today in other primary groups (e.g., biological/family of origin, military, sports teams, etc.). Like the pursuit of multiple and contradictory masculine ideals within other evangelical religious groups, ICOC's approach offered a range of gender assumptions and prescriptions. As Gallagher

(2003), Bartkowski (2004), and Lockhart (2000) have suggested, the evangelical subculture aggressively promotes a wide range of seemingly contradictory masculinities. Evidence for the promotion of these various stances can be found in even a cursory look at evangelical websites (such as Focus on the Family or New Man, www.newmanmag.com). For example, an article written by Donald Miller and posted on the New Man website demonstrates the multiple and contradictory masculine ideals pervasive in the evangelical Christian approach to manhood. Miller recounts a conversation with a female friend: " 'Women don't want to be thought of as helpless,' my friend began, 'It's hard to say that without sounding like a feminist, because so many people think in black and white these days, but it is true. The knight in shining armor figure is a desire for some women, but the female part of that fantasy involves the knight bringing her back to his castle where they walk and talk together, and he adores her. They have a relationship. He is gentle and fun, and he is a good communicator. These are the things women find sexy.' "

Religious organizations that in any way claim to help men become traditionally masculine are in fact forced by the increasing value placed on gender egalitarianism and therapeutic ethics to present, as well, contradictory notions of expressive masculinity in their discourse repertoires. A religious movement today, in the United States and other Western nations, would likely not experience significant growth if they only stressed a traditionalist, strong male patriarch image. Egalitarianism and expressive masculinity have grown too strong as cultural ideals. In most of the research on religious groups that promote a traditionalist masculinity, at least some level of accommodation to egalitarian ideals and men's liberationist beliefs and practices is shown (Bartkowski 2004; Gallagher 2003; Lockhart 2000). Furthermore, evangelical movements with specific conversion goals, like the ICOC and the Promise Keepers, for example, may integrate and waver between gender positions at a higher level than other conservative communities as they seek to appeal to a wide audience (Bartkowski 2004). Including such a broad variety of approaches and beliefs naturally presents a challenge: how are these religious organizations and individuals to promote and manage these contrary ideals as they frame distinctive organizational identities?

James Davidson Hunter (1983), in his study of evangelical Christians in the United States, presents an accommodation model of religious identity construction, that the beliefs and practices of evangelicals are an accommodation of mainstream society, efforts to fit with the "plausibility structures" (Berger 1967) of a secular, pluralistic, and bureaucratic society. Understanding religious groups and subcultures as a process of accommodating and/or resisting contemporary culture leads to support of Hunter's (1991) subsequent "culture wars" thesis: a working theory that presents the United States as divided between the ultimate resistors—conservatives and religious traditionalists—and the accommodators—liberal religious denominations and secular humanists. While the accommodation and resistance model is helpful to a certain degree,[3] it can inhibit grasping the greater complexity that underlies cultural "battles" over, for example, gender, family, and education in modern and contemporary U.S. society. Such a model also stands in the way of understanding the more multilayered processes of, for example, individual constructions of religious and gender identity. Groups and individuals do not just accommodate and resist; they appropriate, challenge, selectively draw from, and recast—they creatively rewrite, use, and then throw away religious and secular culture as they learn and give birth to new strategies for becoming moral communities and selves.

Sociologists of religion have recently called attention to this multiple creative approach that religious organizations and individuals use in crafting moral selves and organizations, stressing that the tools of religious identity construction come from various cultural beliefs and practices and originate from *various* social institutions, groups, and structures (Ammerman 2003; Bartkowski 2004; Gallagher 2003; Smith 1998). This new model of understanding religious identity construction is essential. In the new model, contemporary religious identity and experience is better conceived as a creative engagement with culture, an ongoing piecing together of cultural beliefs and approaches that gives organizations, individuals, and movements vitality (Smith 1998). Geertz (1973) spoke of religious ritual and cultural symbol and practice as producing "lasting moods" and "motivations," instilling beliefs and worldview in the minds of individuals. But these moods, beliefs, and worldview are, in essential ways, always shifting and in conversation with one another. In our contemporary world, moods are disrupted often by local and world events, challenged by governments, organizations, and individuals; moods and motivations are always, as Swidler (1986, 2001) would note, representative of culture *in action*. Thus, when analyzing new religious movements like the ICOC, groups that are, without doubt, engaged in a highly active process of crafting, pulling, grabbing, rewriting, and constructing religious identities culled from shifting cultural ideals and practices, it is crucial to move beyond a model of accommodation and resistance. We need theoretical models that leave room for complex, dynamic, and creative approaches as organizations and individuals shape religious/spiritual identities in our pluralistic marketplace.

Operating under this new model of understanding, Bartkowski (2004, 53–65) crafts a useful analytical tool for thinking about the construction of gender in a world of competing and shifting masculinities and femininities. He argues that Promise Keeper (PK) authors may have different tendencies toward either more traditionalist (the "Rational Patriarch") or liberationist (the "Expressive Egalitarian") gender ideology, but that regardless, PK authors are most times shifting constantly between the two. Using a rhetorical device Bartkowski names "discursive tacking," he describes how PK authors, like a sailboat, move away from their central position or course and then return to this central ground as they explicate what a PK man is and should do. This discursive tacking ultimately establishes gender archetypes that "seem to overlap rather than overtly contradict one another." This rhetorical device, Bartkowski argues, "enables Promise Keeper writers to construct discursive bridges over the chasms that would otherwise place these ideologies at odds. Discursive tacking enables PK writers to produce flexible visions of godly manhood that appear " 'holistic' and 'well-rounded' " (Bartkowski 2004, 65). Discursive tacking is a useful analytical tool because of its ability to leave room for multiple ideological beliefs and practices creatively engaged along the course of the sail.

As I suggest in chapter 2, the ICOC gender discursive path moved in seemingly erratic patterns, back and forth between traditionalist, essentialist, egalitarian, expressive, feminist, and men's liberationist gender ideals and practices. At times, gender discourse, while drawing heavily from the organizational repertoire, seemed determined by individual position, goals, and group status. But throughout all, relationality stayed the center of the rhetorical course; therapeutic ethos was centering, emerging as a straight and reliable position. Returning to relationality and a therapeutic ethic with consistency and fervor made, as Bartkowski suggests above of PK discourse, the ICOC's contradictory and varied positions of muscular and expressive sensitive church brothers appear "holistic" and "well-rounded."

Muscular Brothers

When traditionalist, essentialist gender beliefs and ideals surfaced in ICOC formal discourse, they centered around brothers in the Kingdom becoming muscular men whose physical stamina and strength would enable them to be extremely productive evangelical workers. ICOC emphasis on building muscular, healthy bodies as an essential piece of religious identity formation is indicative of "muscular Christianity," a historical movement that produced the YMCA, the Boy Scouts, public recreation, and playgrounds, as well as our cultural emphasis on sports as forming moral and healthy individuals:

> Between 1880 and 1920, American Protestants in many denominations witnessed the flourishing in their pulpits and seminaries of a strain of religiosity known, both admiringly and pejoratively, as "muscular Christianity." Converts to this creed included Josiah Strong, a Social Gospel minister who thought bodily strength a prerequisite for doing good; G. Stanley Hall, a pioneer psychologist who wished to reinvigorate "old-stock" Americans; and President Theodore Roosevelt, an advocate of strenuous religion for "the Strenuous Life." These and other stalwart supporters of Christian manliness hoped to energize the churches and to counteract the supposedly enervating effects of urban living. To realize their aims, they promulgated competitive sports, physical education, and other staples of modern-day life. (Putney 2001, 1)

Muscular Christianity was a religious movement that took shape at the turn of the twentieth century in the United States, a time when many white Protestant males feared the rising and passionate participation of women in religious activities. They wanted to bring young men back into the church, to rescue them from an industrializing society that they saw as threatening to produce a culture of effeminate men with no physical stamina (Putney 2001; Rotundo 1993). The YMCA and other similar organizations arose around this newly defined "masculinity" that they believed would be able to fight the feminization of religion, the threats of immigrant populations to white Protestant values, and the dangers of an industrializing nation.

This form of aggressive, race-driven muscular Christianity faded somewhat after 1920, but we have seen a recent return in the later quarter of the twentieth century. Most notably we can see major tenets of muscular Christianity in the controversial Promise Keepers movement, an evangelical men's movement known for its meetings in football stadiums across the country. Bartkowski (2004, 32) notes that muscular Christianity in the late twentieth century has appeared, just as it did in the early twentieth, alongside serious shifts and changes in our family and gender landscape. The continued participation of women in the workforce, women engaging in strong political action, the rising attention to women's sports, and significant gay/lesbian/bi/transgender challenges to normative heterosexuality and hegemonic masculinity are just a few late twentieth-century developments that have given rise to current muscular Christian movements.

Early twentieth-century attempts to build strong, healthy bodies for a Christian mission took shape through a promotion of sports and athletics. Putney (2001, 45) notes that muscular Christians at the turn of the twentieth century were "undoubtedly best known for their celebration of bodies." This concern with developing healthy and strong bodies was not just of concern to muscular Christians: "Many nineteenth-century reformers, first in England, then in America, expressed faith in the power of strenuous activity to overcome the perceived moral defects of urbanization, cultural pluralism, and white-collar work." Early muscular Christian clergy were themselves especially active in sports and athletics (Putney 2001, 50–64). Today's muscular Christian men turn to the institution of sports and athletics as well; in the late twentieth/early twenty-first century, these appeals to sports and athletics are framed by our current cultural obsession with shaping "healthy" bodies and promoting health and wellness.

In our society, many individuals see sports as building skills that will help young people succeed in future "team" endeavors, building moral conscience and as providing a love of physical activity that will encourage a lifetime of "healthy" body choices. Connell (2000, 188) notes: "The image of sport is one of healthy bodies in vigorous action. Sport might seem our society's health-giving activity par excellence—exercise, fresh air, good fellowship." Yet sports upholds its own sets of contradictions; for example, given the extreme emphasis on sports as producing healthy bodies, sports, as an institution, supports the normalization of pain and injury (with its own medical subspecialty to deal with the blows) and promotes using bodies as instruments of aggressive and violent action (Messner 1992).

Concern over development of healthy selves and bodies through the shaping of athletic disciples was exemplified in the ICOC's "sports ministry." ICOC male members, whether they were active in sports or not, clearly felt the social pressures of sports as a performance of masculinity; they understood the male dream of succeeding in sport that bears down on young boys and men, and so they came to understand, as ICOC brothers, that muscular bodies were ideal instruments in winning Kingdom goals. Like many other religious groups today, ICOC men would gather to play sports. In the ICOC, these social gatherings had names like "brothers' basketball," "brothers' football," or "brothers' baseball." Formal discourse featured ICOC leaders as healthy and dedicated athletes active in the brothers' sports ministry. In fact, ex-members joked often about the extreme emphasis in group on the sports ministry and how the movement's founder, Kip McKean, bragged about his children's sports accomplishments. For a while in the mid- to late 1990s, a humorous picture circulated on ex-member websites: a digital photo of a brother's basketball team where all players were given the face of Kip McKean. The emphasis on body strength, of building strong muscular men, was a large part of the formal construction of ICOC brotherhood, and its manifestation in group was particular to the developments of our contemporary health and wellness movement.

The ICOC creatively drew from contemporary cultural tools of health, wellness, and dieting as they constructed their version of body as a temple theology. They worked to convince members and potential converts that the ICOC approach to shaping bodies resulted in strong men who lived awesome intimate relationships and who would become productive evangelists for the Kingdom. Their concentration on shaping muscular Christian bodies through diet and exercise was reflective of a long-standing relationship between body, health, and religion.[4] American Protestantism has a particularly rich history of diet as part of Christian discipline and lifestyle. From John Calvin and the Puritans' emphasis on fasting to nineteenth-century physician Edward Hooker Dewey, who "taught that disease was often caused or abetted by gluttonous behavior and excess body weight and advocated both extreme and mild forms of fasting as a panacea for all ills" (Griffith 1999, 220), to John Harvey Kellogg, a late nineteenth-century Seventh-Day Adventist who introduced cornflakes cereal as a substitute for greasy breakfasts full of meats, Protestants have stressed thin bodies as the location of grace and salvation. Griffith notes that "by the early decades of the twentieth century, Anglo-American diet reformers had achieved colossal success in their quest to demonize fat and preach thinness as necessary to personal salvation" (1999, 221).

That mainstream health and wellness diet and exercise fads made their way into ICOC body as a temple theology and discourse is not unusual for modern and contemporary U.S. Christian subcultures. According to Griffith, the first Christian text to "articulate" new "consumer-driven values of slenderness and beauty" in body as a temple theology, and "the first twentieth-century representation of the Christian diet book genre, was *Pray Your Weight Away* by Presbyterian minister Charlie Shedd (1957)." In her study of fasting, dieting, and the body in contemporary Christianity, Griffith calls attention to the proliferation of Christian dieting publications and groups in the evangelical subculture:

> In the fifty years after *Pray Your Weight Away* was published, American Christianity saw the rise (and sometimes fall) of iconic groups and hopeful concepts like Overeaters Victorious, Believercise, the Faithfully Fit program, and the Love Hunger Action Plan. . . . *Devotions for Dieters* was published by pastor Victor Kane, a book that was reprinted in 1973 and again in 1976 . . . as [Charlie Shedd] his 1972 book *The Fat is In Your Head* remained on the National Religious Bestsellers list for 23 months and sold more than 110,000 copies by 1976. Evangelist Frances Hunter produced *God's Answer to Fat* in 1975, a top religious best-seller. . . . Other striking successes in this period include titles such as *Help Lord—The Devil Wants Me Fat!* (1977); *Slim for Him* (1978); and *Free To Be Thin* (1979); the latter sold more than half a million copies and spawned a virtual industry of diet products marketed by the author, including an exercise video and a low-calorie, inspirational cookbook. (Griffith 1999, 223)

Muscular ICOC brothers were playing sports and working out in the gym, just as early muscular brothers of the YMCA were dedicated to building strong bodies for evangelical purpose. However, the ideas and methods for achieving strong and healthy bodies were shaped by contemporary notions of dieting and health and wellness. Today's Christian dieting and health and wellness discourse draws from popular language that stresses contemporary approaches to weight loss: "low-carb" diets, measuring "fat" indexes, striving for "low cholesterol," regulating "metabolism," relaxation through "yoga," an appeal to a wide range of medicalized and weight loss "experts' " prescriptions and terms. Health and wellness is central to the consumer market, with a vast array of exercise programs, food, pharmaceutical products, and professionals. These products and approaches are highlighted in the evangelical publishing industry and were used in various ways to stress the building of strong bodies for ICOC evangelical purpose. Turn-of-the-twentieth-century jumping jacks and healthy diets were replaced by twenty-first-century body shaping techniques like weight-lifting machines, the South Beach Diet, and low-fat, low-carb diet obsession. These cultural approaches made sense to ICOC men and women; they seemed productive actions in the war against weight gain, secular humanism, and the growth of their movement. To become a disciple was to engage in good "healthy" turn-of-the-twenty-first-century body consumerism.

We live in a culture where personal trainers are hired to push women and men to bodybuilding heights, to produce ideal body shapes by holding hands and monitoring progress. Laing and other ICOC leaders' promises to serve as trainers who would actively shape masculine brothers no doubt made sense to many members and potential converts. I was not allowed to attend all-male events, but I did listen carefully and analyze all-male audiotaped events. One tape, given to me by a leader when I requested to attend the yearly regional Men's Day, was of a clearly energetic collective performance like Marriage Enrichment Day and other special events where thousands of members gathered in one space in megachurch style. Sam Laing was the guest speaker on this particular tape; his preaching style and rhetorical emphasis on building a hegemonic masculinity that views the male body as a strong instrument of Christian social mission were indicative of historical and contemporary muscular Christian leaders. Laing began the day with the promise that he would "transform" them into men. His pledge was met with cheers from the men in the conference center.

Not surprisingly, a large part of the ICOC path to shaping masculine bodies for God's Kingdom and to improve personal relationships involved losing pounds. For men, getting stronger meant more muscle and less fat. Recall Laing's statement in chapter 2 regarding husbands losing weight: he didn't want to hear about "metabolism" or "genetics" and promoted the idea that men could and should lose weight if they needed to. Following Laing's promise to transform his audience into men, he offered a personal testimony of weight loss, relational health, sexuality, and masculine power:

> I remember, when I got in my thirties, I realized that for me to get in shape it's going to take a lot more effort than when I was in my twenties. I could go out and play brothers' football without even warming up. . . . I said to Geri [his wife], "I'm going to start going to the gym," and she said, "I like you just the way you are." Well, I started working out and she said, "Oh, I like you even better the way you are." . . . I was an animal. I tore the gym apart. I got motivated, honestly brother. I don't care whether you run or go to the gym or do something, but Abraham and the guys in this book [Bible] are examples of men who stayed strong spiritually and physically. Look at Paul, Joseph, and Jacob, they got stronger as they got older, they got more full of life.

Today, muscular bodies are talked about through a particular health and wellness discourse. When religious communities promise to shape bodies for moral, spiritual, and organizational purposes, they draw from various cultural tools and strategies, in creative ways, as they paint images of ideal gendered bodies. Laing's message that day, and on other occasions, made clear that God was calling men to develop their muscular Christian selves so that they would be better able to serve as evangelists in the Kingdom, as well as improve intimate relationships with spouses and girlfriends. Throughout ICOC discourse, strong and healthy bodies were presented as exceptionally able to tackle the demanding proselytizing goals that leaders had set. In fact, disciples who did not aggressively work to produce converts often emerged in group and individual narratives as "lazy" and "unhealthy."

Muscular ICOC Christian bodies were built to win and to conquer souls, body images that suggested competition and aggression; yet muscular brothers were held to high expectations of relationality. While I was not privy to the individual social conflicts within the group over evangelical power, leaders often felt the need to address such tension during formal events. Laing and City COC leaders clarified to ICOC brothers that not everyone could become an evangelical leader. To get "on staff" as a paid ministry leader was presented as an important, coveted, and high-status position in the movement. The creation of muscular ICOC brothers produced a competitive evangelical environment, generating much disappointment when only a certain number of church brothers were offered a position at the helm of regions, congregations, and missionary posts. In part, to legitimate the reality that not all brothers would be able to "lead," the leadership stressed group imperatives that brothers should be sensitive and caring, listening faithfully to the needs of fellow brothers and able to admit that they may not have "leadership potential." Images of strong, competitive masculine bodies for the Kingdom were often rhetorically softened by images of expressive brothers behind the front lines of the evangelical war. As disciples were likely told growing up and playing competitive sports, they were not in competition with their team brothers, but in a close-knit church family working together for evangelical success. Living this contradiction was familiar, as was the dilemma posed by the expression of male intimacy bounded by the demands of a heterosexual hegemonic masculinity.

In contemporary U.S. culture, stressing the importance of men showing emotions and dedicating themselves to a therapeutic ethos necessarily presents a challenge to hegemonic masculinity. I use the term *hegemonic* here because, despite the pervasive influence of emotionality and expressive masculinity as rising contemporary masculine ideals, and the challenges of gay and transgender movements, normative constructions of the heterosexual male continue to dominate (Connell 1995). When hegemonic heterosexual masculinity confronts expressive masculinity's show of emotion and intimacy among men, individuals and groups must develop strategies for balancing the resulting discord. Part of this balancing can be rhetorical, moving the discursive course back and forth from an affirmation of heterosexuality to the valuing of male expressivity and emotionality. Sometimes this discursive balancing, in upholding heterosexuality, involves the assertion of male dominance in relationships with women. Messner (1992, 85–107), for example, notes how men in locker rooms, as they confront actions and displays of male connectedness and team intimacy, voice sexual conquests of women and deny emotional connection and expressiveness in their relationships with women. Explicit downplaying of emotional connection with women was not an option in the ICOC, as relationality in marriage was so strongly valued. However, one could argue that Laing's story of tearing apart the gym, of becoming an "animal" while working out, was a story of sexual conquest as he implied his wife liked him "even better" after his workouts.

The task of balancing heterosexual masculinity with expressive masculinity was a big challenge in the ICOC. They seemed to balance by returning most frequently to the relational, expressive masculine ethic. ICOC leaders often boasted of how Kingdom brothers were not afraid to hug each other, kiss each other, put their arms around each other, and show emotion. In the City COC congregation, relationality, enacted through the expressive, emotive male, was in the forefront of congregational and individual depictions of Christian masculinity. To "lead" the movement, just as to "lead" in the home, was to be a strong, muscular man—but hegemonic masculine notions of body shaping patriarchal leadership seemed to take up less rhetorical space. It was in formal movement discourse (specifically events, publications, and audiotapes meant for men only) that I heard most about ICOC brothers armed with a physical power that magnified their ability to evangelize the world and push Christian muscle in "building the Kingdom." The call to build muscular men was not as prevalent in my data of mixed gender functions or individual formal interviews. First and foremost in my field notes and interview transcripts were stories and prescriptions of ICOC men able to enact valuable relational skills and who helped their fellow male disciples learn to do the same—this was the central course of the discursive path I witnessed.

The course of the discursive journey, where and when language and symbol pull away from and return to a particular ideological position, depends on audience, space, and individual and organizational performance goals. Perhaps I heard more emphasis on expressive masculinity and relationality because the City COC brothers I formally and informally interviewed thought that I would respond more favorably, as a woman, to their presentation of self as expressive and emotional. And too, perhaps hegemonic, muscular Christian prescriptions did not dominate in mixed-gender events because they knew these prescriptions, and the language used to convey their message, would not fall well on ICOC women's and potential converts' ears. Had I been allowed to participant in male-only social events, I might have heard more assertions of hegemonic masculinity and the claiming of physical superiority and ultimate male power and male headship in family and church.

MUSCULAR SISTERS/ DOMESTIC KINGDOM WORKERS

Kingdom sisters, as evangelical workers, were engaged in a different creative approach to balancing gender ideals as they fulfilled religious duties: melding muscular sisterhood with more traditional notions of domestic womanhood. In chapters 2 and 5, we saw how ICOC's gender discourse regarding roles, attitudes, and practices for women in family relationships wavered from a more traditional (as in female submission and women as caretakers of small children) to a more egalitarian, postfeminist stance (as in mutual submission and individual satisfaction). Throughout, egalitarianism, gender equity, and relationality held rhetorical prominence. The juggling of somewhat contradictory gender prescriptions and ideals was true on the evangelical front as well. In their roles as sisters in the ICOC Kingdom, women were to be strong, physically fit, attractive, and beautiful sisters on the front lines of their movement's evangelical war, speaking out at large public events, publishing in DPI, and living the exemplary life of a productive Christian missionary and evangelist. Yet, this female ICOC evangelical fervor was cast in a language reminiscent of late nineteenth-century domestic Protestantism, where women were relegated to the home to craft pious domestic spaces for the good of their family and church.

Connell (1995, 230–231) reminds us that "though most discussion of masculinity is silent about the issue, it follows from both psychoanalytic and social construction principles that women are bearers of masculinity as well as men. . . . Girls and women participate in masculinized institutions and practices, from bureaucracies to competitive sports," and I would add here, to spiritual endeavors to conquer and wage religious battles. When the first female Palestinian suicide bomber succeeded in killing herself and others, the world seemed shocked that a daughter would engage in such an aggressive act previously committed by sons. But the truth is, women regularly embody and enact what many think of as masculine principles such as aggressive action and competition. When they do so, it often "occurs in a context of patriarchal institutions where the 'male is norm,' or the masculine is authoritative" (Connell 1995, 231). In the ICOC, church sisters were cast as muscular evangelical workers and warriors, just as their Kingdom brothers; the organization made clear that both genders were to develop strong and healthy bodies, to use these bodies as instruments, to go into the world, sometimes on "dangerous missions," and fight for the ICOC evangelization of "the world in one generation."

In his historical look at muscular Christianity, Putney (2001) notes that even though the historical movement was fueled by a fear of the feminization of religion and thus included misogynous rhetoric, many women invested in similar ideals of strong female bodies and athleticism for Christ. At that time, some, like Mary Baker Eddy, founder of Christian Science, started their own religious spaces based on more "feminine" principles and a rejection of the pursuit of body health. But many women, Putney argues, especially those shaping the late nineteenth-century Young Women's Christian Association (YWCA), the Camp Fire Girls, and the Girl Scouts, "embraced" the "Strenuous Life," especially "those aspects of it that advanced health." They promoted the belief that girls, as well as boys, "deserved to draw strength from nature and from strenuous outdoor games" (Putney 2001, 145). Putney names his chapter on women "Muscular Women."

ICOC "sisters," as turn-of-the-twenty-first-century strong female Christian bodies in pursuit of health, echoed the efforts of women during those early years of the YWCA—exercising and shaping bodies with resolve and strength for use in a social evangelical mission. However, ICOC's discursive repertoire was composed of cultural tools and strategies that were particular to late twentieth-, early twenty-first-century U.S. society: language, beliefs, practices, and habits that come from the growth and dominance of our medicalized consumer health and wellness movement concerned with weight loss and "healthy" eating in the face of much medical and social concern over a rising "obesity epidemic."

Several ICOC women talked about how important it was for a female disciple to "take care of herself physically." Exercising daily and eating the right foods would make you a beautiful sister and productive evangelist. At one Marriage Enrichment event the guest female speaker talked about how she had worked out that morning at the wonderful gym in the hotel and how important it was to exercise. Looking "in shape" would benefit your relationship with your spouse and enable you to attract new female converts to the movement. During events, women talked about how being a sister in the Kingdom of God had helped them shed pounds, and how disciplers had helped them stay on goal. Formal prescriptions of health and wellness for ICOC sisters were also found in DPI texts. In *Life and Godliness for Everywoman* (Jones 2000, 112), disciple and medical doctor Helen Salsbury, in a section on growing older, writes:, "If your diet is poor and/or you need to lose weight, get advice. Maybe you could volunteer or get a part time job at a weight loss center or a health food store. You will learn much about living and eating healthier. There are multiple sources on the Internet for medical and dietary newsletters. Just ask around and look. Try growing some herbs or learn organic gardening."

Dr. Salsbury echoes a historical body as a temple theology: God gave you this body, he has uses for it, it is a gift, and so you must do your best to keep it pure. She offers advice for weight loss strategy and warns that obesity could be deadly:

> Do something drastic to change. Losing weight can help you feel better about yourself, no matter what age you are. It helps your attitude and will eliminate some of your physical complaints. There is a reason that that joint hurts. It may not just be arthritis. Diabetes, heart disease, high blood pressure, difficulty breathing, snoring and depression are some of the consequences of obesity. If you are obese, get help quickly and believe you can change. You *can* change. Learn about weight control and do not give up. Fast foods are killing Americans. Unfortunately, we have created a generation of junk food junkies, and it reeks of Roman debauchery. (Jones 2000, 112)

Implicit in Dr. Salsbury's and other formal ICOC lectures on weight loss and health maintenance was that healthy and strong female bodies gave way to productive evangelical lives. Salsbury charges, "If you are overweight, you are not just hurting yourself, you are hurting God"

(Jones 2000, 112). How exactly were they hurting God? McKean and other top leaders made clear that women were to be active church leaders, missionaries, and evangelists. An "obese," "lazy," and "diseased" woman did not fit the ideal soldier for the Kingdom image. They would not have the energy to get the work of the Kingdom done, nor would they serve as examples of ideal womanhood that would draw new converts.

Women in the City COC often spoke informally of the "strong" women's ministry in the church, women as "powerful ambassadors for God," and attributed a large part of the success of the movement to the strength of the women's ministry. Like Dana's call of "Women power!" before the showing of *Secrets of the Heart* (chapter 4), leaders and members were constantly naming and praising powerful church women. Kip McKean, in his manifesto, RR, speaks of the birth of the women's ministry under the guidance of his wife, Elena McKean, and another founding female member, Pat Gempel:

> Another aspect of restoration that enriched the movement was led by Pat Gempel and Elena McKean. That was the creation of formal training for women leaders and the discipling of all women. Thus, a dynamic women's ministry was created. This opportunity for leadership excited the sisters and attracted non-Christian women to God's movement. Many women in the traditional church perceived their role as "second-class" since they simply prepared meals for fellowship dinners. Thus, with no real purpose, many became lazy and/or discouraged in their daily Christianity. . . . Pat, Elena and I, by studying the Word together, came to understand that God commands women to be responsible for and lead the other women. Ultimately, women could then put their all into the church because they saw from Scripture their purpose was exactly the same as the purpose for men—to change the world by making disciples.

In McKean's pronouncement, we can hear loud and clear a postfeminist position: women in other churches that promoted a return to "tradition" were treated as "second-class," while women in the ICOC had *equality* in evangelical purpose and community roles. In that delicate rhetorical floating of traditionalism with egalitarianism, leaders and members may move away from egalitarianism at points to stress an ultimate gender hierarchy that put male leaders in charge of female leaders.

However, egalitarianism and mutuality would always return as essential in gender relationships and informally (female and male) members sometimes reversed the traditionalist positions. Some told me that local women leaders would, even if it was not named as such, disciple and lead men. The breadth of the organization's gendered discursive repertoire gave women and men options for framing group interactions, and the audience, social space, and individual performance goals influenced members' discursive paths.

In organizational discourse, ICOC muscular sisters were caught in a dance of power and influence that has historically been the case in many religious communities. Jualynne Dodson (2002), for example, in her book *Engendering Church: Women, Power and the AME Church,* offers an in-depth look at the formal and informal mechanisms through which black women wielded incredible power and influence in the African Methodist Episcopal Church, an institution that for the first half of the nineteenth century had no formal positions for women. Throughout religious history in the United States, there have been many cases where women's formal power has been limited, yet informal organizational power, influence, and responsibility were great.[5] Women, per the significant body of social research documenting these cases, have historically carried a large portion of the public grassroots community work that sustains religious institutions and communities, even if they have been offered limited public and institutional credit for doing so. The ICOC women's ministry provided women in the movement with a voice and mechanisms for asserting public influence and power.

In formal discourse, ICOC muscular women took their strong bodies and minds on exciting missiological trips, traveling around the world to dangerous places. At times, their descriptions of paid and unpaid ICOC missionary efforts sounded like advertisements for intrigue and adventure. Megan Blackwell writes in Linda Brumley and Sheila Jones's DPI text, *She Shall Be Called Woman,* volume 1 (Jones and Brumley 2000, 39): "As I write this, we are preparing to leave for the Middle East tomorrow morning. Americans are advised not to travel there, but we are convinced that the kingdom must advance." Blackwell, a mother, is aided by the conversion of her biological father to the ICOC family as she prepares to leave her children: "God has comforted me by providing my father, who became a disciple a year ago, to take care of the kids." Kay

McKean, the founder's sister-in-law, writes in the same text, "My life is, indeed, an adventure. With each adventure, God is molding my character to have the Christ-like qualities of love, bravery, strength, patience. . . . It's thrilling to be able to live a life that can make an eternal impact on others. . . . [H]e is with me, leading me, changing me, and giving me the victory!" (Jones and Brumley 2000, 139–140).

ICOC women were encouraged by the organization to be out in the public beating the evangelical war drum. Teresa Ferguson offers Deborah (Judges 4) as a model—she was a biblical woman who "inspired a nation of women to step outside of their household duties and put their hands to the battle." She speaks of her renewing commitment as a high-ranking women's ministry leader: "Like Deborah, I have to keep listening to God daily. I am a woman chosen by God to speak his words to others. . . . I must recite the victories which God has given me and to those other faithful warriors around me" (Jones and Brumley 2000, 65). We hear, in the voices of formal ICOC female testimonies, a clear belief in the woman warrior for Christ, healthy and strong women ready to travel across the world to fight the battle. But these were the glamorous, high-status aggressive missionary assignments: to be chosen to travel to another country, to be a "guest speaker" from state to state, city to city at regional ICOC Women's Days and Marriage Enrichment Days, to be asked to author an essay for a DPI volume. The more common female ground soldiers heeded a call to leadership and missionary work in domesticity.

When women are called to do masculinity in organizations, their adherence and performance of masculine actions are creatively cast through feminine form: institutions may combine sisterly duties and/or motherly duties with aspects of normative masculinity to explain and justify particular organizational goals. Formal, and especially informal, church discourse was driven by ideals that echoed clearly the beliefs of late nineteenth-, early twentieth-century domestic Protestantism. Domestic Protestantism was born of the "separate spheres" doctrine that arose in our industrializing nation from white Protestant culture. Domestic Protestantism was based on the idea that men went out into the dangerous, sinful working world and came home to a pious, Godly home sphere tended by and shaped through women's domestic efforts. The home sphere was to soothe and provide spiritual rejuvenation from a harsh, industrializing working world. Even though ICOC women were expected to keep up with their evangelical brothers as warriors for God's Kingdom, they were also told by leaders and fellow disciples that they were naturally more suited and able to entertain, cook, and keep homes clean, neat, and attractively decorated. One woman declared during a local women's brunch gathering: "Women are naturally looking for things to do. We're bothered by messes." The majority of ICOC married women were charged with the overseeing and upkeep of the movement's domestic conversion spaces.

DPI's 1995 book, *The Fine Art of Hospitality: Sharing Your Heart and Home with Others*, emphasized the potential for members to evangelize the world through inviting neighbors, friends, and acquaintances into their homes and offering them tempting hospitality, a performance of warm home and mouth-watering food. As Kim Strondak writes:

> You may ask, "How can I make an impact in my neighborhood?" "How can I turn a perfect stranger into my new best friend?" "How can I win souls and be abundantly fruitful?" Your home is one of the most important avenues for evangelism that God has given you. Looking back over the past ten years of being a disciple, I realized that every new friend I've made, every soul I have helped to convert and the ministry I have helped to build have been affected by time around my dinner table. Brunches, luncheons, dinner parties, pizza extravaganzas, campus turkey dinners, chili and "chowda" fests, Sunday BBQs, birthday parties, wine and cheese parties, chocolate parties and jam-making gatherings are some of the fond and fun memories of the hospitable ways I've used my home to win hearts and souls for Jesus. (Jones 1995, 70)

Opening homes and providing hospitality was presented in group formal discourse as an evangelical advantage in a world where strong community and social connection was threatened. Kay McKean writes, "God's kingdom must advance, and we as 20th-century disciples will have a great hand in that advancement as we obey the command to be hospitable. As I read in the Bible of souls being saved through hospitality, I am reminded of so many stories of conversions in recent years that began with the question, 'Would you like to come to my home?' As those in our modern world become more and more isolated from one another, we are exhorted to be different and to open our homes to the lost and to the saved" (Jones 1995, 63). Winning souls for the ICOC Kingdom involved meeting cultural expectations of domestic order.

ICOC prescriptions for female hospitality adhered to twentieth-century rigid ideals of domestic cleanliness: "In order to be encouraging and effective in our hospitality, we must be content in the situations (houses or apartments) God has given us. We must have order and consistency in cleaning and decorating our houses, so we can reflect the nature and beauty of God's character" (Jones 1995, 10). Furthermore, women were encouraged to pursue a Martha Stewart, *Better Homes and Gardens* approach in designing their domestic space. Jeanie Shaw advises: "Does your home reflect the glory of God? Does the creative energy you put into it with color, design, sound, light, plants and fun cause those who enter to feel warm, happy, peaceful and 'at home'? . . . Get ideas from others about decorating your house. Take note of styles you see and like in others' homes, and then imitate them. . . . Use colors that complement each other and group pictures attractively" (Jones 1995, 31–32).

In their creative confrontation with late twentieth-century cultural gender assumptions, members and leaders knew that they could not get away with assigning evangelical domesticity solely to the sisters; they had to include brothers in their prescriptions as well. And so, there was a chapter in the hospitality book entitled "Not for Men Only." The author of the chapter, Ron Brumley, admits that the other twenty-one entries are by women and that women in the church are more likely to be readers of this particular DPI text; still, he advises us to read on.

> The statistics are not in yet, but I imagine that, after perusing the Table of Contents of this book, the majority of readers will be women. Quite honestly, if I hadn't been asked to participate in the writing of it, I probably wouldn't have purchased a copy either. . . . My point is that men often leave "hospitality" up to their wives—the same men who believe in 1 Timothy 3:2 and in Titus 1:8 that says "the overseer must be . . . hospitable.' . . . It is my firm conviction that all male disciples can and need to grow in the gift of serving—of being hospitable as we reach out and influence the fragmented world in which we live. . . . So men, let's read and study and grow in our hospitality. It's definitely a subject *not for women only*. (Jones 1995, 65)

During City COC services, events, and in my formal and informal interviews with members, I heard numerous stories about and compliments of men who contributed to the household labor, cleaning, and cooking. For example, one woman proudly noted that her husband cleaned the bathroom and did the dinner dishes, and one female leader told me how her husband cooked for the family and complimented him on his chicken pot pie. When I spoke with him, he agreed that it was superb and offered to give me a copy of the recipe. Member and leader focus on male involvement in domestic chores is reflective of the rising attention in the evangelical subculture to the participation of men in both housework and parenting (Gallagher 2003, 105–126). Still, in all of their presentations and performances, church husbands, fathers, and brothers were "helping" the women. As in secular culture and the wider evangelical Christian subculture, men are asked to be more involved, but the actual work done is still gendered.

The evangelical domestic duties of muscular sisters were essential to the success of the movement and the organization often stressed this point. Indeed, local City COC congregations had no official buildings (the result of an early edict by McKean and top leaders based on the idea that disciples were the brick and mortar of God's Kingdom, not buildings), and so except for weekly services, which were held in rented hotel conference rooms, other church buildings, or auditoriums, much of the social life of the church took place in members' homes. It was important then for potential converts attending Bible studies and social events to have an impression of "healthy" domestic and family life—the domestic female warrior then was a key to Kingdom success. For a movement that claimed to produce "awesome families," the reflection of this exceptional character in the appearance of domestic homes was important. Sisters in the church seemed to bear the brunt of this evangelical task.

BROTHERS AND SISTERS *FOR* THE KINGDOM

Church sisters struggled to meet nuclear family demands of domesticity, child care, and necessary contributions to household income, and some also felt the added pressures of pursuing long-sought individual professional and occupational goals. Their church family status as sisters *for* the Kingdom of God introduced new, yet familiar contradictions. To be an ICOC disciple was, in many ways, to pursue a demanding career choice—to become a strong and productive evangelist, active in church missionary programs, and maintain their homes as welcoming domestic evangelical spaces. The female members I spent the most time with in the City COC, while not high-profile ICOC women missionary leaders, spoke of themselves as strong, outspoken Kingdom workers who managed to balance work, family, home, and church. They saw their role in the Kingdom as equally important, and witnessing the high demands placed on female evangelists and leaders, never spoke of wanting to become an ICOC public face.

ICOC brothers too seemed to struggle to manage wage work, nuclear family, and church family therapeutic demands with such high evangelical demands and pressures from leadership to be productive warriors for the Kingdom. Many talked of demand in the group to develop muscular, slender bodies, to look the role of healthy and strong church members, fathers, and husbands. Like their church sisters, the demands of ICOC brotherhood and discipleship magnified existing work/family dilemmas and introduced new and powerful tensions between church and family gendered roles and responsibilities. Many found the role of muscular brothers as relentless and demanding; for them, the discursive emphasis on expressivity and relationality offered a much more soothing ground and retreat from leadership pressures on "numbers" (converted).

CHAPTER 7

A Kingdom That Promised Too Much

AT THE START OF THIS ethnography, I asked how we might make sense of the contradictory portraits of the ICOC: an ideal family community alongside a dangerous and destructive one. How do we come to understand why individuals join religious groups that seem a direct affront to deeply held social values? My ethnography of this movement is not exhaustive; no doubt there are relationships and institutional dynamics that I was not allowed to see. However, my work does suggest that the answer to this puzzling ICOC family paradox lies somewhere in the recognition that members and leaders were incredibly of this world. Their attraction to the movement, their attempts to shape better selves and relationships in unsettled lives, were not based in radical departures from cultural belief and practice, but on religious, family, and therapeutic strategies and approaches that already permeated their lives. I have shown here, and others before have suggested, that controversial new religious movements are not so much a break from the norms and cultural expectations of the mainstream as they are attempts to order/make sense of our world (Beckford 1985). They are magnified attempts to use and push beyond dominant cultural boundaries.

The sociological study of radical or controversial religious movements must pay rigorous attention to the complexity and ingenuity of groups' creative use of various cultural beliefs and practices even as it develops an analysis of social control within authoritative systems. Researchers of controversial new religious movements have tended, until recently, to be labeled by one another as "cult apologists" (those more sympathetic to groups) or "cult bashers" (those who are highly critical and negative of controversial groups) (Zablocki and Robbins 2001).

These divisions have resulted in somewhat separate camps that argue over theoretical paradigms and language (such as whether to call these groups "cults," given the pejorative nature of the term, or new religious movements). Benjamin Zablocki and Thomas Robbins (2001, 9) rightly call attention to the need for those studying controversial new religious movements or cults to continue to break down these opposing camps, to maintain ongoing dialogue, and to search for cooperative theoretical engagement. To look for answers to the question of why and how people join radical religious movements by focusing primarily on "deceptive conversion tactics" or "brainwashing" is a dead-end analytical street. People do not make such life-altering commitments to controversial groups because they have been duped or have fallen prey to some sort of mind control. Likewise, not recognizing the effects of tightened social controls in religious groups with high levels of creative cultural engagement could be dangerously limiting. Understanding and developing an analytical middle ground, as Zablocki and Robbins (2001) suggest, is essential. This approach will help us further uncover how culture is actively shaped in and through controversial religious/spiritual movements, and teach us more about how organizations and individuals draw from multiple cultural sources as they confront unsettling experiences. Developing such an analytic approach is essential in a world in which we are threatened by religious groups that violently pursue their political and religious goals. It is with this commitment to exploring a middle ground that I wrote this ethnography.

A sociohistorical analytical approach is critical in these efforts as well. In controversial new religious movements, as in all religious groups, old axes of variation and deeply felt cultural cleavages are still at work, just as new ones are introduced. Crafting clarity from cultural ambiguity is hard individual and organizational work; in comparing historical and contemporary groups' performance efforts, processes of institutional and individual resolution are more easily recognized and understood. I have noted here, for example, the similarities of the ICOC and the Oneida community, as well as muscular Christian approaches in contemporary and early twentieth-century U.S. society. Looking at the YMCA and other such organizations highlights the historically complex and persistent nature of gender and the importance of economic and political conditions in shaping religious goals and institutions.

Over the past twenty years, the discursive debate between the followers of McKean, church leaders, and former members and critics of the movement has been fought in pulpits, publications, and on-line with cultural swords of relationality, individualism, dysfunctionality, sickness, and health, through Christian, family, and medical therapeutic discourse. Most of these frontline performances were of members' empowerment and disempowerment, presented as a war of "good" versus "evil." But when we move beyond the front lines and into the experiences of everyday life, ritual practice, and narrative performance, we begin to see that the ideological boundaries that at first seem so clear are indeed gray, the result of dynamic use of many different cultural beliefs and practices. In the ICOC's sustaining of cultural contradictions, we see vibrant "culture in action" (Swidler 1986, 2001) as members and organizational leaders creatively strive to fashion a strategic approach to intimate relationships.

Vertigo

Experience in the ICOC seemed, for many, to result in a disturbing state of cultural vertigo. The capricious individual course of the ICOC discursive journey, supported by an organizational repertoire with perplexing breadth, was often confusing, lacked cohesion, and brought members to a place where they felt unsure of ideological paths and relationships among disciples. Connell (1995), and later Barbara Risman (1998), use the term "gender vertigo" to represent the results of extreme attempts to challenge normative assumptions of masculinity and femininity, to push beyond—as many transgendered and transsexed individuals and groups do—the notion that there are only two genders. The experience of gender vertigo comes from attempts to change, take apart, and creatively alter taken for granted notions of what people (as gendered individuals) "naturally" do and want, and how they are to interact. A call to bring about gender vertigo by sociologists like Connell and Risman is partly a political venture, an effort to bring about social change. For transgendered and transsexed folks the cause is political as well, grounded for many in a commitment to validate individual choice, lifestyle, and subculture. Pursuing these goals in the production of gender vertigo is a different task from what I observed in the ICOC, but the highly active process of challenging, ignoring, and creatively molding cultural ideals, beliefs, and practices to produce a better social environment is similar.

The ICOC organization and individual members, in crafting what they hoped was a more suitable, rewarding Christian family environment, exercised culture in ambitious ways: their discourse and group practices summoned familiar cultural ambiguity, magnified existing contradictory ideals and practices, and introduced new ideological and practical disconcertments. Even though it may seem as if the ICOC was adhering to "traditional" social positions that accommodated and appropriated contemporary notions of equality, egalitarianism, and therapeutic culture, my ethnographic analysis of group performance and individual narratives demonstrates how they were involved in a much more complex and inventive cultural process.

Drawing high boundaries, rendering the ICOC as an exclusive Christian community, and setting extremely high conversion goals pushed the movement to a high level of cultural creativity. They were involved in a process that, as Risman (1998, 11) suggests about gender vertigo, goes "beyond gender whenever we can, ignoring gendered rules, pushing the envelope until we get dizzy." The ICOC pushed to move beyond cultural boundaries, and many members did indeed feel scattered in the creative organizational production of "awesome family" that upheld and magnified existing cultural contradictions and introduced a number of new and deeply paradoxical beliefs and stances. They felt so scattered, in fact, that they had to retreat to familiar cultural ground. It is ironic that a search for clarity in intimate relationships was a major impetus for many joining the movement, and that a search for clarity in intimate relationships was a driving force for many in abandoning McKean's vision.

Familiar, Magnified, and Added Cultural Cleavage

To be a member of the ICOC was to live with a constant affront to U.S. values that support a respect of religious pluralism and acceptance of difference. City COC members never directly said that they were saved and all others who called themselves Christians were not. Some, in fact, were clear about not wanting to "judge" others and cited the Golden Rule defense, "Do unto others as you would have them do unto you," as legitimation for not offering judgment. Their frequent citation of the Golden Rule reflects a heavy contemporary mainstream religious investment in Golden Rule theology (Ammerman 1997, 368). Frequent return to this rule is understandable given its reflection of relationality—the idea that we are to listen and take seriously the ideas, concerns, and beliefs of others just as we would assume that they should do for us. Most members, however, did not directly challenge the official institutional position: to be a Christian meant to be involved in discipling relationships, and the ICOC was the only contemporary Christian community that had gotten discipleship right. One official movement legitimation for exclusivity was repeated often: if you were a true Christian who, in your heart, wanted to follow discipleship as Jesus had commanded, why then would you not join the ICOC community? Clearly, some did not know of God's ICOC "modern-day movement"; they were, of course, to be the target of strong national and international missionary zeal. But if you were a member of another Christian congregation (most of which were talked about as "dying" and lacking true discipleship) and heard the ICOC's message, why would you not want to be a part of God's modern-day Kingdom when introduced to the truth through the First Principles study?

For some, this self-identification with an exclusive movement while valuing religious diversity was not a new dilemma, but a magnification of previous membership in conservative religious denominations that implicitly claimed to have the right religious worldview while tolerating religious pluralism. These institutions (here I am speaking of the more fundamentalist wings of various U.S. religious denominations) may show rhetorical respect for other religious views, while insisting that their moral community is *the way* God intended individuals to live and worship. Living with the paradox of religious exclusivity in a nation that is called to respect diversity and religious difference is a long-standing, familiar social cleavage. Freedom of religion and freedom from religion has always been a precarious balance. Historically, respecting religious diversity and freedom of religion has existed alongside the elevation of particular religious worldviews. Many of our major cultural institutions including medicine, education, and sports, as well as our dominant workplace culture, were shaped by a white Protestant ethos. For ICOC members then, pledging commitment to a social group that claimed ultimate truth in a society where respect of religious difference and diversity was highly valued was not new—it was not necessarily a strange and out of the ordinary religious position, but rather a comfortable paradoxical stance.

As demonstrated throughout this ethnography, ICOC's gender discourse was full of familiar essentialist gender notions that supported traditionalist gender roles in marriage and family alongside contemporary ideals of egalitarian marriage and gender equity. Members and leaders stressed the muscular and relational character of Christian women. They stressed female power and ability in public endeavors and careers in a culture that continues to associate domesticity with women. A strong therapeutic ethos pushed constant rhetorical return to egalitarianism and gender equity. All women and men in our culture are swimming along, challenging at particular points in our lives established ideals about gender and embracing normative notions at other times. Like it or not, we must confront and answer these social forces as we shape ourselves and our most intimate relationships. And, inevitably, much of our performance of "doing gender" (West and Zimmerman 1987) varies according to social status, the particular audience, and our political and individual goals at the moment. Laura and Alicia were able to describe themselves as being "led" by their husbands through asserting their own will because they had group status and inside organizational knowledge. "Baby Christians" did not emerge as such savvy users of the discipling system. City COC women and men, in their storytelling and daily interactions, seemed to move back and forth along a gender course where their exact positions were determined by personal circumstance, social environment, and audience. As discussed in chapter 6, ICOC's creative use of existing gender beliefs and practices added its own level of contradiction: prescriptions of muscular Christian womanhood that magnified the role of both public church worker and domestic evangelist. In many ways, women in the ICOC experienced an extreme form of postfeminism: like Phyllis Schlafly and Beverly LaHaye (voices from the New Right's Concerned Women for America), they preached domesticity, but much of their lives was centered around a public evangelical Christian mission that supported feminist principles.

City COC members and other ICOC former members across the country, as they left the unified movement, voiced a need to return to less intensified gender contradictions. Many talked of the ICOC as moving women too far away from traditional notions of female domesticity by aggressively pushing evangelical and therapeutic church responsibilities. Bartkowski (2004, 65–66) argues, regarding the downfall of the PK movement: the "loose mélange of gender discourses is likely one reason for the Promise Keepers' quick rise to prominence during the 1990s. Given the diversity and flexibility of these gender ideologies, PK was able to appeal to men with a wide variety of gender sensibilities. However, flexible ties are not those that bind . . . the ideological diffuseness of the Promise Keepers probably contributed to the movement's equally fast decline." The sustaining of various gender positions in the ICOC organizational discourse repertoire may have attracted more folks to the movement, but clearly the resulting confusion from prescribing such varied positions with great intensity and evangelical purpose contributed somewhat to the downfall of the unified movement.

Marriage disciplers appeared in group and individual narratives as attractive ideological specialists in their efforts to sift through confusing gender beliefs and practices. Ultimately, however, marriage disciplers presented members with yet another level of cultural tension. Much of the marriage advice and prescriptions described in narratives of marriage discipling efforts in sermons, individual interviews, DPI literature, and KNN productions mirrored secular and other evangelical Christian approaches to healing marriage. In particular, they supported what members understood as a legitimate ambiguous marriage position: spouses were individual selves with rights and responsibilities regarding their own health and happiness, and spouses were supposed to be deeply dependent on one another. This contradiction was a familiar one, supported by divorce and therapeutic culture, as well as major conservative religious ideologies. But the contradictory stance was magnified in the ICOC: you were an individual responsible for your own happiness and "healthy" marriage relationships, but you were also joined in great intimacy with the discipling community, in particular, with your marriage disciplers. The four of you worked together to ensure a satisfying marriage; you had responsibilities and reciprocal ties to one another that secured a family-like bond. When you gave up on a marriage, or were having a difficult time resolving spousal issues, you were seen as abandoning God, your spouse, and those brothers and sisters in the Kingdom who had invested much time and effort in your relationship. Jeremy appropriately described this level of therapeutic involvement when he told me: "We are really in each other's marriages." Former members complained that such intense involvement of a third party in marriage relationships took focus away from the primacy of the marriage relationship.

Such high-level bonds and involvement of disciplers extended to members' relationships with their children as well. The movement appropriated evangelical discourse on child rearing, especially in painting a grim picture of threats to children in the secular world. This story of the world as a dangerous place for kids and teens was familiar. Like Dobson and other evangelical spokespeople, they promoted giving parents more authority, teaching parents to raise obedient children, giving them permission to use corporeal punishment to do so, and relieving the pressure to appeal to medical therapeutic experts. Yet, even as they tried to return power to parents, they introduced a new and even more intrusive moral authority—the discipling system. Group members were autonomous parents, but officially, they were asked to appeal to their disciplers regularly regarding child rearing. If they were confused about a particular interaction or issue with their children, they were to turn to their disciplers right away. When children entered the preteen and teen years, parental authority and responsibility seemed to further diminish as teens found peers and counselors in the preteen and teen ministry programs. Through marriage and child-rearing experiences in the ICOC, we see how members were resocialized to a familiar, yet intensified, contradictory cultural position as free individuals dependent on institutional authority.

Our position as individuals dependent on social institutions has been given a great deal of sociological thought. Classical theorists like Durkheim, Marx, and Weber all puzzled over the pull of social forces and the role of the individual. Contemporary social theorists wrestle with these questions as well. In the United States, individualism is a strong and pervasive belief and social value. Yet many institutional arrangements structure, guide, and limit our individual actions, choices, and life goals. We are responsible for maintaining our own "health and wellness," yet are dependent on the methods and moral diagnoses of medical and therapeutic professionals to do so. We are workers capable of pulling ourselves up, moving up the social ladder, yet we are dependent on government, corporations, and other institutional structures to do so. We are dependent on our families of origin, and yet expected to earn our own way in life, making something of ourselves and becoming independent workers. ICOC members were on familiar ground then when the movement demanded they be responsible for their own actions, self-motivated, successful in family and evangelical endeavors, and at the same time pledge submission to disciplers and leaders who were to guide them and have authority in major life decisions and relationships. The dual position of being independent selves responsible for their own success and satisfaction, as well as dependent on institutional support systems to fulfill their needs, was deepened and made explicit in the ICOC movement.

The pull between individual responsibility and dependence on institutional structure is a contradiction that varies in intensity in spiritual and religio-therapeutic groups. Irvine (1999) notes in her study of self-help groups for "codependents" that individuals join as "victims" of family "dysfunction," of "codependent" relationships, and are determined to learn to spend more time on themselves and do what they need to do as individuals. Yet the irony, as suggested in the title of her book, *Codependent Forevermore*, is that this journey of selfhood takes place through dependence on others. Many self-help groups, of course, like "codependent" self-help groups, downplay group dependence and authority and do not engage in high levels of social control. We tend not to see a great deal of *explicit* authority and control in healing/spirituality groups because of our strong cultural promotion of self and individual therapeutic journey. On the other hand, groups like the ICOC and, for example, in the late twentieth century in Manhattan, the Sullivan Institute, a "psychotherapeutic community," or "quasi-religion," as Amy Siskind (1994) names it, push to incorporate high levels of authority and control with therapeutic beliefs and practices. The ICOC therapeutic structure bore strong resemblance to the Sullivan Institute, where "patients/members were under constant surveillance by other members and by their own therapists, who were obligated to report dissidents to the leadership" (Siskind 1994, 51) The Sullivan Institute faded in the 1980s after media attention around a custody case and the exit of high-ranking therapists/leaders in the group. The ICOC faded in 2004, after much ex-member, media, and therapeutic and religious "expert" criticism, the resignation of Kip McKean and other leaders, and on-line distribution of deep and passionate criticisms from leaders and members throughout the Kingdom.

There is an important lesson to take away from this ethnography and the rich body of literature that sociologists of religion have produced on the contemporary religious/spiritual marketplace: a little bit of authority with individuality works, we live it every day, it is part of our institutional and therapeutic culture, but at the end of the day a dominant cultural emphasis on individualism reinforces that we should feel as if we are in control of our own lives. In fact, the therapeutic edict of the importance of individual selves on journeys of improving self and relationship dictates that individuals must control the wheel. They can take direction from others, but in the end, the individual must at least *feel* and be able to *describe themselves* as in charge of their most important life decisions and relationships. The ICOC movement (and groups like the Sullivan Institute), through its mandatory and authoritative counseling structure, upset this delicate balance too much. Even a most personal, individual level of spiritual and religious experience of the divine, of having "Jesus" in their "hearts," was too often interrupted by authoritative ICOC discipling interventions; disciplers often acted as mediators who would bring you to Jesus, and who would tell you whether or not God was in your heart. Such constant interference with the individual's relationship with God was disconcerting. On the issue of individualism versus dependence, the ICOC pushed disciples to a place of cultural vertigo—resulting in many members feeling scattered, unsure of themselves, their relationships in group, and their relationships with God. In the first years of the twenty-first century, most members were ready to return to more familiar, if ambiguous, cultural terrain.

Another very deeply felt contradiction was the pull they felt between church community and nuclear family/family of origin. Here again, some of the tensions were familiar, but in the ICOC, the responsibility one sustained to one's own nuclear family and family of origin was constantly in tension with church family goals and responsibilities. It was clear, in the formal discourse of the ICOC movement, that "God's family" should be your number one concern. It was also clear that your nuclear family should be a number one concern. Many could only sustain these split allegiances for so long. They were already torn in several directions with wage work, child care responsibilities, domestic duties, and family of origin caretaking—even though they received some assistance from the discipling community network, their church therapeutic and evangelical chores were often consuming. The maintenance of two competing prime kin networks was almost impossible to sustain in the context of other responsibilities like wage work and evangelical duties.

ORGANIZATIONAL DISSOLUTION

Eileen Barker (1992), in her lecture "Behold the New Jerusalems! Catch 22s in the Kingdom-Building Endeavors of New Religious Movements," argues that "the plain truth is that new religious movements do not have a particularly impressive track record when it comes to restructuring society." By this she means not that new religious movements (NRMs) have had no effect on society. "Christianity and Islam, were, after all, NRMs in their time," but that NRMs have not been especially successful when it comes to maintaining the often radical grounding social visions of their charismatic leaders. New religious movements often fade away, or become more mainstream in the religious/spiritual marketplace. As Berger (1967) noted, to survive, radical sects in a modern setting either lose their controversial status and come to resemble one another more and more in bureaucratic structure and theological intent, or come to huddle together under "sacred canopies." McKean's radical vision of discipling, in its attempt to balance to such a high degree of authoritative and submissive demands with egalitarian/therapeutic principles, has followed in the footsteps of other "radical" new religious movements that ultimately retreated or became more like the dominant religious culture. In the Oneida community in the late nineteenth century, John Humphrey Noyes attempted to promote individual expression of sexuality, Christian socialism, and group marriage ideals through a highly monitored, authoritative group structure. Too much dissent from mainstream views combined with introduction of heightened cultural contradiction was not a viable institutional approach. Oneida members eventually returned to romantic love and more mainstream religious structure and approaches to intimate relationships. Most members of the ICOC movement, as the unified movement fell apart, returned to a more mainstream balancing of family, religious community, and therapeutic intervention. Only McKean and a small group of followers, huddled together under a sacred canopy in Portland, Oregon, tried to revive McKean's "radical" vision of Christian discipleship.

The City COC congregation, over the years (1995–2000) during which I conducted field studies, did not seem to grow, appearing to maintain instead a core group that made up at least half or more of its membership. Again, these are my visual estimations; my request to survey the congregation was denied by local leadership. Accurate membership numbers for the unified movement were almost impossible to obtain; numbers were produced solely by the church and often calculated through weekly attendance at services (which would include guests). The unified international movement did have a high dropout rate—ex-members and critics claimed 50 percent of new members left the movement each year, which would, in the first few years of the twenty-first century, suggest that there were a large number of former members. Some former members have admitted to doctoring numbers because of leadership pressure to baptize and see congregations grow. I would suggest then that the majority of ICOC growth appears to have taken place primarily in the years prior to 1996–1998, not long after core leaders signed the Evangelization Proclamation in 1994 (see chapter 1). But for thousands of individuals, being an active part of the discipling community made sense for a number of years. How did the movement keep commitment and belief in discipling alive and sacred for these individuals? What forces led to the unified movement's crumbling at century's end?

Individual narratives, formal group discourse, and powerful collective rituals legitimated the discipling structure and cast the ICOC movement as truly sacred, as "awesome." Heightened group contradictions and ambiguity were rendered meaningful through stories and language that *legitimated* the feeling of being pulled in one direction and then the other—being ultimately responsible for one's children and at the same time the success of the ICOC movement. Institutions have long been adept at legitimating contradictions through storytelling (Berger and Luckmann 1966). In ICOC stories and performances, disciplers were cultural guides, helping members sift through various ideals and approaches and performing heroic relational interventions creatively composed from contradictory approaches. Most important, individual stories and group narrative employed a great deal of discursive movement, shifting back and forth from one belief to another: stressing at one moment discipline and authority and at the next relationality; arguing at one moment that women were naturally domestic and the next that they belonged in front of the congregation, in coffee shops, and on streets evangelizing for the Kingdom; arguing one moment that men were to lead families and sexual encounters, and the next that men needed to recognize and give in to their wives' needs; demanding at one moment that disciples were first and foremost responsible for the growth of the Kingdom of God and at the next that their nuclear families were most important. This dynamic discursive dance was idiosyncratic as well—the only constant step was toward ideals, habits, and practices that emulated relationality and therapeutic ethos as they tried to embrace authoritative social control. This well-performed dance was a major source of legitimation for these intense contradictions—*its choreography made the ICOC seem whole and morally sound.* It also provided a repertoire for a multitude of situations; for example, if it was in the interest of an ICOC woman, at one particular moment, to present herself as submissive to male leadership in family and church, she had the language and script to do so. If she wanted to present herself as a strong evangelical missionary, she had the language and script to do so. If she wanted to present herself as "doing motherhood," she had the language and script to do so.

The movement's dynamic discursive performance was made exceptionally potent through contemporary media venues, mechanisms that made multiple and contradictory approaches and ideals seem natural and purposeful. The ICOC movement, like many other religious institutions today, used the power of film, music, creative arts, and printed publications to sustain and sacralize group beliefs. My findings here stress the importance of media today in religious practice and institutional health. Film, music, publications, and on-line religion are becoming the blood and heartbeat of religion—many religious organizations now depend on these venues to successfully bring alive religious symbol and belief. Religious institutions today, after all, operate in a culture that is saturated by these forms (Brasher 2001; Martín-Barbero 1997; Wuthnow 2003). KNN films like *Secrets of the Heart* and *The Prodigal Daughter*, ICOC's rock band, the Radicals, and their music video, theatrical and comedic scripts, modern dance performed during weekly services and special events, and DPI's long list of ICOC self-help and relationship manuals were powerful ritual media mechanisms. These mechanisms made a significant contribution to the ability of group narrative and sacred symbol to resonate through collective effervescence.

Sociologists of religion should pay greater attention in the future to the interconnectedness of media, various creative expressive venues, and religious/spiritual life. Wuthnow (2003, xiv) notes that there has been "surprisingly little attention" given "to the role of imagination and the arts in Americans' spirituality. Standard treatments of religion and the arts have focused on famous paintings in fine galleries, church architecture, and belles lettres. They fail to tell us how people experience the arts in congregations and communities in everyday life." As Martín-Barbero (1997) suggests, the electronic church, religious films, and other media venues are part of an engaging process of the reenchantment of the contemporary global community. Media, in its broad sense incorporating print, video, music, and web, is an inescapable and powerful contemporary tool of bringing the sacred into everyday religious life.

There was another very important factor that contributed to the ability of the movement to grow and sustain membership in the midst of cultural vertigo: many members developed very real and meaningful social kinship networks during their tenure with the church. If they left the movement, they would most likely, to a large degree, be cut off from those disciples whom they had come to love and care for, and to whom they had entrusted their most intimate relationships. Once a member had developed strong family bonds in the church, he or she seemed less likely to give it up. While there are certainly those individuals who were glad to be rid of church family relationships that were not satisfying and that they described as abusive, many ex-members confirmed that severing these ties was the hardest part of the process of leaving the ICOC. Many former ICOC congregations today still hold strong to the brothers and sisters they made during their tenure in the unified movement.

Another force keeping members within the movement was the successful group process of boundary making. Powerful individual narratives and group performances of tightly knit, intimate social networks succeeded in setting boundaries that deemed those inside the Kingdom as saved and those outside as not saved. Some expressed a deep fear of "going to hell" and eternal damnation as impetus for staying in the group. Many were truly fearful that if they left the movement, they would have to leave God behind.

Despite all of these institutional forces and mechanisms for sustaining membership and keeping cultural confusion at bay, members could only tell the story as long as it made sense: narratives of self and organization have to resonate in some way with real-life experience. To use again Kai Erikson's (1976) classic and exemplary cultural analysis of Buffalo Creek, the West Virginia community ravaged by flood in 1972: the people could only sustain the balance of independence and reliance on the Coal Company so long as they found validation for the contradiction in their everyday lives—when the company betrayed them and the floodwaters raced down filled with black coal, killing over one hundred members of their community and leaving thousands homeless, their orientation as both independent and dependent successful beings fell apart. The ICOC did not kill, but members did come to see the movement as betraying them in many ways. There came a point, as the century turned, when many disciples stopped and realized that they were in a Kingdom that promised and demanded too much. They became seriously dizzy, and felt scattered in trying to balance and negotiate ambiguous cultural tools of right relationship, self-development, gender, parenthood, marriage, and the time-consuming evangelical and therapeutic demands of discipling at every turn.

There is a lesson to be learned in the efforts of organizations to produce a structural panacea (like discipling) for intimate relationships at the turn of the twenty-first century. Religio-therapeutic movements that attempt to embody multiple contemporary understandings of family, gender, and therapeutic relationships may initially attract a wide range of individuals and see growth. Although they might work for a while, eventually the vertigo is likely to take over. One can only pursue this precarious cultural course for so long; cultural cohesiveness will likely unravel, and no amount of ritual legitimation can repair when options are available in a pluralistic society where religious, spiritual, and secular approaches for developing community, faith, family, and health and wellness abound. Sustaining high levels of cultural contradiction then, like charismatic authority, is necessarily precarious.[1] As the dizzying effect took hold in the ICOC, there were other organizational qualities that contributed to its rapid dissolution: the extreme movement emphasis on "numbers" and evangelizing from top leadership became more apparent and seemingly destructive to individuals, families, and local congregations; their founder and charismatic leader faltered; and local leaders and evangelists began to powerfully speak out and name church abuses.

The fall of the ICOC unified movement was no doubt influenced by the unyielding efforts of critics to label the group as a "dysfunctional church" and a "dangerous cult." Barker (1993, 340) suggests that external obstacles play some role in the success of NRMs: "Throughout history, new religions, especially those that aspire to restructure society, have typically been viewed with the deepest suspicion by the rest of society . . . from sensationalist and inaccurate stories in the media and virulent attacks and lobbying from anticult groups, to forcible hospitalization and illegal deprogramming; from refusal to grant peddlers' licenses or permission to hold meetings in church halls, to litigation resulting in financially crippling judgements" (340). The ICOC was a constant target of organized critics; ex-members came to develop their own websites and support groups, producing an anti-cult culture of its own. However, the ICOC movement was strongest at a time when the Cult Awareness Network and anti-cult organizations were faltering somewhat in social influence. The "brainwashing/cult" paradigm and the use of "deprogrammers" had been questioned and delegitimated through court cases and therapeutic "experts." The mid- to late 1990s was, after all, a time when, through bankruptcy purchase, a member of one accused "cult," Scientology, was able to purchase and now controls the Cult Awareness Network name and on-line activity (www.cultawarenessnetwork.org). ICOC leaders and members then had a powerful social backdrop to successfully enact a form of "tertiary deviance" with ready-made discourse from an *anti-anti-cult movement.* "Tertiary deviance," a process named by John I. Kitsuse (1980), represents the efforts of those openly labeled "deviants" to reject these labels and attempt to win acceptance based on their own actions as morally sound. Outside negative labels of family "dysfunction" were most definitely a challenge for the organization, but as I've illustrated throughout this ethnography, they were also used as fuel to legitimate discipling on moral grounds. The downfall of the unified movement must be attributed more to in-group dynamics and structural and ideological obstacles rather than to outside labeling and legal pressure.

Media, print, video, film, and websites, as I've noted, are powerful contemporary mechanisms that are capable of bringing the sacred into everyday religious life. They are also capable of turning the sacred negative, of circulating, with incredible efficiency, dissenting ideas and convincingly composed condemning manifestos. In 2002, the prolific DPI writer and charismatic ICOC preacher, Gordon Ferguson, authored a book with another leader, Wyndham Shaw. This book, *Golden Rule Leadership*, is described on the current DPI web page as "a book on leading others the way you would want to be led. The word is getting out on this book as it challenges leadership paradigms and calls us to build a spirit of team and family in the body of Christ."[2] This book brought criticism from those who adhered strictly to McKean's vision of discipleship and articulated many of the concerns that leaders and members had regarding authoritative "one-over-one" discipling practices.

As I listened on-line and informally interviewed several members as the unified movement fell apart, I heard an often repeated question: "Have you read the Kriete letter?" On February 2, 2003, Henry Kriete, from the London ICOC church, posted a final version of his "open letter" to the "elders, teachers, and evangelists" in the ICOC "fellowship of churches" entitled "Honest to God: Revolution through Repentance and Freedom in Christ" (www.reveal.org). Kriete posted his letter (covered in detail below) at a time when many members and leaders were questioning the authoritative aspects of discipling and the claim that the ICOC was the one true church (OTC) doctrine. McKean and several other leaders had posted resignation letters, and the organization had held a "unity conference" in Los Angeles in November of 2002 to try to address in-group criticisms and bring top evangelists back to common ground. The ICOC movement, from the top to the bottom, was ripe and ready for dissension; Kriete's letter circulated on-line, read by many members and leaders with eager and open "hearts."

Henry Kriete and his wife, Marilyn, were powerful leaders in the ICOC. In his own description of their service to the movement he writes: "We first visited Boston in 1981, and moved there in the Spring of 1982. . . . I have been discipled by all these men: Bob Gempel, Kip McKean, Al Baird, Jim Blough . . . and others. . . . Before moving to London (our second time), we served in the American Commonwealth Region . . . from 1994 till 2001. In various capacities, Marilyn and I have lived and served on four continents, in six countries, two world sectors, ten churches and about 15 different ministries." In his introduction he voices damning revelations about the movement: "Much grace and power has been lavished on all of us by God. . . . However, at this moment in our brief history, I have never been more alarmed, even ashamed of what we have become. . . . Our movement is no longer moving . . . the things we boasted in: our numerical growth, our retention rate, our member to fall away ratio, the faithfulness of our children . . . our unity." Before he begins with his indictment of the "four systematic evils" of the movement, he asks that the "brothers and sisters" in the Kingdom who read his letter will also recognize that several leaders who have resigned in the past have also offered "sincere and conscientious" criticisms.

Kriete captures the feeling of unrest and questioning that permeated the movement in its final years. Under a section entitled "God Says 'Enough' " he writes, "A backlash from years of 'not listening,' insensitivity, abuse, coercion and legalism—as well as cowardice from the full-time ministry leaders to stand up for the truth—is now underway. . . . [H]earts are still breaking, and hearts are being crushed. . . . [I]n spite of all of this, the Christians are feeling liberated, emancipated even." What exactly are they freed from? Reviving the words of national heroes to legitimate his claims, just as McKean had done in his early "Revolution through Restoration" manifestos, Kriete argues: "In London, the upheaval is against systemic evils that have gone unchallenged for too long. Resistance, if not rebellion, is always the fruit of conformity. . . . As JFK once said, 'If you make peaceful revolution impossible, you make violent revolution inevitable.' Please pray for a peaceful revolution." Kriete sets the stage for revolution through sinful repentance as he names the exodus of many ICOC leaders: "Hundreds of leaders, if not thousands, including myself," have been "trapped in . . . systemic evils . . . that is the stubborn reality and nature of our hierarchy. As you will see, many of the issues I am going to raise in this paper are endemic to our 'culture' as a movement—the corruption of power, selfish ambition, the continuing climate of fear and cowardice, the bravado and rank duplicity from our 'top leaders.' Why I am so ashamed and saddened is that I have been as much to blame as anyone. But really, whether more or less is beside the point, because almost all of us are guilty to some extent." The ICOC movement "system" he argues, made the leaders into Pharisees (that group of high-status Jews portrayed in the gospels as hypocrites and legalists who were not able to hear Jesus' message): "We have become proud and blind, just like the Pharisees. And being blind without knowing it is the most frightening kind of blindness of all. This paper is an attempt to open our eyes before it is too late. My goal is not only to break our heart, but in a sense, to slap us in the face as well." Kriete then forcefully lays out the "Four Systemic Evils" as follows:

- our corrupted hierarchy
- our obsession with numbers
- our shameful arrogance (the cause of/by-product of 1 and 2)
- our seduction by money

Evil number one speaks to the high level of authority, dependence, and social control in the movement: "We have become a religious hierarchy that has created, fostered, and sustained a culture of control and dependence on men, rather than freedom." He justifies his usage of the phrase "culture of control": "Consider the facts: we are a hierarchy, and have been led by one man at the top. We have had a 'founder,' complete with personal and 'kingdom-wide' authority that we were expected to respect and follow. We have had World Sector leaders and Geographic Sector Leaders—to consolidate the grip of power and establish a global network of control over every last congregation . . . local church autonomy is practically viewed as heresy." He also accuses some administrators of using "smoke and mirrors" in church accounting and some "wholesale financial mismanagement" due to pressures from top church officials. This control, Kriete makes clear, has led to routine violation of Christians' freedom in religious experience: we "have fostered in them an unhealthy dependence, rather than freedom to grow and mature." Kriete's message fervently addresses the dizzying effect of the movement's contradiction of promoting individual freedom even as they encouraged dependence and much submission to church authority. When members still loyal to the ICOC movement read systematic evil number one, they heard a familiar dilemma and justification of doubts they may have had regarding loss of their individual choice and will.

Systematic evil number two, "our obsession with numbers," also legitimated many of the concerns and frustrations of members. Kriete is harsh in his charge: "Many of our leaders have become so obsessive about 'the numbers' it has retarded them spiritually, made them neurotic, or even idolatrous." He talks of "dishonesty" in reporting statistics, "fudging" and "inflating" attendance, or not "accurately" doing the " 'month end' because 'we have to grow this month' or 'there is no way we are going negative.' "

In Kriete's voicing of systematic evil number three, "our shameful arrogance," members heard a welcome questioning of the one true church (OTC) doctrine. Letting go of this church tenet would enable them to embrace other Christians as "saved." Suddenly, mothers and fathers that members had not been able to convert, perhaps those who, under the OTC doctrine, were damned to hell in Catholic parishes and Presbyterian pews, were actually eligible for salvation and everlasting life. Members could abandon their condemnation of family of origin and their ongoing sense of responsibility to convert their biological/family of origin members.

Kriete's systematic evil number four charged that ICOC clergy took the hard-earned money given by members to "advance the Kingdom," and used it in ways that were inappropriate. The movement had argued that lead evangelists needed higher salaries, a nice house, and health benefits so that they could concentrate on "building the Kingdom." Kriete rejects this as an excuse for granting those high up in leadership with better houses. He charges that leaders, when speaking at local events, would stay in fancy hotels and "presidential suites": "As the 'clergy,' we have allowed for incredible retreats and pet projects: we have had harbor retreats, mountain retreats, castle and Hawaiian retreats, deep-sea fishing expeditions, five star hotels, presidential suites and the like." Kriete's charges are somewhat validated by my observations; for example, during one Marriage Enrichment Day, which took place at a high-end hotel downtown, Kay and Randy McKean said that they were not able to use their fancy suite for the night as they had to get back home to the children. They had a drawing so that another ICOC couple could use the nice room. Furthermore, when one new lead evangelical couple moved to town, they purchased a house where property values were high. Kriete argues, "We have demanded extraordinary monetary sacrifice from our members, but comparatively, it appears we have demanded so little from ourselves." No doubt this indictment rang true to many members who, over the years, had watched some leaders receive special treatment and funding.

Kriete concludes with several points that also legitimated the dizzying effects of ICOC's cultural engagement. With respect to gender, he charges that the movement led to a loss of manhood and womanhood. "So many thousands of men have been effectively emasculated by legalism and compliance to authoritarian leadership," Kriete writes. "The squelching of personal dreams, inner feelings and convictions has had a demoralizing effect across the board. More than several men have lost their manhood." His charge: the demand that men submit unquestionably to church leadership "emasculated" them. For the other gender, Kriete argues that too much power and evangelical duty for women in the ICOC leadership made women overburdened and "conflicted." This strain placed on women resembled, in Kriete's assessment, that of the "western model of the 'total woman' ": "Unfortunately, our western model of the 'total woman' has by and large been forced upon almost all of our women in the full time ministry." Echoing a familiar evangelical antifeminist justification for male church headship, Kriete continues, "We have elevated our partnership with women in the gospel to the role of co-evangelist in many respects, and I am afraid this model has crushed several of them." This articulation of the loss of manhood and rise of feminist model in the church no doubt spoke to members' experience of the heightened gender contradictions. Members and leaders, men and women, were called to an evangelical mission that took away focus from their own families, further complicating and magnifying gender expectations. Kriete's letter named and framed this very real ICOC dilemma.

Kriete's letter also validated members' frustration with the overtaxed therapeutic discipling system. Congregations nationwide seemed to experience the dilemma I observed in the City COC: members sometimes talked about others in the community as a drain to the therapeutic efforts of members and leaders. Members and leaders described these individuals as having "serious" mental health issues. Even though they referred one of these individuals to a professional health care worker, the individual still came to depend on her church sisters in an excessive way—calling all the time and with any "little" problem. There is evidence in formal movement discourse that this was a movement-wide problem. For example, Sam Laing announced during one regional event: "If you are continually having to be helped by disciplers . . . beat up on and discipled and saved out of misery, you are not dealing with your own life. . . . By this time you should be saving other people. By this time some of you should be a Bible talk leader or something." I heard local and national ICOC leaders preach of overtaxing the therapeutic structure several times over my years of fieldwork.

The ICOC's lack of formal training for disciplers as religio-therapeutic experts was another structural condition that likely contributed to this system flaw. They promised a community full of excellent counselors, but had no real system in place to adequately train or monitor one-on-one, two-on-two, or D-group discipling sessions. This left much room for abuse and less than productive therapeutic efforts. With such lofty religio-therapeutic promises and no official training program, it appears that the movement was further weakened when members (whether "officially" diagnosed with a psychiatric disorder or not) continually needed intensive therapeutic treatment.

Certainly not all members agreed with Kriete or read his letter. One former member told me that she intended not to read the letter and would make her own assessment. The important organizational point here is that the "Kingdom" was in large part ready for some explanation of the confusion and disappointment they had experienced in the discipling community. The on-line distribution of Kriete's manifesto contributed to the hurried downfall of the unified movement in 2003–2004. The movement had seen dissension before; for example, in February of 1994, the Indianapolis COC left the ICOC due to leadership disagreement with core ICOC principles, and stories and criticisms about the split circulated on member and former member websites. Leaders' resignation letters and on-line statements before Kriete's played some role in ripening the organization for change—for example, Sarah and Rick Bauer in 1992 and 1993 and David Medrano and Natercia Alves in March of 2000 as they left the Madrid, Spain, COC (reveal.org). Well-articulated and heartfelt letters after Kriete's helped legitimate the decisions of those who were exiting. For example, Patricia and John Engler's resignation statement, May 28, 2004 (http://www.barnabasministry.com/iccresignationp.html), offered an account of their leadership experiences and the "blessings" and problems encountered in the Denver ICOC congregation. Throughout the dissolution of the movement, the Delphi ICOC discussion forum provided active on-line discussion for members and former members. On the ground, members gathered in local congregations for heated and sometimes contentious debate and discussion of past abuses and sins of leadership and the discipling system. Two members told me that they purposely avoided participating in the on-line ICOC-related websites. Nevertheless, clearly these on-line discussions and postings played a major part in the dissolution of the movement.

"A LOOSE BROTHERHOOD"

As I write in the fall of 2004, the unified movement of the ICOC has dissolved; it is difficult to paint an accurate portrait of all its constituent congregations. Kip McKean is in Portland, Oregon, and has founded the Portland International Church of Christ. In 2003, he posted a letter on the ICOC Delphi forum discussion group and Portland church website titled, "Revolution through Restoration III." In this document, which recounts again the birth of the movement and the thirty would-be disciples in the living room in Lexington, Massachusetts, in 1979, he repeats much of the history of the church, stressing numbers and purpose. At places, he adds recent commentary to old texts; for example, at one point he argues that he never supported the one true church (OTC) doctrine, that there are quite possibly other Christians out there who practice discipleship as they should and are saved. He admits again, as he did in his resignation letter and at the 2002 Unity Conference, that he made mistakes in leadership and family, that he was sometimes "cruel" and "humiliating." He talks of his child who, in 2001, struggled spiritually and "fell away" from the church, admitting his young idealism when it came to predicting salvation for Kingdom children: "An older brother and past mentor who has faced similar challenges in raising children recently pointed out to me that I and many people in the movement had taught [about child rearing] . . . incorrectly. We had simply said, 'Train a child in the way he should go and . . . he will not turn from it.' As idealistic young evangelists leading an idealist young movement, we foolishly concluded that all of our children would become disciples, never struggle or fall away."

For the most part, McKean's presentation reads unchanged; he is still balancing much authority in one-over-one discipling with individual choice and will, stressing relationality along the way. He defends the need for a "system," referring indirectly to Kriete's letter and, taking care to define terms, argues that "autonomous" churches and "democratic" church bodies are not desirable. McKean attempts to revive his charismatic authority by presenting himself as having had some sort of divine message and rebirth while on a beach sabbatical. Toward the end of his letter he writes, "In the midst of these troubled times, I still have the dream. I still believe in Jesus' dream to evangelize the world in our generation." In this letter and in more recent postings on the Portland website, McKean presents himself and the movement as revived and recovering from the downfall. As throughout the life of the movement, McKean rarely, if ever, provides hard membership numbers. Portland hosted a "Jubilee" conference in the summer of 2004 where McKean and others preached of reviving the Kingdom, being "radical," and not listening to all that on-line "spiritual pornography" (www.portlandchurch.org). The likelihood of his efforts actually creating a strong new (or reborn) religious movement is doubtful; as I write now, few former churches seem willing to have McKean as a leader.

Trying to make sense of the dissolution and rebuilding is a confusing task. Chris Lee, a former member, posted an ambitious attempt to do so on the REVEAL website in February of 2004. He writes, "How does one capture 'history' as it is making progress? It is a difficult task at best, somewhat akin to shooting a moving target?"—especially, as he notes, when the movement no longer produces publications and "gets more fragmented." In his attempt, he outlines what he sees as three "emerging factions":

1. A reformist group that has taken heed to Henry Kriete and others, who are actively trying to make things better and change. They recognize a number of problems. Some have broken away from the ICC (Salt Lake City) or are making progress toward unity with Mainline Churches of Christ (Tallahassee, Florida). Others have reconciled with "enemies" or ex-members or strived to improve in areas of abuses (Chicago, Atlanta, Triangle).
2. There is a moderate group that, while they recognize that reform is necessary, feel that the current rate of reform is sufficient and believe that the abuses will be taken care of eventually. They do not feel that they need to go to the perceived "extreme" measures of the reformist group, to be radical about reform.

3. There is a conservative or traditionalist group, that feel that Kriete's letter and other criticisms (even positive ones) are just being used by the enemies of the ICC in trying to tear it down, and that the ICC has become "soft" and "weak." They want to return to the glory days of old, when things were more black-and-white and definitive (for instance, mandatory disciplers telling people what to do). This group is divided however, some want a return of high power, Kip, but others do not want Kip to return.

My monitoring of on-line activity related to the ICOC's dissolution and my interviews with a handful of former members in various positions across the country suggest that Lee was correct in his assessment. Since February of 2004, the movement seems to have grown more fragmented; even members who were more "conservative" or "traditionalist" seem to be questioning a return to "glory days," considering major changes in discipling practices and more realistic evangelical goals.

Those individuals I have talked to and listened to on-line in 2003–2004, regardless of their level of dedication or abandonment of previous ICOC doctrine and affiliation, seem to still be involved in an active search to order their lives. Many hold dear to the church family relationships that were born during their time in the movement. Some have been completely disillusioned and, as they often say, "damaged" by their experiences in the ICOC; these are the former members who have joined Mainline Churches of Christ or other denominations, or left Christianity altogether. It is likely that many former ICOC members may find a familiar home in the Mainline Churches of Christ, the denominational church environment that first gave birth to the radical ICOC sect. Some former ICOC leaders attempted to maintain a healing conversation with the Mainline Churches of Christ as the movement was dissolving. Former ICOC leaders Gordon Ferguson, Gregg Marutzky, Al Baird, and Mike Taliaferro went to the Abilene Christian University forum to talk about the history of the ICOC movement and the mistakes that had been made. Lee (2004) mentions the Tallahassee, Florida, COC group as moving toward "unity" with the Mainline COC. Some members have, as Lee suggests, tried to keep their congregational body and ministries together, paying much attention to the criticisms raised in Kriete's letter and fashioning new autonomous, democratic church bodies. Other members with whom I have spoken also seem incredibly confused, tearful, hoping to capture the sacred energy of the discipling movement in congregations that are trying to "soften" and "rethink" discipling. Most of these folks seem quick to distance themselves from McKean. Finally, there is that small group of members who believe, along with McKean, that the fall of the unified movement was just a phase in their divine mission—these are members in Portland and what seem to be a few scattered leaders across the country willing to associate with McKean.

What has happened to the City COC congregation? After the Unity Conference in LA in 2002, like many other congregations, they went through a process of leaders confessing sins, apologizing for the abuses of discipling, and trying to come to some resolution so that they could move forward. The City COC congregation ultimately chose to fashion what they call a "self-governing" church body. Core members are still together, relieved to be cut free from the excessive therapeutic and evangelical tasks the leadership of the International Churches of Christ movement demanded, yet still very much tied to each other—attached to the extended church kin networks they established over the years. They name nearby former ICOC congregations as a kind of "loose brotherhood." Most of the members I interviewed are still in the City COC working to shape this new self-governing church. After reading the bulk of this book, Tom, a member of the new leadership committee, wrote for inclusion in this ethnography: "As the hierarchical leadership structure and internal discipling patterns of the ICOC have been deconstructed, there are wide arrays of differences among the congregations who have come out of this organization. There will likely be no return to a similar structure in the future, but a large degree of brotherhood and cooperation remains and is being rebuilt, and there is a common unifying experience, doctrine, and culture that continues to define churches, and individuals who have spent much time as part of the ICOC." It is clear that members of the City COC want to continue caring for each other and listening to each other, and are concerned about raising their own nuclear families. They want to be Christians who live and practice as they feel Jesus asked them to do. Most important, they seem to be working hard to hold on to the powerful church family relationships they created while in the movement.

I worried about showing this ethnography to my major research participants in the City COC. I worried that these friends I had come to know over the years would be offended by my sociological perspective. I worried that my highlighting of the major contradictions in ICOC ideology and practice would make them angry and might shake their faith. I worried, as sociologists studying controversial new religious movements do, that I would receive harsh words from the formal church organization and an onslaught of e-mails from current members disturbed by my analysis. Much of my worrying was in vain as the downfall of the unified movement offered a unique ethnographic opportunity; I was able to ask my research participants to read my description and analysis of their experience at a time when they were critiquing their own experience. I gave the book to Pat and Tom, and after they had read *Awesome Families* we sat for a couple of hours in front of a warm fire in their living room and engaged in conversation.

Pat noted the absence of her spiritual journey in the book. Her husband Tom agreed, and offered the following written statement in response: "I would like to point out that an academic study from a sociologic point of view does inherently fail to capture some of the spiritual factors in people's lives that transcend sociologic consideration. Therefore, the study fails to give any one looking for a full overview of the ICOC movement some of the spiritual dimensions that defined people's involvement." I suggested to Pat and Tom, after reading the previous comment and talking with them about this issue, that perhaps the reason I did not capture more of their individual spiritual experience was because in formal ICOC group performance, movement growth and therapeutic benefits of discipling were front and center. They agreed that this could well have been the case and that, for some members, such an emphasis on gaining new members and submitting to discipling resulted in barriers to individual spiritual life. The pull between wanting an individual relationship with God that nurtured spirituality and the enforced accountability to ICOC disciplers was representative of the tensions felt in maintaining individuality within such an authoritative structure. Pat and Tom validated that the contradictions and resulting cultural vertigo I speak of in this ethnography were large factors in the downfall of the unified movement. They also offered the following statement: "I acknowledge that the content [of *Awesome Families*] accurately reflects the realities of being a part of the ICOC, especially the larger overarching dimensions. Minor details could be contested on many points but such could be expected by the author interviewing only a sampling of participants in a study group. The sociological picture that is painted is, in my estimation, true to the everyday realities that most people experienced." Pat and Tom spoke of having to come to terms with the pull between individual freedom, choice, and the authoritative characteristics of discipling. They talked about how some current members were now working to purge high dependence on church leaders and structures and promote individual choice in relationship and life issues. For example, Tom talked of a church member asking how they should feel about many of the "moral" issues at stake in the 2004 presidential election. Church leaders answered her by encouraging the member to make her own political decision guided by her individual faith and "heart." Some members missed the old ICOC day-to-day assurance that someone else would take care of their difficult relational, political, and moral decisions. The congregation necessarily confronts the effects of secondary socialization in the old ICOC authoritative structure as they shape their new self-governing community of faith.

This ethnography makes several contributions to understanding how individuals could be drawn to, and remain committed to, social groups that demand high commitment and submission to authority. Members were, as are many in this country who join religious communities, searching for new and fruitful church kin networks and guidance for healing and building intimate family relationships. In their constant presentation of narratives of awesome family relationships, members were able to balance familiar contradictory beliefs and practices through a vibrant use of culture, creatively legitimating seemingly incoherent approaches to healing and constructing family. However, the power of such balancing is short-lived when burdened with too many points of tension in cultural beliefs and practices. On an organizational level, *Awesome Families* calls attention to the precarious nature of social movements who, in their discursive repertoires, commit to extremely broad and contradictory values and cultural approaches. Important too is the way in which this ethnography validates the importance of collective rituals and new media forms for giving life to sacred visions, and calls attention as well to the power of these collective performances and mechanisms in drawing crucial breath from charismatic movements.

Notes

Chapter 1 Sacred Counsel

1. McKean embodied a Weberian sense of divinely sanctioned charismatic leadership and authority (Weber, "The Sociology of Charismatic Authority," 245–252). McKean's authority hinged on the legitimacy of his "personal revelation," and his downfall partly on the precarious nature of charismatic authority (Weber 1946, 262, 248). Many lead ICOC evangelists were also charismatic leaders, meaning individuals with exceptional speaking skills, charm, and the ability to inspire devotion and emotion in members—for example, Kip's brother, Randy McKean, Elena McKean, Gordon Ferguson, Sam Laing, and Geri Laing. In fact, as the unified movement crumbled and McKean's authority faded, some congregations remained loyal to their local charismatic evangelist.
2. See Stanczak, "The Traditional as Alternative: The GenX Appeal of the International Church of Christ," 113–135, for further validation of ICOC's extensive use of contemporary media forms and culture. Stanczak's data is drawn from field study in the Los Angeles ICOC.
3. I found maintaining honest theological criticism and open discussion of religious beliefs as a researcher opened many doors in fieldwork and gave me a clear strategy and coping mechanism for confronting efforts to convince me of ICOC's worldview. See Gordon, "Getting Close by Staying Distant: Fieldwork with Proselytizing Groups," 267. Gordon argues that "open, honest, *disagreement* with the groups' beliefs as well as a *visible* role as a researcher result in increased rapport and acceptance by the groups [proselytizing groups] and reduced psychological stress on the researcher."
4. See Sirianni and Friedland, *Civic Innovation in America: Community Empowerment, Public Policy, and the Movement for Civic Renewal*, for further discussion regarding perceived loss of civic engagement.
5. See Janet Jacobs's book, *Divine Disenchantment*, for validation of high time demands and authority in leadership. Jacobs interviewed a few early members of the discipling movement. Stanczak, "The Traditional as Alternative: The GenX Appeal of the International Church of Christ," validates this high time commitment and level of social interaction as well.
6. For further exploration of this relationship see Rieff, *The Triumph of the Therapeutic*. See also Lasch, *Haven in a Heartless World: The Family Besieged*, 97–110; Conrad and Schneider, *Deviance and Medicalization*, and McGuire, *Ritual Healing in Suburban America*.
7. The medical model represents a dominant paradigm in Western society for understanding health, illness, and deviance. The medical model understands the biological body as a machine that can malfunction and is founded on the

germ theory of disease that stresses each disease as caused by a specific agent. There have been widespread social implications for this dominant model: concentration on the internal body rather than on the external environment. We more often look for causes inside the individual rather than those rising from the social structure and immediate social environment (see Conrad and Schneider, *Deviance and Medicalization*).

8. Evidence of this marriage between religion and psychology is strong in the wider evangelical subculture. For example, the American Association of Christian Counselors Inc. is "an organization of evangelical professional, lay, and pastoral counselors" who claim a dedication to "promoting excellence and unity in Christian counseling" (*Christian Counseling Today* 11, no. 1 [2003]: 6). Their magazine, *Christian Counseling Today*, and their official journal, *Marriage and Family: A Christian Journal*, are distributed quarterly.
9. Weber, *The Protestant Ethic and the Spirit of Capitalism*. See also Ritzer, *The McDonaldization of Society*, 123–145.
10. The heart as a symbol of religio-therapeutic healing is ubiquitous in the contemporary U.S. religious/spiritual marketplace. For example, Griffith (1997, 112) found a similar focus on the heart as a symbol of healing and transformation in Aglow and notes: "The theme of bringing to light those things that have been hidden in the darkness of the human heart is an old one in Christian theology and practice, acted out in various rites of confession and contrition." Griffith explores "the recurrent Aglow depictions of feelings kept 'hidden in the heart' as well as the measures by which such secrets are apparently revealed in the forging of intimate relationships with God and other people."

Chapter 2 An Unsinkable Raft in a Foreboding Divorce Culture

1. The use of the word "traditional" implies that our cultural model of family, the normative nuclear family that includes a mother, father, and children, with mother as domestic caretaker, father as breadwinner and authoritative family figure, is a long-established family structure. This model of family is more correctly understood as an aberrant family form that took shape after the Industrial Revolution. Families then moved from a primarily family-based economy where goods and necessary materials were produced in the domestic sphere, to a wage-based economy where wages were earned outside of the home and necessary materials sold. With the rise of this wage-based, consumer economic model, ideals of female domesticity and male breadwinning took root in dominant white Protestant culture. The normative nuclear family ideal has never been typical and in fact represented less than a quarter of all households in the United States at the turn of the twenty-first century.
2. In covenant marriages, spouses (heterosexual) willingly enter into a legal union that demands, for example, premarital counseling, divorce counseling, and rejection of "no-fault" divorce. Legislation is pending in some states for the creation of such marriage contract options. Covenant marriage is currently legal in Arizona, Arkansas, and Louisiana. Not surprisingly, the covenant marriage movement is backed by many conservative evangelical and fundamentalist Christian leaders and organizations.
3. Nancy Ammerman (1987, 135) in her study of fundamentalist Christians, *Bible Believers: Fundamentalists in the Modern World*, notes that marriages of

Christians or "believers" to nonbelievers were labeled "unequally yoked," a reference to "II Corinthians 6:14" that warns against being matched with unbelievers. R. Marie Griffith (1997, 175–176), in her analysis of evangelical women in Aglow, *God's Daughters: Evangelical Women and the Power of Submission*, notes discourse labeling non-Christian husbands as "unsaved," "backslidden," or "unbeliever[s]."

4. Examples of such recent publications include: Rosenau, *A Celebration of Sex for Newlyweds*; Penner, *The Gift of Sex: A Guide to Sexual Fulfillment*; and Wheat, *Intended for Pleasure: Sex Technique and Sexual Fulfillment in Christian Marriage.*
5. Members acknowledged that other churches tried to counsel individuals before marriage, but stressed that the ICOC was more foolproof because premarriage discipling was mandatory. Like many other tight-knit religious communities, members and leaders presented the discipling community as a "safe dating haven" in a society where dating had become evil, dangerous, and misguided (Kanter 1972; Davidman 1991). Singles talked of how they were blessed to have so many "great brothers" and "awesome sisters" to date in the Kingdom. They presented their potential mating pool as exceptional, better than what you might find in another church or in the secular dating world—better because disciplers were teaching "respect." Some members and ex-members suggested that the ICOC dating pool was exceptional because there were lots of physically "beautiful" and "handsome" brothers and sisters to choose from in the movement. In the words of one young City COC male member, the Kingdom was full of "awesome, powerful, and beautiful women of God." Members noted that one of the reasons the ICOC was so successful in producing great marriages was that members could not get married until marriage disciplers felt they were "ready."
6. This universal process varies cross-culturally. We can name cultures that complicate our gender dichotomy of male/female, such as Native American cultures that might recognize a third gender in those we would label as homosexual, transsexed, or transsexual. See Fausto-Sterling's *Sexing the Body: Gender Politics and the Construction of Sexuality*, in particular chapters 1–5, for an in-depth discussion of the social construction of sex and gender. See also Lorber, *Paradoxes of Gender*, which stresses gender as a social construction. See also the ethnomethodological approach in West and Zimmerman's "Doing Gender," 1125–1151. For discussion on third genders see Herdt, "Third Sexes and Third Genders," 21–84.
7. See Collins, *Black Feminist Thought: Knowledge, Consciousness, and the Politics of Empowerment*; Landry, *Black Working Wives: Pioneers of the American Family Revolution*; and Jones, "My Mother Was Much of a Woman."
8. I explore these contradictions further in chapter 5 drawing from Townsend's book, *The Package Deal*, in his concise and detailed explanation of the ambiguity and tension fathers face today in adhering to emotionality and breadwinning ideals. See also Garey's work, *Weaving Work and Motherhood*, for an ethnographic illustration of late twentieth-century tensions that women face in juggling wage work and "doing motherhood." See also Rosanna Hertz and Nancy L. Marshall's edited volume, *Working Families*, a collection of quantitative and qualitative works that highlight tensions and workplace efforts. See also Arlie Hochshield's work, *The Second Shift.*
9. See Gallagher, *Evangelical Identity and Gendered Family Life*, for an excellent analysis of the gender beliefs and practices of evangelicals in the United States. Gallagher draws on Swidler's (1986) tool kit analogy to help illustrate the

sources of evangelicals' varied gender ideology and how specific gender beliefs and practices are maintained and negotiated.

10. Ex-members, to no surprise, told a radically different story of women silenced through submission, of domestic violence left to flourish, and of gender confusion. The complexity of experience regarding female submission has been documented in the evangelical subculture as well. For example, Sally Gallagher (2003, 165), in *Evangelical Identity, Gendered Family Life*, notes that a "handful" of women in her sample "talked about living in abusive relationships," and that "those who did described how the idea of husbands' headship helped justify the abuse and made it difficult for them to leave."
11. See Gallagher (2003, 155–174) for an excellent discussion of why evangelicals continue to hold discursively to female submission and male headship in marriage. Most important, she argues that this gender stance is a "key marker" of the "embattlement" through which "evangelical subculture maintains its distinctiveness."
12. Here I refer to a subtle yet persistent "madonna/whore" dichotomy at work in adolescent culture and many mainstream media representations of female sexuality. Regarding persistence in adolescent culture see Lees, *Losing Out: Sexuality and Adolescent Girls*; and Tolman and Debold, "Conflicts of Body and Image: Female Adolescents, Desire, and the No-Body."
13. See Roof, *Spiritual Marketplace: Baby Boomers and the Remaking of American Religion*, especially 39–41 and 67–72. See also Nolan, *The Therapeutic State: Justifying Government at Century's End*, 150–169, for an excellent review of therapeutic ethos at work in education.
14. There were also several celebrity members of the church who were put front stage in ICOC performances of awesome church family and who, I suspect, were not disciplined as harshly as other members. For example, one member was a musician with a well-known popular rock band, and he and his wife were featured speakers at large events. Another couple, Megan and Cory Blackwell (she a model and he a former professional basketball player), were asked to help the arts/media/sports ministry (Jones and Brumley 1994, 38). Ex-members charged early on that the group worked hard to convert people with high status as members and they were looking for "beautiful people" who would legitimate the movement.

Chapter 3 Collective Performances of Healing

1. The ICOC's use of the name "Marriage Enrichment" underscores movement incorporation of widespread secular and religious therapeutic approach and language; Marriage Enrichment is the name of a national marriage/family organization that has held workshops in churches and community organizations across the United States.
2. The list continued: "Build a fire in the fireplace, turn out the lights and talk. Take a horse-drawn carriage ride. Go swimming in the middle of the night. Write a poem for your spouse. Remember to look into your spouse's eyes as he/she tells you about the day. Tell your spouse, 'I'm glad I married you!' Hug your spouse from behind and give him/her a kiss on the back of the neck. Stop in the middle of your busy day and talk to your spouse for 15 minutes. Create your own special holiday. Do something your spouse loves to do, even though it doesn't interest you personally. Send your spouse a love

letter. Build a snowman together. Watch the sunset together. Sit on the same side of a restaurant booth. Picnic by a pond. Give your mate a foot massage. Put together a puzzle on a rainy evening. Take a moonlight canoe ride. Tell your spouse, 'I'd rather be here with you than any place in the world.' Whisper something romantic to your spouse in a crowded room. Have a candlelight picnic in the backyard. Perfume the bed sheets. Serve breakfast in bed. Reminisce through old photo albums. Go away for the weekend. Share a milk shake with two straws. Kiss in the rain. Brush his/her hair. Ride the merry-go-round together. Dedicate a song to her/him over the radio. Wink and smile at your spouse from across the room. Have a hot bubble bath ready for him/her at the end of a long day. Buy new satin sheets. Tenderly touch your spouse as you pass one another around the house. Reminisce about your first date. Plant a tree together in honor of your marriage. Go kite flying. Attend a sporting event you've never been to together. Take time to think about him/her during the day, then share those thoughts. Drop everything and do something for the one you love—right now!"

Chapter 4 In with the Old and the New

1. For example, in the early 1970s parents of converts formed the anti-cult group, Free Our Sons and Daughters from the Children of God, FREECOG.
2. Irvine (1999) notes the ambiguity in her study of codependent self-help groups. As victims of family "dysfunction," of "codependent" relationships, they talk about needing to spend more time on themselves and accomplish goals as individuals. The irony, as suggested in the title of her book, *Codependent Forevermore,* is that this journey of selfhood takes place through dependence on others in this therapeutic community.
3. See, for example, Lalich, "Pitfalls in the Sociological Study of Cults." Lalich argues, "There is no way to know how many times researchers have been successfully 'fooled' by such groups, in the sense that the researchers were shown a version of reality that either differed from the typical daily life or hid from view the negative or controversial aspects" (124). In the section entitled "Tricks and Set-ups" she lists "Selected Interviews," "Selected Topics of Discussion," and "Staged Events" as dangerous pitfalls of data gathering in such groups (126–127).
4. Wuthnow (2000, 126) points out that "in a national survey, Poloma and Gallup (1991, 90–96) found that 65 percent of Americans thought it 'very important' 'for a religious person to make an effort to forgive others who have deliberately hurt them in some way.' "
5. For one example of the ease with which forgiveness is given, and little subsequent action taken, see Emerson and Smith (2000, 52–68), *Divided by Faith,* for their discussion of racial reconciliation efforts by white and black evangelicals in the United States.
6. See Flora Keshegian, *Redeeming Memories: A Theology of Healing and Transformation,* for theological discussion of the implications of forgiveness in healing processes.
7. For example, see Larry Crabb, *Connecting: Healing for Ourselves and Our Relationships: A Radical New Vision,* for examples of an evangelical Christian approach to replacing secular therapy with healing Christian communities and counselors.

8. See chapter 7, "Homosexuality: From Sin to Sickness to Life-Style," in Conrad and Schneider, *Deviance and Medicalization: From Badness to Sickness*. See also Neil Miller's journalistic social history, *Sex-Crime Panic: A Journey to the Paranoid Heart of the 1950s*, which tells the story of a group of gay men labeled as "sexual psychopaths," locked up in a mental hospital (to be "cured" of homosexuality) for crimes they did not commit.
9. Use of genetic language by organizations and groups interested in legitimating products, worldview, and family itself is pervasive in U.S. society (Nelkin and Lindee 1995). And there has been an increasing location of a range of individual problems in genetic structure (Lippman 1992).

Chapter 5 Awesome Kids

1. See Amy Siskind, "Child-Rearing Issues in Totalist Groups," 415–451.
2. For overview of arguments see Christian Smith, "Religious Participation and Network Closure among American Adolescents," 259–267.
3. There is a movement within the Christian evangelical subculture to accept the single lifestyle as a valid choice alongside the promotion of marriage as the ideal family unit. This ICOC adoption example and the movement's efforts to build and strengthen their "singles ministry" reflect the acceptance of singlehood in both secular culture and the evangelical subculture. Evidence can be seen for approval of the single life in the growing evangelical publishing industry, for example, Michelle McKinney Hammond's *Sassy, Single, and Satisfied: Loving the Life You're Living*.
4. Micaela Di Leonardo, "The Female World of Cards and Holidays: Women, Families, and the Work of Kinship," has shown the constant "kinwork" women do with regard to constant upkeep and planning of family holidays and events, birthdays, and religious holidays.
5. For example, as Marjorie Devault illustrates in her book, *Feeding the Family*, women spend a significant amount of time budgeting and planning family meals that may never be visible to other family members.
6. Discourses of multiculturalism, multiracialism, color blindness, individualism, and relationality combined in the ICOC to present the discipling network as a powerful and virtuous relational body able to cure individuals of racism and achieve a kind of institutional racial harmony that outside organizations had failed to produce. Multiculturalism and multiracialism are imprecise and historically fluid concepts, too easily recognized by many as the mere presence of individuals from different racial and ethnic backgrounds coming together in a single group. As a result, these concepts often manifest in simplistic organizational and individual approaches to complex social problems and racial/ethnic dynamics (Hollinger 1995). Nevertheless, these concepts are powerful and persistent ideals in U.S. mainstream discourse, used with frequency alongside concepts like diversity and inclusiveness to legitimate organizations and groups.
7. In the ICOC, mandatory close and frequent social interaction forced members to develop strong cross-racial and ethnic networks. In addition, members and leaders drew from this picture of tight-knit diverse networks as they repeatedly performed *intimate diversity scenes*, the enactment and/or narration of close and caring relationships among a racially and ethnically diverse membership (Jenkins 2003).

8. For example the visible efforts of organizations like EPOCH-USA (End Physical Punishment of Children) and NCACPS (National Coalition to Abolish Corporeal Punishment in Schools).

Chapter 6 Brothers and Sisters for the Kingdom of God

1. See, for one strong example, Southwest Airlines' presentations of employees and corporation as family in Freiberg and Freiberg, *Nuts: Southwest Airlines' Crazy Recipe for Business and Personal Success.*
2. Carol Stack introduces this concept of "fictive kin" in her well-known *All Our Kin*, an ethnography that explores the reciprocal nature of constructed kinship among those living in poverty in a black urban community.
3. See James L. Nolan's edited volume, *The American Culture Wars: Current Contests and Future Prospects*, for arguments regarding the usefulness of the culture wars thesis in understanding contemporary U.S. society.
4. See Griffith, *Born Again Bodies: Flesh and Spirit in American Christianity*. Griffith provides a rich social historical exploration of the role of religion in shaping bodies and sexuality.
5. See, for example, Brasher, *Godly Women: Fundamentalism and Female Power*. Also see Griffith, *God's Daughters: Evangelical Women and the Power of Submission*.

Chapter 7 A Kingdom That Promised Too Much

1. See Max Weber's (1921) discussion of the characteristics of charismatic authority and its instability: "By its very nature, the existence of charismatic authority is specifically unstable. The holder may forego his charisma; he may feel 'forsaken by his God,' as Jesus did on the cross; he may prove to his followers that 'virtue is gone out of him.' It is then that his mission is extinguished, and hope waits and searches for a new holder of charisma" (Gerth and Mills, 1946, 248).
2. Discipleship Publications International (DPI), after the fall of the unified movement, is still in operation. It appears that they have dropped books from their list that stress McKean's version of Christian discipleship.

Bibliography

ICOC and ICOC-Related Websites

Delphi Forums Discussion Groups: http://www.delphiforums.com

Hope Worldwide: http://www.hopeww.org

ICOC: http://www.icoc.org

McKean Portland Church of Christ (2004): http://www.portlandchurch.org

Ex-member Websites

REVEAL: http://www.reveal.org

RightCyberUp: http://rightcyberup.org

Achtemeier, Paul J., general ed. 1985. *Harper's Bible Dictionary*. New York: HarperCollins.

Ammerman, Nancy T. 1987. *Bible Believers: Fundamentalists in the Modern World*. New Brunswick, NJ: Rutgers University Press.

———, with Arthur E. Farnsley II et al. 1997. *Congregations and Community*. New Brunswick, NJ: Rutgers University Press.

———. 2003. "Religious Identities and Religious Institutions." In *Handbook of the Sociology of Religion*, ed. Michele Dillon, 207–224. New York: Cambridge University Press.

Bankston, William, Craig Forsyth, and H. Hugh Floyd. 1981. "Toward a General Model of the Process of Radical Conversion: An Interactionist Perspective on the Transformation of Self-Identity." *Qualitative Sociology* 4: 279–297.

Barker, Eileen. 1993. "Behold the New Jerusalems! Catch 22s in the Kingdom-Building Endeavors of New Religious Movements." *Sociology of Religion* 54 (4): 337–352.

Barnett, Maurice. 1989. *The Discipling Movement: A Study of the Neo-Crossroads Philosophy Among Churches of Christ*. Phoenix: Maurice Barnett.

Bartkowski, John, P. 1995. "Spare the Rod . . . or Spare the Child: Divergent Perspectives on Conservative Protestant Child Discipline." *Review of Religious Research* 37 (2): 97–116.

———. 2000. "Breaking Walls, Raising Fences: Masculinity, Intimacy, and Accountability among the Promise Keepers." *Sociology of Religion* 61: 33–53.

———. 2001. *Remaking the Godly Marriage: Gender Negotiation in Evangelical Families*. New Brunswick, NJ: Rutgers University Press.

———. 2004. *The Promise Keepers: Servants, Soldiers, and Godly Men*. New Brunswick, NJ: Rutgers University Press.

Bauer, Rick. 1994. *Toxic Christianity: The International Churches of Christ/Boston Movement Cult.* Bowie: Freedom House Ministries.

Bauman, Zygmunt. 2000. *Liquid Modernity.* Cambridge: Polity Press.

Becker, Howard. 1963. *Outsiders: Studies in the Sociology of Deviance.* London: Free Press.

Becker, Penny Edgell. 1998 "Making Inclusive Communities: Congregations and the 'Problem' of Race." *Social Problems* 45 (4): 451–471.

Beckford, James, A. 1985. *Cult Controversies: The Societal Response to the New Religious Movements.* London: Tavistock.

"Believe It or Else." October 15, 1993. ABC News *20/20* Transcript #1344, 2–3.

Bellah, R., W. Madsen, W. Sullivan, A. Swidler, and S. Tipton. 1985. *Habits of the Heart: Individualism and Commitment in American Life.* 2nd ed. Berkeley: University of California Press.

Berger, Peter. 1967. *The Sacred Canopy: Elements of a Sociological Theory of Religion.* Garden City, NY: Doubleday.

Berger, Peter, and Thomas Luckmann. 1966. *The Social Construction of Reality.* Garden City, NY: Anchor.

Brasher, Brenda. 1998. *Godly Women: Fundamentalism and Female Power.* New Brunswick, NJ: Rutgers University Press.

———. 2001. *Give Me That Online Religion.* San Francisco: Jossey-Bass.

Bromley, David. G. 1998. "Transformative Movements and Quasi-Religious Corporations." In *Sacred Companies: Organizational Aspects of Religion and Religious Aspects of Organizations,* edited by N. J. Demerath III et al., 349–363. New York: Oxford University Press.

Bromley, D., and D. Oliver. 1982. "Perfect Families: Visions of the Future in a New Religious Movement." In *Cults and the Family,* edited by F. Kaslow and M. B. Sussman. New York: Haworth Press.

Bumiller, E. 2002. "President Notes Dissent on Iraq, Vowing to Listen." *New York Times,* vol. CLI, A1.

Chancellor, James. 2001. "The Family and the Truth?" *Religion and the Social Order* 9: 37–51.

Chaves, Mark. 1998. *National Congregations Study.* Data file and code book. Tucson, AZ: University of Arizona, Department of Sociology.

Clark, Candace. 1997. *Misery and Company: Sympathy in Everyday Life.* Chicago: University of Chicago Press.

Clarke, Adele, Janet K. Shim, Laura Mamo, Jennifer Ruth Fosket, and Jennifer R. Fishman. 2003. "Biomedicalization: Technoscientific Transformations of Health, Illness, and U.S. Biomedicine," *American Sociological Review* 68: 161–194.

Collins, Patricia Hill. 1991. *Black Feminist Thought: Knowledge, Consciousness, and the Politics of Empowerment.* New York: Routledge.

Coltrane, Scott, and Michele Adams. 2001. "Men's Family Work: Child-Centered Fathering and the Sharing of Domestic Labor." In *Working Families: The Transformation of the American Home,* edited by Rosanna Hertz and Nancy Marshall, 72–99. Berkeley: University of California Press.

Connell, Robert W. 1995. *Masculinities.* Cambridge: Polity.

———. 2000. *The Men and the Boys.* Berkeley: University of California Press.

Conrad, Peter, and Joseph W. Schneider. 1992. *Deviance and Medicalization: From Badness to Sickness.* St. Louis, MO: C. V. Mosby.

Crabb, Larry. 1997. *Connecting: Healing for Ourselves and Our Relationships: A Radical New Vision.* Nashville: W Publishing Group.

Davidman, Lynn. 1991. *Tradition in a Rootless World: Women Turn to Orthodox Judaism.* Berkeley: University of California Press.

Demos, David, H., and Alan C. Acock. 1993. "Family Diversity and the Division of Domestic Labor: How Much Have Things Really Changed?" *Family Relations* 42: 323–331.

DeVault, Marjorie. 1991. *Feeding the Family: The Social Organization of Caring as Gendered Work.* Chicago: University of Chicago Press.

di Leonardo, Micaela. 1987. "The Female World of Cards and Holidays: Women, Families, and the Work of Kinship." *Signs* 12 (3): 440–453.

Dobson, James. 1970. *Dare to Discipline.* Wheaton: Tyndale House Publishers.

———. 2000. *Complete Marriage and Family Home Reference Guide.* Wheaton: Tyndale House Publishers.

———. 2003. "Men and Women: More Confused than Ever." Adapted from *Straight Talk.* Focus on the Family Resources Center: Word, 1991. Article from www.family.org/married/romance/a0009666.cfm.

Dodson, Jualynne E. 2002. *Engendering Church: Women, Power and the AME Church.* Lanham: Rowman and Littlefield.

Dunphy, Dexter C. 1972. *The Primary Group: A Handbook for Analysis and Field Research.* Upper Saddle River, NJ: Prentice-Hall.

Durkheim, Emile. 1893. *The Division of Labor in Society.* Translated by W. D. Halls. Reprint, Basingstoke [England]: Macmillan, 1984.

———. 1912. *The Elementary Forms of Religious Life.* Translated by Karen E. Fields. New York: Free Press.

Eddy, Mary Baker. 1875. *Science and Health with Key to the Scriptures.* Boston: First Church of Christ, Scientist.

Ehrenreich, Barbara. 1983. *The Hearts of Men: American Dreams and the Flight from Commitment.* New York: Anchor Press/Doubleday.

Ehrensaft, Diane. 2001. "The Kinderdult: The New Child Born to Conflict between Work and Family. *In Working Families: The Transformation of the American Home,* edited by Rosanna Hertz and Nancy Marshall. Berkeley: University of California Press.

Eiesland, Nancy L. 1997. "Contending with a Giant: The Impact of a Megachurch on Exurban Religious Institutions." In *Contemporary American Religion: An Ethnographic Reader,* edited by Penny Edgell Becker and Nancy L. Eiesland, 191–200. Walnut Creek, CA: AlatMira Press.

———. 2000. *A Particular Place: Urban Restructuring and Religious Ecology in a Southern Exurb.* New Brunswick, NJ: Rutgers University Press.

Eldredge, John. 2003. *Waking the Dead: The Glory of a Heart Fully Alive.* Nashville: Thomas Nelson.

Emerson, Michael O. 2000. "Beyond Ethnic Composition: Are Multiracial Congregations Unique?" Paper presented at the 2000 SSSR meeting, Houston, TX.

Emerson, Michael O., and Christian Smith. 2000. *Divided by Faith: Evangelical Religion and the Problem of Race in America.* New York: Oxford University Press.

Emerson, M.O., G. Yancey, and K. Chai. 2000. *Multiracial Congregations Project.* Houston, TX: Rice University.

Erikson, Kai. 1966. *Wayward Puritans: A Study in the Sociology of Deviance.* New York: Wiley.

———. 1976. *Everything in Its Path: Destruction of Community in the Buffalo Creek Flood.* New York: Simon & Schuster.

Farrell, Warren. 1975. *The Liberated Man.* New York: Bantam Books.

Fausto-Sterling, Anne. 2000. *Sexing the Body: Gender Politics and the Construction of Sexuality.* New York: Basic Books.

Ferguson, Gordon F. 1997. *Discipling: God's Plan to Train and Transform his People.* Woburn: Discipleship Publications International.

Ferguson, Gordon, and Wyndham Shaw. 2002. *Golden Rule Leadership.* Woburn: Discipleship Publications International.

Ferré, John P. 1990. "Searching for the Great Commission: Evangelical Book Publishing Since the 1970s." In *American Evangelicals and the Mass Media: Perspectives on the Relationship between American Evangelicals and the Mass Media,* edited Quentin J. Schultze, 99–117. Grand Rapids, MI: Zondervan.

Fischer, Charles S. 1991. "Ambivalent Communities: How Americans Understand Their Localities." In *America at Century's End,* edited by Alan Wolfe, chap. 4. Berkeley: University of California Press.

Foucault, Michel. 1978. *The History of Sexuality: An Introduction.* Vol. 1, 98. New York: Vintage Books.

Freiberg, Kevin, and Jackie Freiberg. 1996. *Nuts: Southwest Airlines' Crazy Recipe for Business and Personal Success.* New York: Broadway Books.

Fried, Mindy. 1998. *Taking Time: Parental Leave Policy and Corporate Culture.* Philadelphia: Temple University Press.

Gallagher, Sally K. 2003. *Evangelical Identity and Gendered Family Life.* New Brunswick, NJ: Rutgers University Press.

Gallagher, Sally K., and Christian Smith. 1999. "Symbolic Traditionalism and Pragmatic Egalitarianism: Contemporary Evangelicals, Families, and Gender." *Gender and Society* 13 (2): 211–233.

Gamson, William. 1992. "The Social Psychology of Collective Action," In *Frontiers in Social Movement Theory,* edited by Aldon D. Moris and Carol McClung Mueller. New Haven, CT: Yale University Press.

Gamson, William, A. David Croteau, William Hoynes, and Theodore Sasson. 1992. "Media Images and the Social Construction of Reality." *Annual Review of Sociology* 18: 373–393.

Garey, Anita I. 1999. *Weaving Work and Motherhood.* Philadelphia: Temple University Press.

Geertz, Clifford. 1973. "Religion as a Cultural System." In *Interpretation of Cultures: Selected Essays.* New York: Basic Books.

Gerth, H. H., and C. Wright Mills, eds. 1946. *From Max Weber: Essays in Sociology.* New York: Oxford University Press.

Giambalvo, Carol, and Herbert L. Rosedale. 1996. *The Boston Movement: Critical Perspectives on the International Churches of Christ.* Bonita Springs, FL: American Family Foundation.

Giddens, Anthony. 1991. *Modernity and Self-Identity: Self and Society in the Late Modern Age.* Stanford: Stanford University Press.

Glaser, Barney G., and Anselm L. Strauss. 1967. *The Discovery of Grounded Theory: Strategies for Qualitative Research.* New York: Aldine de Gruyter.

Goffman, Erving. 1959. *The Presentation of Self in Everyday Life*. New York: Doubleday.

———. 1974. *Frame Analysis: An Essay on the Organization of Experience*. Cambridge: Harvard University Press.

Gordon, David. 1987. "Getting Close by Staying Distant: Fieldwork with Proselytizing Groups." *Qualitative Sociology* 10 (3): 267.

Gray, John. 1992. *Men Are from Mars, Women Are from Venus: A Practical Guide for Improving Communication and Getting What You Want in Your Relationships*. New York: HarperCollins.

Greil, Arthur, and David Rudy. 1984. "Social Cocoons: Encapsulation and Identity Transformation Organizations." *Sociological Inquiry* 54: 260–278.

Griffith, R. Marie. 1997. *God's Daughters: Evangelical Women and the Power of Submission*. Berkeley: University of California Press.

———. 1999. "Fasting, Dieting, and the Body in American Christianity." In *Perspectives on American Religion and Culture*, edited by Peter W. Williams, 216–227. Malden: Blackwell Publishers.

———. 2004. *Born Again Bodies: Flesh and Spirit in American Christianity*. Berkeley: University of California Press.

Hackstaff, Karla B. 1999. *Marriage in a Culture of Divorce*. Philadelphia: Temple University Press.

Hammond, Michelle McKinney. 2003. *Sassy, Single, and Satisfied: Loving the Life You're Living*. Eugene, OR: Harvest House.

Heilman, Samuel C. 1973. *Synagogue Life: A Study in Symbolic Interaction*. Chicago: University of Chicago Press.

Herdt, G. 1994. "Third Sexes and Third Genders." In *Third Sex Third Gender: Beyond Sexual Dimorphism in Culture and History*, edited by G. Herdt, 21– 84. New York: Zone Books.

Herman, Ellen. 1995. *The Romance of American Psychology: Political Culture in the Age of Experts*. Berkeley: University of California Press.

Hertz, Rosanna, and Nancy L. Marshall, eds. 2001. *Working Families: The Transformation of the American Home*. Berkeley: University of California Press.

Hewitt. John, P. 1989. *Dilemmas of the American Self*. Philadelphia: Temple University Press.

Hochschild, Arlie. 2001. *The Time Bind: When Work Becomes Home and Home Becomes Work*. New York: Owl Books.

Hochschild, Arlie, and Anne Machung. 1989. *The Second Shift: Working Parents and the Revolution at Home*. New York: Viking Press.

Hollinger, David A. 1995. *Postethnic America*. New York: Basic Books.

Hubbard, L. Ron. 1950. *Dianetics: The Modern Science of Mental Health*. Los Angeles: Bridge Publications.

———. 1983. *Scientology: The Fundamentals of Thought*. Los Angeles: Bridge Publications.

———. 1990. *Clean Body Clear Mind: The Effective Purification Program*. Los Angeles: Bridge Publications.

Hunter, James Davison. 1983. *American Evangelicalism: Conservative Religion and the Quandary of Modernity*. New Brunswick, NJ: Rutgers University Press.

———. 1991. *Culture Wars: The Struggle to Define America.* New York: Basic Books.

Iannaccone, Laurence, R. 1994. "Why Strict Churches Are Strong." *American Journal of Sociology* 99: 1180–1211.

Ingersoll, Julie. 2003. *Evangelical Christian Women: War Stories in the Gender Battles.* New York: New York University Press.

Irvine, Leslie. 1999. *Codependent Forevermore: The Invention of Self in a Twelve Step Group.* Chicago: University of Chicago Press.

Jacobs, Janet. 1989. *Divine Disenchantment: Deconverting from New Religions.* Bloomington: Indiana University Press.

Jacobs, Jerry, and Kathleen Gerson. 2004. *The Time Divide: Work, Family, and Gender Inequality.* Cambridge: Harvard University Press.

Jenkins, Kathleen E. 2003. "Intimate Diversity: The Presentation of Multiculturalism and Multiracialism in a High-Boundary New Religious Movement." *Journal for the Scientific Study of Religion* 42 (3): 393–409.

Johnson, Miriam. 1988. *Strong Mothers, Weak Wives: The Search for Gender Equality.* Berkeley: University of California Press.

Jones, Jacqueline. 1998. "My Mother Was Much of a Woman." In *Families in the U.S: Kinship and Domestic Politics,* edited by Karen V. Hansen and Anita Ilta Garey. Philadelphia: Temple University Press.

Jones, Sheila, ed. 1995. *The Fine Art of Hospitality: Sharing Your Heart and Home with Others.* Woburn: Discipleship Publications International.

Jones, Sheila. 2000. *Life and Godliness for Everywoman: A Handbook for Joyful Living.* Woburn: Discipleship Publications International.

Jones, Sheila, and Linda Brumley, eds. 1994. *She Shall Be Called Woman,* Vol. 1, *Old Testament Women.* Woburn: Discipleship Publications International.

———. 1995. *She Shall Be Called Woman.* Vol. 2, *New Testament Women.* Woburn: Discipleship Publications International.

Jones, Thomas, and Sheila Jones. 1996. *Glory in the Church.* Woburn: Discipleship Publications International.

Kaminer, Wendy. 1993. *I'm Dysfunctional, You're Dysfunctional: The Recovery Movement and Other Self-Help Fashions.* New York: Addison-Wesley.

Kanter, Rosabeth M. 1972. *Commitment and Community: Communes and Utopias in Sociological Perspective.* Cambridge: Harvard University Press.

Kennedy, Randall. 2003. *Interracial Intimacies: Sex, Marriage, Identity, and Adoption.* New York: Pantheon Books.

Keshkegian, Flora, A. 2000. *Redeeming Memories: A Theology of Healing and Transformation.* Nashville: Abington Press.

Kim, Frank, and Erica Kim. 1998. *How to Share Your Faith.* Woburn: Discipleship Publications International.

Kingdom News Network. 2000. *Jubilee 2000: Even Greater Things* 7 (November/December): 8–10.

Kitsuse, John. 1980. "Coming Out All Over: Deviants and the Politics of Social Problems." *Social Problems* 28: 1–13.

Klaw, Spencer. 1993. *Without Sin: The Life and Death of the Oneida Community.* New York: Penguin Books.

Kriete, Henry. 2003. "Honest to God: Revolution through Repentance and Freedom in Christ." REVEAL, February 2, 2003. http://www.reveal.org.

Laing, Sam, and Geri Laing. 1994. *Raising Awesome Kids in Troubled Times.* Woburn: Discipleship Publications International.

———. 1996. *Friends and Lovers: Marriage as God Designed It.* Woburn: Discipleship Publications International.

Lalich, Janja. 2001. "Pitfalls in the Sociological Study of Cults." In *Misunderstanding Cults: Searching for Objectivity in a Controversial Field,* edited by Benjamin Zablocki and Thomas Robbins. Toronto: University of Toronto Press.

Landry, Bart. 2000. *Black Working Wives: Pioneers of the American Family Revolution,* Berkeley: University of California Press.

Lasch, Christopher. 1977. *Haven in a Heartless World: The Family Besieged.* New York: Basic Books.

Lasch-Quinn, E. 2001. *Race Experts: How Racial Etiquette, Sensitivity Training, and New Age Therapy Hijacked the Civil Rights Revolution.* New York: W. W. Norton.

Lees, Susan. 1986. *Losing Out: Sexuality and Adolescent Girls.* London: Hutchinson Press.

Lemert, Charles. 1999. "Social Theory: Its Uses and Pleasures." In *Social Theory: The Multicultural and Classic Readings,* edited by Charles Lemert, 1–20. Boulder, CO: Westview Press.

Lippman, A. 1992. "Led (Astray) by Genetic Maps: The Cartography of the Human Genome and Health Care." *Social Science and Medicine* 35: 1469–1176.

Lockhart, W. 2000. " 'We Are One Life,' but Not of One Gender Ideology: Unity, Ambiguity, and the Promise Keepers." *Sociology of Religion* 61: 173–192.

Lorber, Judith. 1994. *Paradoxes of Gender.* New Haven, CT: Yale University Press.

Loseke, Donileen R. 2003. *Thinking about Social Problems.* New York: Aldine de Gruyter, 51–73.

Lowney, Kathleen S. 1999. *Baring Our Souls: T. V. Talk Shows and the Religion of Recovery.* New York: Aldine de Gruyter.

Martin, Emily. 1987. *The Woman in the Body: A Cultural Analysis of Reproduction.* Boston: Beacon Press.

Martín-Barbero, J. 1997. "Mass Media as a Site of Resacralization of Contemporary Cultures." In *Rethinking Media, Religion, and Culture,* edited by Steward M. Hoover and Knut Lundby. Thousand Oaks, CA: Sage Publications.

McAdoo, Harriette Pipes, ed. 2002. *Black Children: Social, Educational, and Parental Environments.* 2nd ed. Thousand Oaks, CA: Sage Publications, 47–175.

McDonnell, J. T. 1998. "On Being the 'Bad' Mother of an Autistic Child." In *"Bad" Mothers: The Politics of Blame in Twentieth-Century America,* edited by M. Ladd-Taylor and L. Umansky, 220–229. New York: New York University Press.

McGuire, Meredith B. 1988. *Ritual Healing in Suburban America.* New Brunswick, NJ: Rutgers University Press.

McKean, Kip. 1992. "Revolution through Restoration Part I: From Jerusalem to Rome, from Boston to Moscow." *Upside Down Magazine* (Kingdom News Network).

———. 1994. "Revolution through Restoration Part II: The 20th Century Church." *Upside Down Magazine* (Kingdom News Network).

———. 2003. "From Babylon to Zion: Revolution through Restoration III" (posted on @www.portland.ucd.net).

Messner, Michael A. 1992. *Power at Play: Sports and the Problem of Masculinity.* Boston: Beacon Press.

Miller, Neil. 2002. *Sex-Crime Panic: A Journey to the Paranoid Heart of the 1950s*. Los Angeles: Alyson Books.

Money, John. 1948. "Delusion, Belief, and Fact." *Psychiatry* 11: 36, 38.

Morgan, David. 2002. "Protestant Visual Practice and American Mass Culture," In *Practicing Religion in the Age of the Media*, edited by Stewart M. Hoover and Lynn Schofield Clark, 37–62. New York: Columbia University Press.

Nelkin, Dorothy, and M. Susan Lindee. 1995. *The DNA Mystique: The Gene as a Cultural Icon*. Ann Arbor: University of Michigan Press.

Nichols, Jack. 1975. *Men's Liberation: A New Definition of Masculinity*. New York: Viking Press.

Niebuhr, G. 2001. "Baptists Convene, and Turn to Family." *New York Times*. June 14, A22.

Nolan, James L. 1998. *The Therapeutic State: Justifying Government at Century's End*. New York: New York University Press.

Nolan, James L., ed. 1996. *The American Culture Wars: Current Contests and Future Prospects*. Charlottesville: University of Virginia Press.

Palmer, S. J., and C. E. Hardman. 1999. *Children in New Religions*. New Brunswick, NJ: Rutgers University Press.

Paulson, M. 2001. "Campuses Ban Alleged Church Cult." *Boston Globe*. February 23, 8B1.

Penner, Clifford, and Joyce Penner. 1981. *The Gift of Sex: A Guide to Sexual Fulfillment*. Dallas: Word.

Philipson, Ilene J. 1993. *On the Shoulders of Women: the Feminization of Psychotherapy*. New York: Guilford.

Pleck, Joseph H. 1981. *The Myth of Masculinity*. Cambridge: MIT Press.

———. 1983. "The Theory of Male Sex Role Identity: Its Rise and Fall, 1936–Present." In *In the Shadow of the Past: Psychology Portrays the Sexes: A Social and Intellectual History*, edited by M. Lewin, 205–225. New York: Columbia University Press.

———. 1987. "American Fathering in Historical Perspective." In *Changing Men: New Directions in Research on Men and Masculinity*, edited by Michael S. Kimmel, 83–97. Thousand Oaks, CA: Sage Publications.

Putnam, Robert. 2000. *Bowling Alone: The Collapse and Revival of American Community*. New York: Simon & Schuster.

Putney, Clifford. 2001. *Muscular Christianity: Manhood and Sports in Protestant America, 1880–1920*. Cambridge: Harvard University Press.

Richardson, James T., Robert Balch, and J. Gordon Melton. 1993. "Problems of Research and Data in the Study of New Religions." In *Religion and the Social Order: The Handbook on Cults and Sects in America*, Part B, edited by David G. Bromley and Jeffrey K. Hadden. Greenwich, CT: JAI Press.

Rieff, Philip. 1966. *The Triumph of the Therapeutic*. New York: Harper & Row.

Ries, Janet K. 1977. "Public Acceptance of the Disease Concept of Alcoholism." *Journal of Health and Social Behavior* 18: 338–344.

Risman, Barbara J. 1998. *Gender Vertigo: American Families in Transition*. New Haven, CT: Yale University Press.

Ritzer, George. (2000). *The McDonaldization of Society*. Thousand Oaks, CA: Pine Forge.

Rodgers-Melnick, A. 1996. "A Calling in Question; International Churches of Christ Seen as Aggressive, Authoritarian." *Pittsburgh Post-Gazette*. November 11, B-1.

Roof, Wade Clark. 1993. "Religion and Narrative." *Review of Religious Research* 34: 297–310.

———. 1999. *Spiritual Marketplace: Baby Boomers and the Remaking of American Religion*. Princeton, NJ: Princeton University Press.

Root, Maria P. P. 2001. *Love's Revolution: Interracial Marriage*. Philadelphia: Temple University Press.

Rose, Susan. 1987. "Women Warriors: The Negotiation of Gender Roles in an Evangelical Community." *Sociological Analysis* 48 (3): 245–258.

Rosemond, John. 1989. *John Rosemond's Six-Point Plan for Raising Happy, Healthy Children*. Kansas City, MO: Andrews McMeel.

———. 1991. *Parent Power!* Kansas City, MO: Andrews McMeel.

Rosenau, Douglas E. 2002. *A Celebration of Sex for Newlyweds*. Nashville: Nelson Books.

Rotundo, Anthony, E. 1993. *American Manhood: Transformations in Masculinity from the Revolution to the Modern Era*. New York: Basic Books.

Rubin, Julius H. 2001. "Contested Narratives: A Case Study of the Conflict between a New Religious Movement and Its Critics." *In Misunderstanding Cults: Searching for Objectivity in a Controversial Field*, edited by Benjamin Zablocki and Thomas Robbins. Toronto: University of Toronto Press.

Sarbin, Theodore, and Nathan Adler. 1970. "Self-Reconstruction Processes: A Preliminary Report." *Psychoanalytic Review* 57: 609–616.

Sarbin, Theodore, and Larry Nucci. 1973. "Self-Reconstruction Processes: A Proposal for Reorganizing the Conduct of Confirmed Smokers." *Journal of Abnormal Psychology* 81: 182–198.

Schor, Juliet B. 1991. *Overworked Americans: The Unexpected Decline of Leisure*. New York: Basic Books.

Searl, Natalie. 1994. "The Women's Bible Study: A Thriving Evangelical Support Group." In *"I Come Away Stronger": How Small Groups Are Shaping American Religion*, edited by Robert Wuthnow, 97–123. Grand Rapids, MI: Eerdmans.

Sirianni, Carmen, and Lewis Friedland. 2001. *Civic Innovation in America: Community Empowerment, Public Policy, and the Movement for Civic Renewal*. Berkeley: University of California Press.

Siskind, Amy B. 1994. "The Sullivan Institute/Fourth Wall Community: 'Radical' Psychotherapy as Quasi-Religion." *Religion and the Social Order* 4: 51–77.

———. 2001. "Child-Rearing Issues in Totalist Groups." In *Misunderstanding Cults: Search for Objectivity in a Controversial Field*, edited by Benjamin Zablocki and Thomas Robbins, 415–451. Toronto: University of Toronto Press.

Smith, Christian. 2003. "Religious Participation and Network Closure among American Adolescents." *Journal for the Scientific Study of Religion* 42 (2): 259–267.

Smith, Christian, with M. Emerson, S. Gallagher, P. Kennedy, and D. Sikkink. 1998. *American Evangelicalism: Embattled and Thriving*. Chicago: University of Chicago Press.

Snow, David, and Robert Benford. 1988. "Ideology, Frame Resonance, and Participant Mobilization." In *International Social Movement Research*, Vol. 1, edited by Bert Klandermans, Hanspeter Kriesi, and Sidney Tarrow. Greenwich: JAI.

———. 1992. "Master Frames and Cycles of Protest." In *Frontiers in Social Movement Theory*, edited by Aldon D. Morris and Carol McClung Mueller. New Haven, CT: Yale University Press.

Sontag, Susan. 1979. *Illness as Metaphor.* New York: Vintage.

Stacey, Judith. 1991. *Brave New Families: Stories of Domestic Upheaval in Late Twentieth Century America.* New York: Basic Books.

———. 1994. "Scents, Scholars, and Stigma: The Revisionist Campaign for Family Values." *Social Text* 40: 51–75.

Stacey, Judith, and Susan E. Gerard. 1990. " 'We Are Not Doormats': The Influence of Feminism on Contemporary Evangelicalism in the United States." In *Uncertain Times: Negotiating Gender in American Culture*, edited by Faye Ginsburg and Anna Tsing, 452–477. Boston: Beacon Press.

Stack, Carol. 1974. *All Our Kin.* New York: Basic Books.

Stanczak, Gregory. 2000. "The Traditional as Alternative: The GenX Appeal of the International Church of Christ." In *GenX Religion*, edited by Richard W. Flory and Donald E. Miller, 113–135. New York: Routledge.

Swidler, Ann. 1986. "Culture in Action: Symbols and Strategies." *American Sociological Review* 51: 273–286.

———. 2001. *Talk of Love.* Chicago: University of Chicago Press.

Terry, Jennifer. 1998. " 'Momism' and the Making of Treasonous Homosexuals." In *"Bad" Mothers: The Politics of Blame in Twentieth-Century America*, edited by M. Ladd-Taylor and L. Umansky, 169–190. New York: New York University Press.

Tolman, Deborah, and Elizabeth Debold. 1993. "Conflicts of Body and Image: Female Adolescents, Desire, and the No-Body." In *Feminist Treatment and Therapy of Eating Disorders*, edited by M. Katzman, P. Fallon, and S. Wooley. New York: Guilford.

Townsend, Nicholas. 2002. *The Package Deal: Marriage, Work and Fatherhood in Men's Lives.* Philadelphia: Temple University Press.

Uttal, Lynet. 1996. "Racial Safety and Cultural Maintenance: The Child Care Concerns of Employed Mothers of Color." *Ethnic Studies Review* 19: 1.

Vaughan, John N. 1993. *Megachurches and America's Cities: How Churches Grow.* Grand Rapids, MI: Baker Books.

Weber, Max. 1946. "The Sociology of Charismatic Authority" In *From Max Weber: Essays in Sociology*, edited by H. H. Gerth and C. Wright Mills, 245–252, 262, 248. New York: Oxford University Press.

———. 1904–1906. *The Protestant Ethic and the Spirit of Capitalism.* Reprint, Los Angeles: Roxbury Press, 1998.

Wegar, Katarina. 1998. "Adoption and Kinship." In *Families in the U.S.: Kinship and Domestic Politics.* Philadelphia: Temple University Press, 41–51.

West, Candace, and Don H. Zimmerman. 1987. "Doing Gender." *Gender and Society* 1: 125–151.

Wheat, Ed, and Gayle Wheat. 1997. *Intended for Pleasure: Sex Technique and Sexual Fulfillment in Christian Marriage.* 3rd ed. Burlington, NJ: Revell Press.

Wilcox, Bradford W. 1998. "Conservative Protestant Childrearing: Authoritarian or Authoritative?" *American Sociological Review* 63 (6): 796–809.

Wuthnow, Robert. 2000. "How Religious Groups Promote Forgiving: A National Study." *Journal for the Scientific Study of Religion* 39 (2): 125–139.

———. 2003. *All in Sync: How Music and Art Are Revitalizing American Religion.* Berkeley: University of California Press.

———, ed. 1994. *"I Come Away Stronger": How Small Groups Are Shaping American Religion.* Grand Rapids, MI: Eerdmans.

Yamane, David. 2000. "Narrative and Religious Experience." *Sociology of Religion* 61 (2): 171–189.

Zablocki, Benjamin, and Thomas Robbins, eds. 2001. *Misunderstanding Cults: Searching for Objectivity in a Controversial Field.* Toronto: University of Toronto Press.

Zola, Irving. 1972. "Medicine as an Institution of Social Control." *Sociological Review* 20: 487–504.

Index

About the Author

Kathleen E. Jenkins is an assistant professor of sociology at the College of William and Mary.